Worlds
Within a
Congregation

WORLDS WITHIN A CONGREGATION

Dealing with Theological Diversity

W. PAUL JONES

Abingdon Press
Nashville

WORLDS WITHIN A CONGREGATION:
DEALING WITH THEOLOGICAL DIVERSITY

Library of Congress Cataloging-in-Publication Data

Jones, W. Paul (William Paul)
    Worlds within a congregation : dealing with theological diversity / W. Paul Jones.
        p. cm.
    Includes bibliographical references (p.).
    ISBN 0-687-08434-2 (alk. paper)
    1. Parishes.   2. Theology, Practical—Methodology.   I. Title.
    BV700 .J66 2000
    250—dc21   99-059933

00 01 02 03 04 05 06 07 08 09—10 9 8 7 6 5 4 3 2 1

To
Dr. Martha Marie Fly,
educator, mathematician, and musician,
whose courage
makes clear what it means to live in the "now"

And to
Father Robert Matter, OCSO,
my "hermit on the hill,"
who in wanting nothing else
than to grow old loving his God,
has shown me that
nothing else matters

Fear not that thy life shall come to an end,
but rather fear that it shall never have a beginning.
—J. H. NEWMAN

When I arise in the morning,
I am torn by the twin desires
to reform the world and to enjoy the world.
This makes it hard to plan the day.
—E. B. WHITE

I must be true to the grain of my own wood.
—AFRICAN AMERICAN PROVERB

CONTENTS

LIST OF DIAGRAMS

PREFACE

Transcending the
Liberal-Conservative Impasse

W*orlds Within a Congregation* emerged from the deep crisis enveloping almost every Christian denomination, from Roman Catholicism to mainline Protestantism. In each case, there is a conservative wing whose proponents insist upon a deep but narrow personal commitment to the gospel. In tension with them, a liberal contingent insists upon a hospitable tolerance for diversity, but one in which serious commitment is shy. Out of this apparent impasse, in both local churches and within denominations as a whole, threats of schism become increasingly heard, disclosing the depth of pain that is present. The urgent need is to create an understanding of the church by which to transcend this apparent impasse.

This book is an attempt not to take sides but to raise the issue to another level. By discerning the underlying theological assumptions at stake, a model can emerge by which each perspective will be affirmed in what it insists upon, while exploring how what they reject can be rendered optional. Some readers will have read my *Theological Worlds: Understanding the Alternative Rhythms of Christian Belief.* A number of pastors have asked for a sequel, one which would spell out concretely how the church of the future could be created now, in which alternative theological worlds can take seriously both commitment and diversity. *Worlds Within a Congregation* is that sequel, containing many years of experience and research.

Pastors and priests, parishioners and denominational leaders, seminary professors and students—all are invited to explore the concrete nature of this postmillennial, though largely unrecognized, church which is emerging now. Each book stands on its own, but together relate much as theory does to practice. This present volume applies the image of the variegated church to a variety of situations and environments, as well as different sizes and types of congregations, so as to envisage how this emerging understanding of the church will result in a new approach to Christian religious education, worship, preaching, administration, evangelism, and counseling.

Our task begins by exploring theologizing as the dynamic method involved in the human search for meaning, resulting in a theological World that is autobiographic—exemplifying a deep but often unrecognized commitment on which one's life depends. This search is not only individual, but involves the craving for a communal context in which one's pilgrimage can receive mirroring, accountability, and vision. Rather than insisting, as once it did, on a universal and abstract content, the church of the future will understand its role as beginning within this universal search for meaning. Its task is that of graphically offering the viable alternative Christian life options, together reflecting the church's seamless robe as gloriously multicolored.

The center of our study is the Theological Worlds Inventory—a vehicle developed to identify one's theological orientation. It has been tested with various persons and groups in a diversity of church and secular situations, establishing itself as an excellent tool by which individuals, local churches, and denominations can discover their underlying theological perspective. Brought into self-consciousness, the primary activities of a church can begin to reflect creatively the theological diversity which is present in all churches. In so doing, the intent is to lure individuals and groups into forced options, in which the inevitability of commitment becomes operative. There is every reason to believe that variegation will be the primary ingredient in the church of the future. Whether implemented in small churches or large, this book offers a concrete way whereby evangelism and theological nurture can intersect so that there emerges a new structure and task as blueprint for the postmodern church. I particularly appreciate the comment by a reader of this manuscript: "This book is a discussion of congregational and denominational life, with theological commentary, rather than a theological work illustrated with asides from the spheres of church and culture."

CHAPTER ONE

A Frightened Glance Forward, with Excitement

The Church's Search for a Reason to Be

Individuals attend mainline churches today for reasons previously recognized as neither significant nor valid. Doctrine, denomination, parental loyalty, or childhood rearing are no longer key factors. Instead, research shows that church choosing is largely a pragmatic process. Primary factors are geographic proximity, professional advantage, social opportunities, activities for children, plus the personal charisma of the pastor—enclosed within a sense of belonging. This significant motivational change reflects, as well, a basic shift in how the church is to be understood. Instead of perceiving the church as somehow unique, it has become one institution among many, competing to meet the individual's psychosocial needs.

Even more crucial, theology no longer appears as a significant factor. Whether one considers the conservative or the liberal wings, one common factor emerges. In a society increasingly individualistic and segmented, the "successful" churches are those that provide a sense of active belonging. As one pastor put it, "In a bored and lonely society, the church makes life more livable by offering activity and fellowship." But so defined, the church is reduced to competing with a host of other institutions that promise similar opportunities.

The uniqueness with which the church of the twenty-first century will likely find its identity, is in a deeper understanding of belonging. The need to belong is rooted in the human need for meaning, in a craving for significance and purpose—a desire to participate in "that which counts." Yet this individual sense of meaning involves a reaching out for others with which to share a common theological

World, where one can live and move and have one's being, with profound commitment. The personal price we are paying for the individualistic and competitive society in which we live is the contagious disease of loneliness. As Henri Nouwen insisted, "Loneliness is one of the most universal sources of human suffering today."[1]

It is significant that within the last decade or two the church has begun to awaken to this deeper level in a phenomenon called spirituality. Yet while this hunger has found little point of contact with traditional theology, it is, in fact, a profoundly theological search. Put another way, the hunger to belong involves more than being included. Authentic belonging entails so knowing one's self, as part of a larger scheme of things, that there emerges a profound sense of "coming home." In truth, spirituality means living knowingly one's theology.

For most of the nineteenth century, the church foundered over the apparent loss of its *unique raison d'être*. But in our time, we are on the edge of claiming our unique calling. By discerning theology as the process by which the human search for meaning is done, we are rediscovering the church's unique reason for being. By emphasizing this inevitable process, rather than being threatened by the theological diversity that characterizes the contemporary church, we can begin to develop a model for the church as we enter the twenty-first century. More than simply tolerating this phenomenon of variegation, we are called to find a way to affirm it gratefully, in such a way that deep commitment becomes a forced option.

The church's point of contact with the postmodern world is that of hunger, when "why not?" no longer slakes one's daily "whys." "Most young adults, whether theologically conservative or liberal, are searching for meaning, significant relations with others, a purpose for their lives, and a place in a world that is becoming very crowded for some of them."[2] The resulting restlessness takes many forms. Some know it as having everything—except peace, or when a pink slip crucifies one's life goals, or when troubled dreams are the cost of a promotion gained, or when one becomes wary lest a hidden past might be known. Whatever the form, it is a variation of more and more feeling like less and less. Restlessness can become a yearning, as one is baited by thoughts of death, whether lurking at the door at the end of one's hallway, or aggressively ambushing the young, or in the lonely hours, when one even doubts that there is a motel that will "keep the lights on" for them. However it appears, and no matter when it is recognized, spirituality entails being addressed by the mongrel feel of one's life, like last week's newspaper that missed the porch.

The Postmodern Search for Meaning

Whereas classical Christianity tended to explore spirituality in terms of the self as *depraved*, in our day the evil of our world has, as its reverse side, the self as *deprived*. From birth on we have been suckled by a host of fraudulent promises concerning possessions, status, world, and middle-class belonging. The self that is ripe for understanding the emerging church is one that admits a wistfulness for a community which gives permission to dream dreams of another kind. From the ashes of our spoiled individuality is coming a strange fascination with discipline, for an accountability without commitment is little more than a veiled convenience. Although rarely recognized, this craving is for the church. As Callahan puts it, "We know *who we are* in relation to the community in which we have found home."[3]

Part of the church's difficulty in claiming its unique calling is its encounter with "plural shock."[4] How can the church any longer claim to provide *the* answer, when all absolutes and universals are being dissolved by a diversity of options, within both culture and the church? Buechner identifies our evangelical point of contact with our era. "At its heart most theology, like most fiction, is essentially autobiography. Aquinas, Calvin, Barth, Tillich, working out their systems in their own ways and in their own language, are all telling us the stories of their lives, and if you press them far enough, even at their most cerebral and forbidding, you find an experience of flesh and blood, a human face smiling or frowning or weeping or covering its eyes before something that happened once."[5]

Thus the spiritual stirrings that we can detect all around us are in reality a disclosure of the nature of theology at its heart. These searchings are no more and no less than efforts to birth a soul, by addressing one's own unsettling stories. Rather than seeing diversity as an anemic reduction of the theological task, it is a rediscovery of how the church once came into being, and how its heritage is a continuation. Evangelism can no longer rest simply in defending what appears to be the church's conclusions, but in identifying the theologizing process—concerned, at least initially, on the "how" rather than the "what."

We begin by exploring two recognitions. (1) Theologizing is the meaning-search necessitated by the human fact of existing, enclosed within the yearning to belong, whatever content may result. (2) As a result, the modern church's reason for being is *itself* as an organic whole, within which alternative subcommunities serve as vehicles of disclosure, support, and accountability. Life is a pilgrimage. A tremendous aid in that search is the church's history, like a tapestry of perspectives, held together by the warp of a common origin.

Diversity and Authentic Commitment

A key quandary appears here in our exploration. Even if the church were to affirm internal diversity as legitimate, is this not simply an acquiescence to the liberal insistence, disregarding the conservative demand for deep commitment? The answer is best seen through two stories.

I remember attending the funeral of a friend some years ago. The service was well constructed, well executed, well attended. From beginning to end, it was a liturgy of fond remembrance. There was a tape of some of his favorite music, a table adorned with his fishing equipment, the picture of the last mountain he had climbed, and his red and yellow Kansas City Chiefs hat. When I left, I felt strangely empty and dissatisfied. That night I had a dream of that event, but this time it was my funeral. At the midpoint, I rose from the coffin and left in disdain by the side aisle. To make things worse, I awoke to a friend's phone call, declaring that the funeral was a "rare event," concluding that it was "the kind of funeral I want when I die."

Within the month, I was a guest at a Benedictine convent. While there, there was a death, and I was invited to the funeral, even though I had never met that sister. The words used, although rooted in scripture and tradition, were secondary. I was drawn into the event that was being acted out. Her baptismal gown was placed over the simple pine box, and the priest vigorously sprinkled it, declaring that since Sister's baptism had been an immersion into Christ's death and into Christ's resurrection, Sister was already on the other side of death. "Christ has died her death for her." In dramatic insistence, her body was led by the Easter candle down the central aisle, as in happy defiance we rose and sang, "Christ the Lord Is Risen Today." Her body was stationed so that she too would be facing the altar. Then together, surrounded by beautiful mosaics of the risen Christ gathered with his disciples, we invoked by name a host of saints. The whole community ate with their sister a final Eucharist, as foretaste of the divine promise. The farewell was a recessional out into her world. We followed on foot, as she took her last ride in the battered station wagon in which she had driven to town weekly for groceries. At the graveside, Sister was commended to God. Recalling the ashes with which she had been anointed when she left the secular world for a monastic one, each sister now placed a handful of dirt on the body, covering her as she left for still another world—the final one. As the bell tolled in reminder to us who remained, we returned to the monastery. Reentry was through the laundry room, where her few possessions were being laundered. These tokens of the tradition in which Sister died were being prepared for use by a new member who would follow. At soul depth, I was home.

It was several years before I understood more fully what was at stake in these contrasting acts. The first funeral centered in a thankful remembrance of things past, a eulogy of fond remembrance. The person was central, and the rhythm giving meaning to his dying was right, for it was the rhythm characterizing his life. His theological World was one of emptiness and fulfillment.[6] For him, the funeral had been deeply right, celebrating the varied dimensions of his fullness. His memory would last.

At the monastery I had entered a contrasting theological World. Here too, the funeral and the life shared a common rhythm. This liturgical celebration was one that I came to recognize as the movement from separation to reunion.[7] For Sister, in heavy contrast with that of my friend, the funeral had been deeply right, celebrating her "going home." The insight that has deeply changed my own life began with this awareness that even though these two celebrations were "Worlds" apart, both were very Christian and both were very right. They contrasted two deeply committed life perspectives, both of which were viable alternatives. Neither was better. Yet, if the services had been reversed, it would have been tragically wrong.

Their juxtaposition helps make clear the arena to which the modern church is being called. The current spiritual stirrings, deep in each of us, are, in truth, the call to recognize one's life as a pilgrimage toward meaning. The current yearning for belonging to an

accepting community is in fact a yearning for identifying and nurturing one's true self, through caring accountability. What could
have greater power for such discovering and nurturing than a variegated church, in which both the aforementioned funerals (and others), as well as varied baptisms and weddings, would have their
valid place? Their individual pilgrimages can be clustered in alternative meaning-Worlds. Serving as subgroups or congregations, each
would provide contrasting but lively and viable faithful perspectives, luring each person into an informed leap of faith. It is in such a
variegated church, characterized by self-conscious and organic
diversity, that ecumenism will come of age—not as mergers or even
ingenious linkages of denominations, but as an ecumenism of internal diversity within each denomination and local church. As the
local church is losing its denominational reason for being, the Spirit
would seem to be leading toward an internal ecumenism. The
diverse theological understandings that once gave mainline denominations their reason for being, may now be redeveloped so that they
become viable alternatives offered within the local church itself. This
approach recognizes the wisdom in Paul's theology of ministry—not
to be theological chameleons, but to become all things to all persons,
that we might by all means save some (1 Corinthians 9:22). This
requires a positive recognition that "some judge one day to be better
than another, whereas others judge all days alike," for the real task is
no longer that of forced conformity, but an approach which will "let
all be fully convinced in their own mind" (Romans 14:5, paraphrase).
The unity to weld together this diversity is the conviction that the
power of the gospel is its ability to engage creatively the yearnings
that render each person unique.[8] Neither baptism nor ordination is
the creation of clones. It means training ministers and priests who
know the Christian terrain so well that through the church's activities can provide tours into the backcountry, knowing firsthand those
powerful vistas which together exhibit the richness of alternative
Christian living.

This approach will demand a significant change within all levels
of the church's life. Pastors must reclaim themselves as theological
creatures. By distinguishing between one's public (or pulpit) theology and the process characterizing one's private theologizing, the
minister must lay self-conscious claim to the theological World in
which she or he does in fact live and move and have one's being.
This, in turn, must bring the difficult foreclosure of one's own theo-

logical World as *the* perspective for shaping worship, constructing homilies, designing educational events, understanding pastoral care and counseling, and providing overall administration. The clearer one becomes about one's own theological foundation, the less threatened one will be by developing the art of variegated ministry. In a new way, ministry must be seen as spiritual formation, in which one does not claim to know *the* answers, but is acquainted with how to render vibrant the live options. Put another way, what is required is not so much learning theological content as it is birthing theological eyes. Awakened and honed, one is able to see the alternative theological Worlds silently evoked by the architecture of the sanctuary, the subtle nuances of liturgical furnishings, the distinction in worship between a call to worship and an invocation, the ambience of the church kitchen, the placement of one's desk in the study, how memories are stored in the furnace room, the smell of the fellowship hall, the favorite pew of each worshiper, and the importance of house visitation as exploring each home as a theological statement.

In learning the multilingual face of theological diversity, the pastor can better understand how certain words and doctrines have such contrasting meaning for different parishioners, why congregations keep diversifying into cliques, and why the minister's yearning for a church characterized by an easy consensus will always come away empty. Yet this functional ecclesiology of the variegated church dare not be seen as a liberal cafeteria of indifferent eclecticism, catering to personal whims. The goal is not only to support persons in discovering and living their contrasting pilgrimages, but also to test them in depth and breadth. The underlying thesis of our study is that spiritual formation must be the prime rationale for the church of the future, luring and forging persons through alternative subcommunities into that quality of commitment which requires wagering one's life.

Our task is to render the present theological diversity visible, acceptable, intentional, and thus creative. This means further exploring the liberal-conservative impasse that is threatening most mainline denominations with division and conflict. The creative option which gives most promise of transcending this impasse is one that not only tolerates theological diversity, but glories in it. This means seeing that the seamless robe of Christ, intended to adorn the church as his body, is in fact gloriously woven as a pattern of many colors. This book is intent on giving local church pastors and lay leaders concrete handles by which to understand their diverse congregation theologically, and then, step by step, to bring it on an exciting journey into being the church of the future. This exciting vision of the variegated church brings with it new and creative ways of doing all the major tasks of ministry—Christian education, preaching, worship, administration, evangelism, and counseling.

CHAPTER TWO

Theological Diversity in Today's Church

The Liberal-Conservative Impasse

Christianity has struggled for its life before. Externally, there has always been conflict with atheism in all its various forms. Internally, disputes have been the church's steady diet through the centuries. But the church's present crisis is of a depth and breadth rarely known before. It emerges from the near-bankruptcy of two contrasting perspectives. Liberalism has produced such a broad relativism of options, and has encouraged such a tolerance for openness, that faith teeters on the edge of theological indifference. The result is a Christianity largely robbed of any uniqueness capable of evoking a deep and positive commitment among the many competing self-interests of contemporary society. In contrast, the conservative sectors within Christianity have been growing, providing a content which demands serious commitment. Yet this content is often drawn so narrowly that it tends to contradict the very gospel it confesses, for its claims tend to be so inflexible that the resulting dogmatism appeals only to a small segment of society.

Yet liberalism is wrapped within a deeper dilemma. For several centuries now, the legitimacy of religion as experience, discipline, and theology has been eroded by the scientific method. Skepticism is deep as to whether persons of faith can possibly know what they claim to know, at least with anything resembling the certainty needed for deep commitment. Meanwhile conservatives are foundering over their own deeper dilemma—that of motivation. The early church, as well as most denominations, had its inception in much the same way as did Methodism. Several persons came to John Wesley, requesting that he help them "flee from the wrath to come." Such a wrenching concern is hardly the preoccupation of most persons in modern society. Thus, whereas hostility toward the church formerly centered in skepticism about its "answers," the crisis today centers in a skepticism concerning even its "questions." Thus the issue: do the questions central to modern life intersect in *any* significant way the answers once called religious? In wholesale fashion, the tenor of modern life is increasingly indifferent to, even bored by, the church's motives, its methods, and its reality. We are in an era in which the cosmos has been thoroughly secularized, depleted even of daily metaphors ripe for religious musings. This desacralization of religion, in turn, has brought us to what is best characterized as a post-Christian world. William Hamilton dated the emergence of the "death of God" movement with the day he was a guest panelist on a television show. As theologian, he found that he had nothing to add to what experts in psychology, sociology, and economics had already offered. Bereft of uniqueness, Christian theology would seem to be an endangered species, or well on its way to death by slow reduction.

There are no longer absolutes of any kind—in philosophy, politics, or at the local cafe. Garrison Keillor, spokesperson for the hometown values of mid-America, was forced to confess this in a recent Fourth of July eulogy, calling what our founding fathers wrote as being propaganda, even though it was written "so well that it became our shining ideal." And although that ideal can be polished to a sparkle, after the fireworks are over, Keillor goes with several friends to lie in a field. With only a slight concern for snakes, they stare up at "The South Wall of the Unimaginable Everything." Then "our most profound comments sounded like peas dropped in a big empty bucket," as we realized deeply that "America was a tiny speck of a country, a nickel tossed into the Grand Canyon, and American culture the amount of the Pacific Ocean you bring home in your swimsuit. The president wasn't the president out there [in the sky beyond our clotheslines], the Constitution was only a paper, and what newspapers wrote about was sawdust and coffee grounds."[1] Sentimentality? Or humility? This is closer to an uncomfortable secularism, where when all absolutes are gone, one still yearns to give away one's life to something. Ironic though it might seem, it is somewhere near such a star-spangled field that theology might have its rebirth. Likewise, the church can claim its reason for being among those who ponder, for radical diversity spawns the search for community, for a dependable belonging, without which the pilgrimage for inner integrity is impossible or too costly. [2]

Yet this phenomenon, instead of being received by the church as a unique invitation for creative engagement, shows itself to the world as being wrenched asunder by internal quarreling. The issue around which these battle lines are being drawn is diversity—the code word for which is "pluralism." As we have already alluded, liberals are pained by what they perceive as the inflexibility of conservative dogmatism, for "the sabbath was made for humankind, and not humankind for the sabbath" (Mark 2:27 NRSV). Conservatives, on the other hand, are incensed by a liberal tolerance that savors of indifferentism, "because you are lukewarm, and neither cold nor hot, I am about to spit you out of my mouth" (Revelation 3:16 NRSV). Liberalism, although theologically open, appears incapable of evoking the passion of profound conviction. Conservatism, although capable of forcing deep commitment, does so at the price of a content so parochial, and a defense so divisive, as to seem derelict of compassion.

Consequently, the portrait of the church that casts its shadow dimly upon society is that of competing factions, composed of institutions that are becoming polarized, paralyzed, and neutralized. A church torn, drifts within a society fractured by its own competitive relativisms. Underlying the church's fighting over diversity, are hidden two desperately needed perspectives, but so formulated as to be made incompatible. What is needed, and neither side seems able to provide it, is passionate conviction within a Christianity authentically variegated. Is it possible to discern a theological diversity within Christianity so that viable alternative Worlds can be exhibited? Such Worlds would lay claim in their own way to persons who are quite diverse, rendered so by their unique autobiographies within a particularized sociocultural context.

Such an effort would have as its goal a transforming faith that is without inflexible content, and a diversity of content without the indifference bred of relativism. Yet this is impossible in terms of the way in which the present impasse is defined. It would require impossible combinations by which to confirm the openness of the liberal and the commitment of the conservative. The goal could only be expressed paradoxically, as "open conviction," "formed passion," "disciplined freedom"—brought within hailing distance by the emergence of "spiritual liberals," and "evangelical pluralists."

In his monumental work on the church done over half a century ago, Ernst Troeltsch identified the beginnings of the crisis which is full-blown today.[3] As answer, he identified a typology for the alternative expressions of Christianity operative throughout its history. These are the church (inclusive), the sect (exclusive), and mysticism (individual). He concluded that the church-type was best able to avoid the growing crisis, for it differentiates between grace and human effort so as "to include the most varied degrees of Christian attainment and maturity." This, he surmised, could create a better impact on the general population by involving a great variety in its membership. He recognized that such a solution necessitated a principle of far-reaching adjustment and compromise. This principle could be called diversity. He saw that the days of a church-type based on compulsion and dogmas were numbered, as was the sectarian alternative, which was inclined to establish unity and cohesion by rigid conformity. His hope was that the church-type could be so developed that it could provide "homes within which Christians of very varying outlook can live and work together in peace."[4] Such an approach would have to assume "an historical substance of life which is common to all [Christians]," while capable of being "expressed, partly in one group and partly in another, which would preserve the whole from stagnation."[5]

But the liberalism of which Troeltsch was a part has failed to create the variegated church for which Troeltsch had hoped. The result has been not a creative tension of deep commitment within a community of diversity, but a conflict of antagonists in deep polarization. Jürgen Moltmann has identified this same crisis as the polarization of relevance and identity. He too calls for a third way, one emerging between "absolutist theocracy and unproductive tolerance."[6]

United Methodism: Case Study of the Dilemma

Before developing such a model for the church, we need to make concrete this crisis infecting the present day churches. Jerry L. Walls, representative of the conservative perspective within United Methodism, identifies the dilemma as diversity, confusing "what the church believes" so that we are on the edge of losing all identity.[7] His working assumption is that there is a content recognizably Christian, one capable of being the norm for the church's identity.

This is given to us in "classical creedal affirmations . . . as traditionally understood." [8] These essential doctrines and beliefs (e.g., the Triune God and the deity of Christ) profoundly limit theological diversity. [9] Thus his judgment falls heavily upon liberals as incapable of maintaining the identity and continuity of the Christian message. [10] When "factual discourse about direct divine action" is abandoned, "the Christian tradition as it is generally known" is destroyed. [11] Christianity's truth claims are basic, normative, and nonnegotiable, for scripture is "theologically normative" and "historically reliable." [12] Tradition, experience, and reason function simply to interpret and confirm scripture. [13]

Fifteen years ago Dean Kelley's empirical study concluded that decline within liberal churches is due to a lack of strictness in matters of faith and belief, resulting in a lukewarm relativism that loses members. [14] Walls's conclusion is that "toleration of diversity itself needs to be justified theologically if it is able to claim any kind of integrity." [15] He is convinced that this cannot be done. Our present book is an effort to show how it can and must be done, acknowledging all the while that if one stays within the parameters of the present liberal-conservative standoff, there is no escaping Walls's conclusion. The polarization that is resulting has the danger of dogmatism and inflexibility at one pole, tolerance and indifferentism at the other. [16] The conservative choice is clear: indifferentism is a much greater threat in the church today than dogmatism. Yet whereas this conservative retreat is to scripture as the final revelation, biblical scholars make it clear that scripture itself is the product of theological diversity.

Bishop Richard Wilke's response to this dilemma is from within the denominational structure, stressing strategies, insisting that participation in the church's life is necessary before conversion and church membership can occur. Identifying the urban scene as characterized by emptiness, fragmentation, and aloneness, evangelism needs to be a centripetal force, pulling people into *koinonia* groups as arenas of hospitality. Here persons find others who can identify with them. This is useful insofar as it goes, but Wilke provides little content for the gospel that he insists must be made available to "heal a lost and hurting world." And he is just as vague in describing what happens after people enter these small groups. While good news can be given in the times of pain and transition, as moments when people reach for God, he gives a homogeneity to his small groups by forming them according to similar experience of age and marital status—not the similarity of theological pilgrimage. [17]

Professor Douglas Meeks, cochair of the recent world meeting of the Oxford Institute, spoke for far more than United Methodists when he said that the three primary starting points, which Wesley held together, have been torn apart, giving rise to the present division of tradition, personal conversion, and the experience of the poor. [18]

The Cleavage as Widespread

This dilemma is parabolic of the situation throughout mainline churches. Speaking from within the United Church of Christ, W. Widick Schroeder identifies their crisis as "the quest for denominational identity and the limits of pluralism." [19] His concern is how a denomination can regain distinctiveness sufficient to evoke cohesive loyalty, when what one finds instead is diversity influencing everything. This impasse is pitting the liberal stress on method/process against the conservative emphasis on the content of faith. Bewildered by this wilderness of diversity, clergy, laity, and theologians alike are tempted to call for statements of faith. But this only exacerbates the dilemma, for the UCC church cannot provide these and still be faithful to itself.

A similar situation appears in Reformed circles. Anthony Robinson laments that in reading church self-profiles of clergy persons the most frequent response to questions of "theological stance" are "open" and "diverse." He suspects that such words mask the church's "inability to articulate the faith, too little sense of ownership of the faith, and a difficulty in relating Christian faith to life." He finds missing all traditional theological terminology such as grace, sin, mercy, and judgment. [20] Most responses, he concludes, are "corrupt openness" as variations on the theme of contentless diversity.

Meanwhile such fundamentalists as John MacArthur confess the scandal of a divided church, but at the same time insist that there can be no "sacrifice of the truth or a compromise of the faith or a departure from righteousness." [21] Edward Dobson likewise identifies the church's crisis today as "unity and diversity," but he too remains clear that the only acceptable basis for unity is the defeat of diversity by "correct doctrine." [22] Even in Mennonite circles, this same dilemma appears. Rodney Sawatsky describes it as the need to hold together informed critique with commitment.[23] He identifies diversity as the primary issue, leading to a championing of secularization. Religious pluralism fosters religious relativism, which is a victory of individualism.[24] For him, the dilemma is clear, but not the answer. Christianity is forced to be defined "within pluralism and over against pluralism."[25]

This dilemma polarizing mainline churches is not escaped by self-claimed conservative churches either. Even when they agree on the priority of scripture, what is being discovered is that scripture is no defense against diversity—unless one particular literal interpretation of scripture is made mandatory. Thus the momentum of the intra-conservative battle is moving inevitably toward total scriptural inerrancy. Once any part of scripture is questioned, they hold, the whole is in jeopardy. Diversity is the name for the inevitable path, once this first step is taken. Even within the Southern Baptist Convention, a denomination traditionally rooted in independence and dissent, the polarization is increasingly deep and bitter. As one participant put it, the "tension between those who knew the truth and those of us still searching for it has now escalated into open warfare."[26]

This struggle has become so widespread that evangelical executives within eight mainline denominations have recently been drawn together by their common struggle. They have issued a declaration to all the churches as the only solution to membership loss. They see the present polarization as a call to arms. The task of the church is to spread the good news of salvation by word and deed to a lost and despairing humanity. It is not the self-development of persons or the political liberation of oppressed peoples. The impasse is clear.

Threshold of a New Perspective

If such cleavages continue unresolved, either of the two most likely possibilities will be tragic. On the one hand is external schism; on the other is the internal divisiveness of an increasingly disloyal minority. Yet what else can be done in the face of the growing frustration, with a sense of impotence on both sides inciting bitterness?

Carl Lindquist's response provides a first step. He declares that finding something to replace our disintegrating liberalism must begin with a frank and honest acknowledgment: that in reality the church is one of broad diversity, representing a pluralism of theological perspectives. Far from being a dirty word, diversity is an enduring fact within the Body of Christ. [27] The church's major task follows: to search for a postliberal theological foundation for diversity. F. Gerald Downing suggests what could be a second step. The church's "biggest heresy," he insists, is that while acknowledging individual differences, it still tries to "say the same things and do the same things in the same ways for everyone." [28] By taking seriously the diversity of conceptual, educational, cognitive, personal, cultural, and maturational factors, we must develop diverse methods and perspectives within the Christian faith. Diversity requires that "theology needs to be done in ways that start where we are, and so affirm what we are and who we are, [enabling] our movement on to what and who we are to be." [29]

This idea of a variegated church would have two strengths. On the one hand, it would allow non-Christians to experience Christianity by participating in viable alternatives, each one of which could offer growth and conversion. On the other hand, it could bring the excitement of greater depth, growth, and mission to those already in the church, many of whom are bored and untouched because of the present single approach to Christianity. Evangelism and church renewal will happen together, or not at all.

Statistics support such a direction. Forty years ago only several hundred congregations averaged more than seven hundred persons in attendance. Today there are more than five thousand such congregations. Furthermore, there are a disproportionate number of members born before 1930 in smaller congregations, whereas those born after 1940 are mostly found in larger ones. [30] Even on the grounds of expedience, the situation is ripe for authentic theological diversity. Whereas this calls for the restructuring of large congregations, this experimentation entails important attitudinal and programmatic implications for smaller churches as well.

A Cultural Point of Contact

Daniel Yankelovich, a pollster of American trends and values, perceives that in contrast to the previous consumptive values of our society, he detects a growing desire for commitment within a tolerance for diversity and pluralism. [31] His warning is, in truth, an invitation to the church. Unless we can discover an alternative to non-committed pluralism, he insists, our society will become increasingly fragmented and anomic, the family a shambles, the work ethic collapsed, the economy uncompetitive, our morality flabby and self-centered, with even less personal freedom than we have had under the old order. This explains in large part the attractiveness of the fast-growing conservative churches. They promise an alternative order to a world experienced as complicated and chaotic. Half of their members are converts, increasingly professional people. These persons find in scripture, interpreted by clear authority, a distinguishable alternative to the worldliness and greed experienced daily. What claims their commitment is not really content, in spite of what conservatives declare. The appeal is the process of a face-to-face community sufficiently strong to resist the authority of the bureaucratic structures in and around which they experience their lives as arbitrarily defined. [32]

Even among persons usually regarded as unchurchable, there is increasing evidence that life is proving to be less than they had hoped. This is especially true for those who reach a threshold in age or career where it is irrefutable that one only goes around once. In the time left, there is a growing desire to make a contribution, or to become different, or to belong where one can be accepted, down deep, for who one is. What is silently sought is an alternative World worth gambling one's life upon. [33] Although what is needed is becoming increasingly clear, the conservative single option is too contracted for the majority of searchers.

Toward an Internal Ecumenism

Every denomination, at its inception, made claim to be a (or *the*) faithful expression of the gospel. Today this basis has eroded into a theological minimalism. A Calvinist would today be regarded as odd in most Presbyterian churches; and quotes from the Mercerburg theologians would strike most United Church of Christ members with the charm belonging to one's parents' county newspaper, a month late. Rather, denominational differences mostly result from polity, class, geography, charisma, and convenience. Whereas rival theologies once pitted Calvinists against Wesleyans, and both against

Baptists, such conflict is anachronistic, with opposition largely
reduced to a competition for members.

Against past ecumenical efforts that had as the goal a unity based
on a least common denominator, or on racial or class homogeneity
J. Robert Nelson insists that the church must be fundamentally
different from all such grouping. Our sisters and brothers in Christ
are given to us rather than chosen, just as it is in one's biological
family.[34] Against an ecumenism of reductive and repressive homogeneity, we are proposing an *internal ecumenism*. The needs which
once gave rise to *separate* denominations must now be given free
play *within* the structures of each denomination as a whole, and as
the formative dynamic of each congregation. This can lead to a variegation that is theologically diverse, and at the same time profoundly
committed.

In one sense, such an ecumenism has already begun, unofficially.
In taking social justice stands on hard issues, one's faith companions
are almost always cross-denominational. Thus, for example, a task
force opposing United States involvement in Central America is likely to be ecumenical, while the pro-life pickets down the street represent an intriguing spectrum, from Roman Catholics to Southern
Baptists. In another sense, these issues and others, such as capital
punishment or the lottery, are divisive in any existing denomination.
Such informal ecumenism illustrates that genuine commitment and
theological diversity can intersect in promising fashion. Our task,
then, is to glory in this emerging phenomenon, and attempt to
ground it theologically as the threshold of a postliberal church within each local church and denomination.

The New Testament scholar Oscar Cullmann provides a biblical
grounding for the variegated church, "The Holy Spirit creates unity
not only in spite of diversity, but precisely *through* it."[35] The full
measure of the Holy Spirit's workings is evidenced in the emergence
of that kind of plurality characteristic of the human body, "Whoever
does not respect this richness and wants uniformity instead, sins
against the Holy Spirit." Cullmann's own proposal is a community
of churches crossing denominational lines, for it is a false ecumenism
to consider the different confessions as examples of human bungling.
His model for theological diversity suggests the historic pattern of
alternative monastic orders within the unity of the Roman Catholic
Church. The real sin, he insists, is transforming this richness of the
church's diversity into hostile, fighting church groups.[36] Although

this idea of a community of churches has important cross-denominational possibilities, what is more deeply needed, and on which
our attention will focus, is a correlative model—the church of communities.

Moltmann, too, suggests a viable theological grounding for our
work. Since "a being is revealed only in its opposite, then the church
which is the church of the crucified Christ cannot consist of an
assembly of like persons who mutually affirm each other, but must
be constituted of unlike persons." [37] The power for this church of the
future, then, will not reside in friendship, based on love for the similar *(philia)*. It will be a creative love for what is different, and thus for
what often appears to be alien and ugly *(agape)*. This requires our
serious consideration of a church in which communal support is in
tension with hard diversity.

As we proceed, we will do well to bear in mind the image of
today's church as a threadbare hammock, stretched precariously
between two dated options. One is the liberal openness to a broad
diversity, but so tolerant that the passion for faithful commitment is
dissipated in competitive convenience. The other is a conservative
perspective demanding deep commitment, but so formed by a nar-
rowness of interpretation that the passion can be as judgmental as it
is idolatrously closed. The need is for a variegated church, so characterized by genuine theological diversity that it can offer powerful
alternatives—sufficient to render deep a forced option. This is the
meaning of "worlds within a congregation."

CHAPTER THREE

The Variegated Church:
A Model for Models

Christianity as Diverse

There is no such thing as *the* Christian faith, in the sense of anything resembling a common, agreed upon substance of belief, held as a uniform center by those calling themselves Christian. Currently there are more than two hundred fifty recognized denominations, which together weave the tapestry called American Christianity. Vatican II has brought the surprising awareness that Roman Catholicism is also anything but monolithic. Rather it functions as a liturgical umbrella for a diversity spanning the spectrum from the archconservative Sister Angela to the radical social witness of the Berrigan brothers, from inner-city Catholic worker houses to desert hermits. As for Catholic orders, to put a Jesuit and a Trappist in the same room is to enact hostility once thought possible only within Protestantism. Even in the supposedly monolithic periods of church history, alternative religious orders kept lively witness to Christianity as a composite of alternative contrasts in both belief and practice. The church's history cannot even support the image of a tree with one main trunk, with increasingly varied branches. Far more accurate is the image of creative grafting, cross-fertilization, and natural selection within a dense and spreading grove.

This should not come as a surprise, for our earliest descriptions of the church evidence a rivalry of evangelists, congregations, cultural contexts, and personalities. In fact, Christian diversity is amply evidenced in the four Gospels themselves, Gospels which are theological composites from earlier diverse sources. The conclusion that must be drawn is this: *There has never been either a unified Christian church, or a common Christian theological position, in the light of which diversity can be faulted.* What is new in our era, then, is not the fact of diversity, but the call of the church *to celebrate this diversity in a gesture of rare and expectant honesty.*

The Present Theological Situation

This approach to diversity is strongly supported by the contemporary theological scene. We are passing over a threshold in which significant truth can no longer lay claim to total objectivity. Objectivity at best is subjectivity identified. Truth claims must be seen as existential wagers in the face of viable alternatives. All around us, individual and collective subjectivities are competing to define us. Persons in the same theater never watch the same motion picture. Multiple Worlds of meaning, resulting from contrasting but workable perspectives, define the nature of the situation in which all of us out of necessity live—and must, from now on. Yet one cannot be neutral or uninvolved. There is no option but to live out of some orienting point of view. And whatever else truth may mean, at ground level it designates the degree to which a person is conscious of one's orientation, and the consistency with which that orientation is lived out, as a World. The result is that faith becomes the most basic characteristic of the human person, wagered in the face of life's unavoidable question: *Why?* The truth of one's faith-perspective as a Christian is its livability, tested in the midst of a supportive and accountable community. Here one can discern how deeply and broadly the resulting theological World allows, encourages, and enables one to accept one's self and others as being who they are.[1] The primordial task of being human, then, is to forge and be forged by a World of meaning sufficient to warrant the gambling of one's life. Such orientation is not optional, only the degree to which it functions consciously. This World is birthed autobiographically, as each person endeavors to domesticate the chaos. The fact that this shaping begins months before birth, and is significantly in place before one takes much thought, is the meaning of "original sin." It stands for the degree to which one's metaphorical base is largely imposed, by the individual's umbilical attachment, and the prescribed space and cultural time in which birth becomes an occurrence.

Truth, then, is relational, as a variation of this confession: "Once I was blind, and now I see." This makes the theological process functional, with God the generic name for that which so functions in one's life that it is better to live than to die. The variegated church finds its calling within this process. By relinquishing the temptation to believe that one has *the* truth, or that there even *is* one truth, one is opened to theological diversity as a joyously divine gift. Life is gloriously covenantal, relational, and incarnational, as rich intersections of personal and communal diversity.

The norm for such variegation is the multiform Christ event, appearing mysteriously as a composite confession of multiple and converging metaphors, evoking in a variety of ways the power to heal the uncommonly diverse wounds of the world. Take, for example, the key event called resurrection. It is fact in the sense that it expresses the new and diverse lives of those transformed by the Christ event. Scripture is central because it is a magnificent source book, describing the favorite, yet contrasting, vistas whereby its writers and editors invite us to stand in order to see. Commitment comes in identifying which perspective or World is rendering one whole. The event called Pentecost says it well. The Spirit is experienced when one is enabled to witness "in our own tongues the mighty works of God" (Acts 2:11).

The tragedy of the church's history is that very often these contrasting vistas no longer become invitations, but instead, each becomes a lone option of a single denomination or movement. What is needed today is a distillation of these major vistas into viable alternative space-time Worlds. This can happen through dialogue with diverse cultural situations, serving as a base for the church as variegated. This means shifting from the present unproductive competition of denominations *against each other*, to the competitive claim of theological Worlds *within each congregation*. The variegated church might be molded as subcongregations of alternative celebration and practice, intent on forced choice and disciplined faithfulness. Congregational unity will be built upon respect for the commitment of those with whom one is committed to disagree, because of the One to whom each is attempting to be faithful. This approach renders as its goal the church as a richly inclusive environment, evoking pride in one's conviction, while fostering eargerness to share in the diversity.

Theological Worlds

Whereas in one sense there are as many theological Worlds as there are individuals, in everyday life they overlap in different configurations. The variegated church we will be prescribing results from discerning the nuclei of greatest density, identifying these as the major alternatives in the Christian faith. The church is indispensable, for our longings for meaning are inseparable from our need to belong. Without a primal community, loneliness so eats at one's life-gamble that the burden of doubt becomes unbearable. Functionally, the church is where one is nurtured by sharing one another's joys and sorrows, and where one is held accountable by hearing and speaking the truth in love. For such trust to emerge, it is necessary that each subcommunity have a defining perspective at the point where theological Worlds overlap. Research indicates, as we shall further see, that these overlapping theological Worlds tend to cluster in five composite, alternative Worlds. All five are viable, with none more faithful, more preferable, or more mature—except to each person.

A significant problem arises precisely at this point. One's functional theological World is most often unconscious, unrecognized, and therefore basically unknown. Thus a fundamental task for the church is to help each person discern and render self-conscious the World in which he or she is *already* living, for better or worse. Such recognition is best done through action-reflection. Through spiritual direction one's World is detected through its observable fruits, and the variegated church incarnates each distinct World in its alternative worship and activities, so that in participation a deep resonance can indicate that which is "home."

Bishop Rueben Job insists that God has chosen to be revealed in community. Thus, "every local congregation should be this community or made up of many of these smaller communities." [2] He laments that there are so few such groups. Actually, I am amazed that so many of them exist. I am still mystified by how members of such groups find each other, for their members usually stand under the same horizon of meaning. No doubt there are factors such as age, gender, marriage, singleness, and vocational type—but the kind of bonding which is being sought goes deeper. Unfortunately, the basic attraction today is the result of a modern society in which there is increasingly less "normal" time and opportunity for folks to meet, discern common patterns, and magnetize into distinct Worlds of meaning that can evoke lasting commitment. The lack of intentionality about this process is what makes the responsibility of the church so urgent. What is needed is a process in place whereby individuals, who are largely deprived of arenas in which to meet in any deep manner, are exposed to each other around the search for meaning. It is no surprise, then, that baby boomers (born 1946–64) are church shoppers, attracted by larger churches where alternative meaning-communities are already beginning to emerge and invite choice. [3]

Variegation as Need, Fact, and Motivation

Although the variegated congregation as a self-conscious creation is relatively new, it can draw upon the congregational diversity which already exists. I can now recognize it in the local church of my youth. Architecturally, it was an Akron plan layout, which cut the building diagonally into two distinct arenas. The Sunday school met in one of two large semicircular spaces, rimmed with class alcoves closed off with curtains. The "pastor" of this church was the Sunday school superintendent. He conducted opening exercises, with most of the elements being the same as the order of worship for the other church—hymns, prayer, offering, scripture, and sermon. When dismissed, this alternative church broke into a number of different classes, each one different, depending on the teacher and the composite of members. A bell brought us back together for a closing hymn and benediction. After this, we were expected to go into the other semicircle, called the sanctuary, where the paid pastor brought his own orientation to bear as norm for everyone. These two actually functioned as alternative Worlds, and whereas the loyal persons went to both, each appealed to a contrasting clientele.

As I look back now, the whole church was a composite of theological Worlds. There were the older persons who hung onto the dwindling Sunday evening service; they overlapped in part with the Wednesday evening prayer meeting folks. In addition, there was the Thursday morning conservative World for women as "prayer partners in healing." They, in turn, were quite suspicious of the Tuesday morning women's study groups that focused on social justice issues such as world hunger and the plight of the homeless. Meanwhile, youth groups continued to divide and reassemble, usually in terms of the sponsors at any particular time. The most contrasting groups were those favoring altar calls and abstinence pledges, and the skating party and car wash type. At first glance, the Friday night Boy Scouts appeared more united. Yet even here, after being kept awake all night by the trivia of the Beaver Patrol, I knew after the next camporee that the Eagle Patrol was where I belonged. And after borrowing several pots from the church kitchen, we quickly learned the unifying hegemony of the kitchen women. In my mother's Sunday school class, the lesson was a gentle sharing of their lives as parents. My father's class was a Bible lecture, complete with chalkboard. The singles class met at the local restaurant. And the Excelsiors, the Gideons, and the Fishers met side by side, but each was a World unto itself. I can understand better now the mutiny that occurred when an unsuspecting new pastor suggested a rearrangement of meeting rooms. These were Worlds not lightly tampered with. And as a young adult I was introduced to the strange World over which the trustees possessively presided. Indicatively, not only were the church and Sunday school budgets and income distinct, but each class had its own treasurer, as did the memorial fund, the women's society, and the men's fellowship. Variegation is not new. What *is* new is the need to render it *intentional*.

This variegation has become more pronounced in the contemporary church. Paying attention mostly to numbers, church leaders are discovering that it is less expensive to have multiple services than to build larger buildings. But with multiple services, an interesting dynamic is emerging. A growing number of congregations schedule two different worship services every Sunday morning with two different sets of hymns and two different orders or formats for worship—in some cases with different preachers. Most often the adult chancel choir appears at the eleven o'clock hour, and the youth choir at the earlier service. This difference alone leads inevitably to significantly contrasting ambiences.

Roman Catholic parishes have had a long history of multiple Sunday masses, more recently adding Saturday evening. While multiple clergy formerly lent a distinct flavor to each of the masses, the present clergy shortage has forced a lone priest to provide all of what he regards as being identical masses. As I pressed priests in a number of interviews, it became clear to me, and a surprise to them, that whereas the homily had the same theme at all of the masses, it was adapted to each mass because of those who habitually come to particular services. Illustrations, humor, tone, volume, intensity of delivery—all of these were significantly modified without the priests being very conscious of doing so.

Time after time I heard the same basic story. The parochial school youth choir service means an earlier Sunday mass oriented toward young families—using the "Glory and Praise" hymnal, a folk mass complete with guitars—where birthdays are reason enough for singing. And people like to sit together. At the still earlier Sunday morning mass, however, priests often give up trying to introduce congregational singing. These members are more traditional but ranging in age. They thrive on more silence and solitude, trusting an unspoken promise that this mass will not require corporate participation of any kind. Instead, many of them say the rosary during the mass, for their World is one of personal relationship with God, thriving on such staples as candles, incense, and quiet Gregorian chant. "Passing the peace" in the family service takes the risk of not being able to get the hugs stopped. At the early mass, however, worshipers need their space—making that clear with their bodies scattered all over the sanctuary—so in time, the passing of the peace has been wisely omitted. The Saturday evening mass, by contrast to both of these other masses, tends toward doing—often sandwiched between a fellowship dinner and an evening of young adult activities. The last Sunday mass is for the more sacramentally minded, those who thrive on hearing and smelling and seeing. These tend to be the movers and shakers, those who are usually community minded. It is where the fiftieth anniversary resaying of the vows are said, and Mother's Day and Memorial Day dare never to be neglected. They dress properly, whereas Saturday night is casual. Sometimes there is even a mass at noon, which is for the remnant, those who did not make it before, probably because they do not seem to belong anywhere.

This same dynamic of variegation emerged in interviewing Catholic staffs. I asked what determined their choice as to who would do which masses. "I suspect it is a matter of where each of us feels most at home." This was a phrase that recurred in almost all interviews. A conclusion that a number of priests drew, to their surprise, was the degree to which these masses had evolved, largely on their own, into significant alternatives. At the beginning of our conversations most priests had thought that the difference between masses was largely a matter of age, "Guess that isn't it; all the masses are of mixed ages. Must be something else."

The phenomenon I kept experiencing was of unconsciously variegated subcongregations, which had distilled for both parishioners and priests into latent theological Worlds. I asked one staff person if he experienced masses as different theologically. "If you had begun with that question, I would have said 'I certainly hope not.' But I suspect now that they are. The seven o'clock and nine o'clock masses are probably variations of pre-Vatican II theology." Another priest drew this conclusion: "Clearly if we moved the guitar mass to a different time, the people who come would just move to the new time. I always thought that attendance at different masses was a matter of convenience—it has become far more than that now." My conclusion was that in almost all of these interviews, diversity tended to be a phenomenon that "just kind of happened, so that we're unclear what it all means." Several priests promised to plan their masses self-consciously as intentional and genuine alternatives. But a basic question remained—*what* authentic alternatives are there?

Research among mainline Protestant churches disclosed a similar emergence, with a surprising number of smaller churches experimenting with Saturday evening services. Although the rationale given was one of convenience, some acknowledged that they were responding to experiences in Cursillo, modeling the extra service around folk singing, lay participation, and often the Eucharist. "The folks even dress differently." One minister said of her two services that whereas she tried to make both services the same, "it wasn't long before the two services took on a theological life of their own. I tried to make both services the same, but even my preaching came out differently. You could just feel the different expectations, so that the reactions of each congregation were characteristically different." Another pastor contrasted his multiple services this way. "In one service I learned quickly that the folks want me to speak with authority, behind the pulpit with the huge Bible between me and them. In the other, it only feels right if my preaching is a sharing, standing right down there with them. They asked for a choir—a small one."

In contrast to the assumption of most church leadership, it is increasingly clear that most congregations have multiple personalities. Most pastors see this as an unhealthy schizophrenia, requiring a firm leadership style that enforces a working unity. But the same question kept arising: what if these pastors became committed to identifying theologically these existing audiences, building upon this diversity?

After discussing with pastors their experience with variegation, most of them had one question. As one pastor put it, "Multiple services do feed the different needs of people. But how are we able to discern what folks *really* need, when they have had so little experience in truly knowing themselves? They know better what they don't like, but that is not enough." It was from this quandary that the Theological Worlds Inventory (TWI) had its inception. It has since been tested widely as an aid in almost every dimension of the church's life—dimensions we will explore in the following chapters.

Chapter 4 is, itself, the Theological Worlds Inventory. It is designed so that it can be photocopied and used as a self-contained unit. As an instrument for theological self-discovery, it is designed for use at six levels:

1. To discover one's own theological stance
2. As an aid for the reader to participate personally in the meaning of theological variegation
3. As an instrument for the pastor to use in working with individuals, such as in counseling and spiritual direction
4. As a tool for discerning the theological complexion and creating a profile of one's congregation
5. As an instrument for developing a new approach to such ministerial tasks as preaching, worship, confirmation classes, teacher training, evangelism preparation, administration, and new member incorporation
6. As an inventory for reorganizing one's church as a variegated congregation

Even if reforming the church is of little interest to the reader, or even less, an openness for significant change in one's ministerial styles, still all is not lost. The inventory will be an enjoyable way of walking into alternative Worlds—seeing how the newspaper reads from someone else's overstuffed chair by the west window, or peering out their backdoor at the horizon, just beyond the garbage can. You might even realize, as you drive someday to your house, why you call it "home," and why, in fact, your neighbor with the push mower seems so strange.

CHAPTER FOUR

The Theological Worlds Inventory: Discovering One's Self and One's Congregation

I. INTRODUCTION: THE MEANING OF A THEOLOGICAL WORLD

Because we alone of all creatures can ask "Why?" we are unique. But because our answers are often unclear, we never know with certainty who we are or what we are to do. This is what makes life a struggle for meaning. Whether we recognize it or not, then, we are functional theologians, beginning months before our birth.

Rather than reflecting a perspective decided in advance, most often our answers are working assumptions carved out unconsciously through the process of living. Thus the World that results as home is often unknown to the self. There are as many Worlds as there are persons. Yet these individual Worlds overlap, forming communities—latent and manifest. Those with whom we share a World are those whom we can understand almost intuitively, able even to finish their sentences for them. There are other persons, however, with whom we live Worlds apart. These are not only the ones we have difficulty understanding, but with whom it is difficult to find a point of contact. My research has identified five such Worlds, serving as a typology of pure possibilities.

A World results from the interaction between two poles. The first is one's *obsessio*, that lived question, need, ache, or dilemma, which has its teeth into us at the deepest level. Other concerns are variations on that basic theme, standing in line behind its importance. The second pole is one's *epiphania*, that which through one or more events, moments, and/or persons brings sufficient illumination, satisfaction, or healing to provide a lived answer worth wagering one's life upon. One's *epiphania* is what touches promisingly one's *obsessio,* either as fact or as hope.

The dynamic establishing one's World, then, is this ongoing inter-action of *obsessio* and *epiphania.* One's disposition is determined by whether this dynamic is seen more from the perspective of one's *obsessio,* or if the *epiphania* is the more weighted pole. Whichever, each knows itself only in relation to the other.

Christianity does not create yet another World. Rather, those who affirm Jesus of Nazareth as *epiphania* for their World do so because of the healing pattern of meaning resulting from its unique engagement with one's concrete *obsessio.* Thus there are as many Christian Worlds as there are Christians. But they also converge in communities, resulting in five Christian variations on the themes of the universal theological Worlds.

One's theological World, then, tends to be unconscious, unknown, and/or unrecognized. Therefore, theological growth begins with first discerning the World in which one is living. This *Theological Worlds Inventory* is designed to assist in that task. As a vehicle for articulating one's theology self-consciously, it can lead one to explore what it means to live more faithfully within one's World, help sense if one's World is stifling and in need of abandonment for another one, and help one enter into dialogue with members of other theo-logical Worlds.

II. THE THEOLOGICAL WORLDS INVENTORY

Instructions

For *each* of the following questions, choose the answer which fits you best and put a "3" next to that answer. For the same question, choose the answer that is second best for you and put a "2" next to that answer. Then choose the answer that fits third best and put a "1" next to that answer. Respond honestly to as many as you can. If a question, or its options, makes no sense to you, omit it. There are no right or wrong answers as such. An answer is "correct" if it reflects your *own* feelings. It is "wrong" if it reflects either what you *think* you should prefer, or what you *guess* may lead to a particular out-come for the Inventory. In answering, let your mind roam quickly over your life experiences. Remember your own joys and struggles, as early as you can. Let your answer characterize the "feel" of life for you over the "long haul."

1. My uneasiness increases when I feel:
_____ a. out of control
_____ b. tempted
_____ c. disconnected
_____ d. exhausted
_____ e. empty, rootless

2. Life for me is a:
_____ a. mysterious pilgrimage
_____ b. basic right
_____ c. courageous act
_____ d. new gift
_____ e. quest for self-fulfillment

3. My spiritual life is best characterized as:
_____ a. requesting forgiveness with empty hands
_____ b. meditating on ideals for my life
_____ c. praying for others
_____ d. contemplating, centering, uniting with
_____ e. ascetic, strength for the dark night

4. A scripture passage with which I can identify is:
_____ a. "We can rejoice in our sufferings, knowing that suffering produces endurance."
_____ b. "For God so loved the world that He gave His only begotten Son."
_____ c. "Thou hast made us but a little lower than the angels."
_____ d. "The wolf shall dwell with the lamb, and a little child shall lead them."
_____ e. "I have uttered what I did not understand, things too wonderful for me, which I did not know."

5. I tend to view death as:
_____ a. a reality to be faced steadfastly
_____ b. deserved and rightful
_____ c. a foe to be resisted
_____ d. opening to another world
_____ e. part of life's rhythm

6. The human condition is most characterized by:
_____ a. alienation

_____ b. pain
_____ c. personal guilt
_____ d. injustice
_____ e. invisibility

7. I am renewed when I experience:
_____ a. awe, wonder
_____ b. exoneration, justice
_____ c. fullness, self-worth
_____ d. humility, forgiveness
_____ e. compassion, integrity

8. When things are not going well, I sometimes feel:
_____ a. condemned
_____ b. powerless
_____ c. isolated
_____ d. shut out
_____ e. victimized

9. Who is Jesus?
_____ a. suffering companion
_____ b. disclosure of that which is not recognized
_____ c. a definitive human word about who God is
_____ d. God's definitive word about who we are
_____ e. foretaste of what is promised to be

10. When I experience limitations, I tend to:
_____ a. feel overwhelmed, passive
_____ b. become arrogant, self-serving
_____ c. act judgmentally, sometime violently
_____ d. feel impotent, hollow
_____ e. feel exiled, separated, rejected

11. To improve things, my efforts should focus on changing:
_____ a. structures
_____ b. attitudes
_____ c. beliefs
_____ d. relationships
_____ e. perspectives about the whole

12. That which I find painfully real in life is:

_____ a. conflict

_____ b. disappointment

_____ c. shallowness

_____ d. isolation

_____ e. judgment

13. "Center stage" for making sense out of my existence is:

_____ a. the cosmos

_____ b. the self

_____ c. the demonic

_____ d. history

_____ e. life itself

14. What is most likely to disrupt life?

_____ a. seduction

_____ b. institutions

_____ c. weariness

_____ d. homelessness

_____ e. self-doubt

15. I tend to focus on:

_____ a. elsewhere

_____ b. past

_____ c. future

_____ d. expansive present

_____ e. each day as it comes

16. I have been haunted by a sense of:

_____ a. emptiness, worthlessness

_____ b. longing

_____ c. being at fault

_____ d. being threadbare

_____ e. anger

17. Life is a joy when I feel:

_____ a. vindicated

_____ b. loved

_____ c. at rest

_____ d. harmony/unity
_____ e. cleansed

18. An image for "home" is:
_____ a. tomorrow
_____ b. spring housecleaning
_____ c. a day off
_____ d. a room of my own
_____ e. the ocean

19. In my life I have struggled most with feeling:
_____ a. unimportant, worthless, trivial, undeveloped
_____ b. guilty, sinful, incompetent, wrong
_____ c. separated, homeless, adrift, lonely
_____ d. used, hopeless, fragile, futility
_____ e. competition, injustice, inequality, exploitation

20. What tends to give you hope?
_____ a. changes in this world that will make it better
_____ b. support that encourages me to become who I am
_____ c. experiences that hint of the meaning of the whole
_____ d. trust in God's graciousness
_____ e. divine companionship to see it through together

21. I can best contribute to the Reign of God by:
_____ a. fighting for the oppressed
_____ b. being obedient to God's will
_____ c. standing with the rejected
_____ d. maximizing the potentialities in me and others
_____ e. striving for harmony between nature and humans

22. When I am not at my best, I can feel:
_____ a. trapped
_____ b. wandering
_____ c. driven
_____ d. wrong
_____ e. unfocused

23. The rhythm that best describes conversion for me is from:
_____ a. guilt to pardon

_____ b. suffering to integrity
_____ c. alienation to homecoming
_____ d. nothingness to self-identity
_____ e. oppression to liberation

24. I invest much time in efforts to:
_____ a. discover myself
_____ b. forgive myself
_____ c. realize myself
_____ d. give of myself
_____ e. be true to myself

25. The words best describing the human condition are:
_____ a. wanderer, orphan, stranger
_____ b. victim, wounded, undone
_____ c. self-doubt, impotence, ache
_____ d. duplicity, selfishness, forbidden fruit
_____ e. enslaved, oppressed, violent

26. Freedom means:
_____ a. no hunger or thirst for anyone
_____ b. going home
_____ c. a chance to start over
_____ d. to outlast
_____ e. to lose self-doubt in becoming who I am

27. How does reconciliation with God occur?
_____ a. By entering the world, God conquers the forces opposing us
_____ b. Christ pays the price for our sin
_____ c. In following Jesus, we come to a closer relationship with God
_____ d. There are moments in which the veil is lifted, and we belong
_____ e. God identifies with us as companion through it all

28. Which pair of words best describes the dynamic of living?
_____ a. emptiness/fulfillment
_____ b. suffering/endurance
_____ c. separation/reunion
_____ d. conflict/vindication
_____ e. condemnation/forgiveness

29. In reflecting on my past, I remember times of feeling:

_____ a. invisible

_____ b. tempted

_____ c. engulfed

_____ d. powerless

_____ e. lost

30. Evangelism is effective if someone:

_____ a. is awakened to try

_____ b. encounters the plight of the oppressed

_____ c. finds the courage to persevere

_____ d. senses the priority of being over doing

_____ e. is brought to belief

31. God is the One who:

_____ a. brings into deeper harmony

_____ b. takes sides

_____ c. lures forth possibilities

_____ d. atones for us

_____ e. experiences our needs with us

32. Why do good?

_____ a. to make amends for my actions

_____ b. in response to the kindness and encouragement I have
          received

_____ c. power and energy overflowing from deep within

_____ d. empathy with others

_____ e. to fight injustice

33. I am afraid lest in the end:

_____ a. I might give up

_____ b. There won't be anything more

_____ c. Things will not have been made better

_____ d. I will be unliked/unwanted

_____ e. I will be found wrong

34. I identify with:

_____ a. Israel's forty years braving the desert

_____ b. Sara who was barren

_____ c. Adam and Eve who became homesick for Eden
_____ d. Peter who betrayed
_____ e. Moses who ran away from taking the hard stands

35. A noble purpose for my life would be to:
_____ a. evoke harmony
_____ b. obey God
_____ c. fight the good fight
_____ d. persevere with integrity
_____ e. respect each person as sacred

36. Jesus is best understood as:
_____ a. pioneer, prophet
_____ b. threshold, model
_____ c. companion, sympathizer
_____ d. illuminator, evoker
_____ e. savior, Lord

37. The problem with so many of us is that we don't:
_____ a. risk
_____ b. last
_____ c. care
_____ d. know
_____ e. confess

38. Who is the Christ?
_____ a. redeemer
_____ b. Messiah
_____ c. revealer
_____ d. suffering servant
_____ e. teacher/example

39. One needs to focus on:
_____ a. the long run
_____ b. depth
_____ c. breadth
_____ d. motivation
_____ e. goal

40. As I understand suffering:

_____ a. it can become an instrument in personal discovery

_____ b. it is wrong, to be fought

_____ c. God's ways are not our ways

_____ d. it is part of life

_____ e. it can be a testing or penance

41. Faith is trusting in:

_____ a. the future as promise

_____ b. the unknown

_____ c. a new beginning

_____ d. me

_____ e. the inevitable

42. I could be faulted for expecting:

_____ a. too much

_____ b. to lose

_____ c. to be inadequate

_____ d. to be wrong

_____ e. too little

43. I am drawn by picturing Jesus:

_____ a. alone with God in the mountains in prayer

_____ b. with the woman at the well

_____ c. overcoming temptation in the desert

_____ d. casting out the money changers

_____ e. agonizing in Gethsemane

44. Life entails:

_____ a. guilt to be removed

_____ b. victory to be won

_____ c. mystery to be unveiled

_____ d. duty to be lived

_____ e. fulfillment to be realized

45. Which of these activities would make you feel alive?

_____ a. experiencing reconciliation after a bitter fight

_____ b. helping a homeless family

_____ c. doing a retreat in the mountains
_____ d. having deep meal conversation with a friend
_____ e. being acknowledged by friends at work

46. Redemption for me comes from experiencing Jesus as:
_____ a. nurturer
_____ b. comrade
_____ c. liberator
_____ d. illuminator
_____ e. savior

47. When things get difficult, in order to survive I sometimes:
_____ a. turn secret
_____ b. turn away
_____ c. turn off
_____ d. turn inward
_____ e. go away

48. I live life as if it has about it the feel of:
_____ a. fantasy, mystery
_____ b. tragedy
_____ c. lyric poetry
_____ d. pathos
_____ e. "comedy" (successful resolution)

49. Relationships sometime become strained because of:
_____ a. intensity, heaviness
_____ b. reluctance to venture
_____ c. failure, selfishness
_____ d. factors external to the relation
_____ e. misunderstandings in communication

50. God is the One who:
_____ a. identifies with us
_____ b. forgives us personally
_____ c. promises a new earth
_____ d. draws us into union
_____ e. adopts us as family

51. One must learn how to deal with:

_____ a. one cause at a time

_____ b. one world at a time

_____ c. one day at a time

_____ d. one life at a time

_____ e. one episode at a time

52. A biblical image that appeals to me is:

_____ a. Jesus and the woman accused of adultery

_____ b. Job's patient strength in adversity

_____ c. The Emmaus reunion

_____ d. Exodus to the Promised Land

_____ e. The thief forgiven on the cross

53. I need:

_____ a. approval

_____ b. strength

_____ c. to experience myself as part of a greater Whole

_____ d. to become worthy

_____ e. to have a cause

54. I can identify with the Psalmist who said:

_____ a. "As a hart longs for flowing streams, so longs my soul for thee, O God."

_____ b. "Parent of the parentless and protector of widows, you lead out the prisoners to freedom."

_____ c. "In the shadow of your wings I will take refuge, 'til the storms pass by."

_____ d. "Too heavy for us are our offenses, but you wipe them away."

_____ e. "You have made us little less than a god; with glory and honor you have crowned us."

55. Sin is:

_____ a. a condition that defines us even before we act

_____ b. misdirected good

_____ c. part of life's struggles

_____ d. closing one's eyes to the mystery

_____ e. compromising too soon

56. The ideal Christian is a:
_____ a. martyr
_____ b. saint
_____ c. witness
_____ d. visionary
_____ e. spiritual mentor

57. My experience of sin is:
_____ a. unrealized potential
_____ b. separation
_____ c. indifference
_____ d. perversity
_____ e. weakening

58. The gospel means:
_____ a. remaining faithful to the end
_____ b. denying myself for others
_____ c. giving myself for a cause
_____ d. learning to love myself
_____ e. losing myself in God

59. It is fine to:
_____ a. enjoy
_____ b. try
_____ c. begin again
_____ d. soar
_____ e. win

60. A worthy end for my life would be:
_____ a. to reunite with all of life
_____ b. to change the way things are
_____ c. to endure, with integrity
_____ d. to become a whole person
_____ e. to do good

61. Christian experience centers in:
_____ a. "mystic" oneness
_____ b. focused growth
_____ c. strength to persevere

_____ d. common cause
_____ e. new birth

62. It is important for persons to:
_____ a. get in touch with their feelings
_____ b. keep on keeping on
_____ c. confess their shortcomings
_____ d. risk the unknown
_____ e. get involved

63. A group of words that characterizes Christ's work is:
_____ a. vision, victory, completion
_____ b. justification, reprieve, salvation
_____ c. survival, sojourner, companion
_____ d. unity, homecoming, oneness
_____ e. model, wholeness, freedom to be

III. THE THEOLOGICAL WORLDS DESCRIPTION AND SELF-RATING

Instructions

Before scoring the inventory you have just taken, read the descriptions of the five Theological Worlds below. Then put the number "1" next to the World that best fits your perspective, a "2" next to the one that fits second best, and so on, through all five descriptions. This will give you an opportunity to select a World and give an order of preference for the other Worlds. A comparison of your choices here with your scores (as determined in Section IV) will help indicate your degree of theological self-awareness.

_____ **WORLD ONE: SEPARATION AND REUNION**

For inhabitants of this World, there is often a sense of abandonment. Within this huge cosmos, we feel isolated, small, lonely, a speck in a vast and staggering space. At times we seem to be aliens, or orphans. Life tends to be a quest to understand the mystery of this Whole. Our longing is to find our way home, as it were. We yearn wistfully for a harmony to all things, while being haunted by the sad thought that there may be nothing behind it all. Resolution as the promise of homecoming can begin through experiencing the fact of our existence as itself a gift. In sensing this mystery of being, one can be touched with awe. Such sensitivity often comes in sacramental moments in which we are grasped in oneness with the ground of our being. It is as if a veil is lifted, if only for a moment, and we know that we truly do belong. Such moments serve as center point for the turning wheel, the unchanging in the changing, the eternal in the flux.

The cycle of nature reflects, almost liturgically, the cycle of life itself: birth, death, rebirth. Experiences of this ongoing rhythm are foretastes of a hoped-for cosmic harmony, that final reunion of everything that is separated. Even on this side, touches of paradise can be sensed around us. It is when we do not understand this, or forget, that we get in the way. But we are nonetheless bitten by eternity, so that neither this life nor this earth can ever really feel like home. The meaning of our craving is to return from whence we came, losing ourselves in God. Day by day authenticity is in becoming transparent to that God, living so that we point beyond ourselves to the Power of Being in which we are all grounded.

_____ WORLD TWO: CONFLICT AND VINDICATION

In this World, history and its various institutions are tainted with self-interest. Conflict seems to be at the heart of life, even of nature, with many persons deprived of the means needed for living. Wherever one turns, the scene is a drama of winners and losers. Death is the final enemy, symbolizing the hostility that resists the crucial goal of humanizing this world. The foe is widespread, for even the cosmos is beset by entropy, so that such hemorrhaging seems to give to each part a sense of being violated. Thus threatened by the possibility of chaos, persons are tempted to grasp for power, escalating into a threat of nuclear destruction. Nations seem willing to "bring it all down" rather than lose. At one level or another, then, one keeps being pushed into being a warrior or a victim. Our reaction is often one of anger, sometimes even rage. Reform is called for, even rebellion. Yet even though one is determined to change the world, such efforts sometimes feel like a never ending defeat.

Hope for resolution is rooted in the vision of a new heaven and a new earth, to be realized as liberation within history. In Shakespeare's words "all's well that ends well." Otherwise, history is "a tale told by an idiot, full of sound and fury, signifying nothing." Since death in all forms is God's foe, resurrection provides promise not only to the individual but to history itself. In behalf of that goal, God takes sides, being committed to the poor, the captive, the blind, and the oppressed—and so must we. God calls us to be cocreators in this completion of creation. History will be vindicated by its completion, flowing back to give meaning to each part as means to that end. "Thy Kingdom come on earth, as it already is in heaven." One way to work toward that vision is to live as if the end were already here. Such hope in the God of the future makes us never satisfied with what is. This is why the prophet believes in a hope worth dying for.

____ WORLD THREE: EMPTINESS AND FULFILLMENT

Those who inhabit this World are concerned with the self, for the dilemma that has taken hold of them is self-estrangement. One is uneasy that "if people really knew me, they wouldn't like me. It isn't so much that I'm bad, it's as if there may not be much there. If my mask were to slip, it would all be over. But perhaps that wouldn't change things much after all, since often no one seems to care." The problem for many of us in this World is that often we are made to feel invisible, impotent, unheard, or insignificant. We are after-thoughts, like outcasts, as it were. And inside there is this emptiness, a void, an ache that resides in one's mid-section—the fear of being nobody, which in turn hinders action for fear of being rejected. "So I try to be who others want me to be, until I don't know who I am. And yet still, I don't belong. My life seems like a deception, as I become increasingly alienated even from myself. The result is a paralysis, an aimlessness, a floundering—trapped by myself within myself. My reward is a strange comfort in inertia, where it is too late for action, too soon for regrets."

Resolution begins by being awakened to one's possibilities, usually by the support and promise of a caring friend or group. In being accepted, one is lured toward wholeness and fulfillment. For the Christian, such meaning emerges not only through the nurture of a Christian community, but through the One who in scripture models life as giving and receiving love. In being loved for who I am, I can be and can become my true self. Knowing from within that real selfhood means to love and be loved, I am empowered to realize my potential. Such faith involves believing in myself so that I dare to feel again, unable to love others if I do not love myself. The delicious mystery of living is growth, expansiveness, fulfillment—the dynamic of redeemed life. It entails a cycle that nature models for us. Death is part of the life process, just as rebirth is part of the death process. Throughout, the focus is self-discovery, self-growth, self-risk. Therein God is not distant, but experienced as present in a world that becomes friendly in its orderliness and hospitable in its potentiality.

_____ WORLD FOUR: CONDEMNATION AND FORGIVENESS

This World is characterized by the struggle with temptation and sin. Within each of us is a tendency toward arrogance, to play god by idolizing who we are and what we possess. While we prefer to see our questionable behavior as rooted in ignorance, more often than not we deliberately choose what is wrong, often because it is "forbidden fruit." In the silent hours, it is hard to quiet a sense of guilt, evoked often by fear of judgment. We can feel like fugitives. This condition has to do not simply with what we do, but with an inner disposition. In trying to change, we experience an impotence to be otherwise, as if we are diseased. It is as though there is a deep need within me to justify my life, to convince myself and others that I am worthy of being alive. Thus life becomes an unending chore to be done. Yet I can never do enough, and so this drive flirts heavily with self-deception—in regarding myself as being far better than I am. But the truth is that the good I want to do, I don't do; and what I shouldn't want to do is precisely what I end up doing. So I am caught, with even my efforts at selflessness being selfishly motivated.

Since I cannot get out of my own way, resolution becomes possible only through God's intervention, centering in the gift of forgiveness. Repentance, leading to conversion, exhibits faith as trust that we have received reprieve, even though in no way do we deserve it. In spite of our unacceptability, God adopts us, not simply as children, but as heirs of life eternal. This is why the word "grace" is so important, for the gospel is the miracle of the empty hands. The Christian's life is one of paradox in which God forgives the unforgivable, loves the unlovable, and accepts the unacceptable. Our call is to respond in faithful obedience to this proclamation. Emphasis is not on self-realization but on self-sacrifice. Good works are done not in order to receive, but are spontaneous and joyous responses to being already justified by God's graciousness. Thus life becomes the ongoing pendulum between repentance and forgiveness, characterized by thankful humility.

____ WORLD FIVE: SUFFERING AND ENDURANCE

The dilemma that focuses life for citizens of this World is life itself, the way things are. There is a heaviness to daily living, so that it seems that whatever can go wrong, will. And whatever was troublesome yesterday will surely happen again and again. While the characters and settings change, the plot remains basically the same, as variations on the theme of "victim." Whether the examples are a poor person who knows deprivation from without, or a successful one who is being eaten by cancer from within, there is the same sense of being engulfed, controlled, wronged—as if a refugee. Suffering is the one constant, the sign of living near the edge. Unable to exist without being scarred, one often feels like life is a predator. So one is tempted not to feel anymore, to trade in trying for a cynical fatigue. Worn down in one's courageous fortitude, distrust is often the best defense against being done in. This is a hard world, one not readily chosen, for sadness edges even the joys.

Although one cannot really change the way things are, one does have a choice of how to live life. Resolution, ironically, can come through suffering, as a refining fire, as it were. Travail, rightly faced, can bring healing, in which integrity is birthed. Integrity is a determined willingness to outlast, to persevere, no matter what. Spirit is that strange power which strengthens one to press on, even when one can think of no better reason than just keeping on keeping on. For the Christian, such faithfulness, no matter what the consequences, is rooted in the belief that we are not in it alone. Because the companion God is suffering with us, we can endure to the end. On Golgotha, God screams in agony with us, drinking deeply of all that we too go through. Therefore nothing can separate us from the love of such a God.

Redeemed life has little to do with grand designs or miraculous reversals. It is the integrity born of tenacity on the daily road, respecting the small and the commonplace. A knowing glance and a sharing hand are the manna which feed. What gives dignity to life is the quality of never quitting, facing without deception whatever happens so that it becomes a moral victory. What matters is not the quantity of life but the quality of living. Thus life is to be drunk to the dregs, for one only goes around once. This can be done if one takes life "one day at a time."

IV. SELF-SCORING THE THEOLOGICAL WORLDS INVENTORY

Instructions

Transfer your responses to each question onto this page. Note that the letters a, b, c, d, e are NOT in alphabetical order. Then total each column. The highest number indicates the theological World which most fits you; the second highest indicates the second best fit, and so forth. Compare the results with your "Self-Rating."

1.	c____;	a____;	e____;	b____;	d____
2.	a____;	b____;	e____;	d____;	c____
3.	d____;	c____;	b____;	a____;	e____
4.	e____;	d____;	c____;	b____;	a____
5.	d____;	c____;	e____;	b____;	a____
6.	a____;	d____;	e____;	c____;	b____
7.	a____;	b____;	c____;	d____;	e____
8.	c____;	b____;	d____;	a____;	e____
9.	b____;	e____;	c____;	d____;	a____
10.	e____;	c____;	d____;	b____;	a____
11.	e____;	a____;	d____;	c____;	b____
12.	d____;	a____;	c____;	e____;	b____
13.	a____;	d____;	b____;	c____;	e____
14.	d____;	b____;	e____;	a____;	c____
15.	a____;	c____;	d____;	b____;	e____
16.	b____;	e____;	a____;	c____;	d____
17.	d____;	a____;	b____;	e____;	c____
18.	e____;	a____;	d____;	b____;	c____
19.	c____;	e____;	a____;	b____;	d____
20.	c____;	a____;	b____;	d____;	e____
21.	e____;	a____;	d____;	b____;	c____
22.	b____;	c____;	e____;	d____;	a____
23.	c____;	e____;	d____;	a____;	b____
24.	a____;	d____;	c____;	b____;	e____
25.	a____;	e____;	c____;	d____;	b____
26.	b____;	a____;	e____;	c____;	d____
27.	d____;	a____;	c____;	b____;	e____

28. c____;   d____;   a____;   e____;   b_____
29. e____;   d____;   a____;   b____;   c_____
30. d____;   b____;   a____;   e____;   c_____
31. a____;   b____;   c____;   d____;   e_____
32. c____;   e____;   b___;   a____;   d_____
33. b___;   c____;   d___;   e____;   a_____
34. c___;   e___;   b___;   d____;   a_____
35. a___;   c___;   e___;   b____;   d_____
36. d___;   a___;   b___;   e____;   c_____
37. d___;   c___;   a___;   e____;   b_____
38. c___;   b___;   e___;   a____;   d_____
39. b___;   e___;   c___;   d____;   a_____
40. c___;   b___;   a___;   e____;   d_____
41. b___;   a___;   d___;   c____;   e_____
42. a___;   b___;   c___;   d____;   e_____
43. a___;   d___;   b___;   c____;   e_____
44. c___;   b___;   e___;   a____;   d_____
45. c___;   b___;   e___;   a____;   d_____
46. d___;   c___;   a___;   e____;   b_____
47. e___;   b___; ' d___;   a____;   c_____
48. a___;   e___;   c___;   b____;   d_____
49. e___;   d___;   b___;   c____;   a_____
50. d___;   c___;   e___;   b____;   a_____
51. b___;   a___;   d___;   e____;   c_____
52. c___;   d___;   a___;   e____;   b_____
53. c___;   e___;   a___;   d____;   b_____
54. a___;   b___;   e___;   d____;   c_____
55. d___;   e___;   b___;   a____;   c_____
56. e___;   d___;   b___;   c____;   a_____
57. b___;   c___;   a___;   d____;   e_____
58. e___;   c___;   d___;   b____;   a_____
59. d___;   e___;   a___;   c____;   b_____
60. a___;   b___: d___;   e____;   c_____
61. a___;   d___;   b___;   e____;   c_____

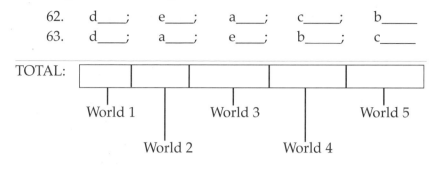

62. d___;   e___;   a___;   c___;   b____
63. d___;   a___;   e___;   b___;   c____

TOTAL:

World 1   World 3   World 5

World 2   World 4

World 1: Separation and Reunion
World 2: Conflict and Vindication
World 3: Emptiness and Fulfillment
World 4: Condemnation and Forgiveness
World 5: Suffering and Endurance

V. THEOLOGICAL WORLDS: AN EVALUATION

Each theological World can be a valid arena in which to live, move, and have one's being. No one World, as such, is better or more true than another. Neither can these Worlds be arranged so as to view some as elementary, others as more mature. The first task enabled by this inventory is to identify the World in which you already live. The result may be a feeling of satisfaction, for your self-identity may be as you would want. Thus you are ready to understand that World more coherently, furnish it more fully, articulate and share it more fluently, and live it more faithfully. Or you may be surprised by the result and enjoy exploring that World. On the other hand, you might receive the description of your self-identity with negative feelings. This might mean that you are living in an inherited World rather than residing in your own home. Or you may be living your World at its weak edges. Or, in seeing your World rendered self-conscious, you may begin to experience it as suffocating or inhibiting, inviting the honesty of crisis.

Whichever your reaction, the next task is to explore the alternative Worlds. This may be done for several reasons. It can enrich your own World by incorporating coherently dimensions of the others. It may well test the viability of other Worlds as the beginning of your own conversion. It can help you understand better other persons, and why you and they interact as you do. It can help to provide a profile for a particular congregation, giving clues to its inner dynamics. Or it may provide the base for restructuring your church.

What follows is an invitation to begin such a dialogue, indicating a few of the strengths and weaknesses possible within each World.

WORLD ONE: SEPARATION AND REUNION

Strength: Persons inhabiting this World are attracted by wholeness and harmony, valuing the inclusiveness of all. The cosmos and nature share this organic and mysterious totality. There is a quiet and often patient acceptance of human foibles by placing things within this larger perspective. There is a tendency to be sacramental, whether in the formal sense or through delight in participating in the rhythms of nature. Whichever, meaning is celebrated in the simple gift of existing. Although life is often experienced in terms of polarities or dualities, ultimately these are unreal. Unity is rooted in God, in whom we live and move and have our being. Because God, as all in all, grounds and holds all things in being, it is possible to transcend the separation of subject and object in contemplation and the mystic experience. This may make one sympathetic to Eastern thought in particular and the unity of all religions in general. The basic posture in this World is to stand before life as mystery, invited to live as a reverent guest. The Reign of God means the unifying of all things in God, experienced now in foretaste, as moments of transparency. In such timeless moments, one is touched by the still point of the turning wheel. Ethics emerge from this organic vision, ecologically sensitive that "in as much as you do it to the least of these, you do it to me."

Weakness: Mystic experience can undercut the passion for action. Becoming resigned to the rhythms of separation and reunion, one can overlook destructive problems by seeing them as relatively insignificant from the perspective of eternity. Social, economic, and political dimensions of life can be treated as if they are not fully real. Since harmony is intuited as cyclic rather than linear, history can take on an uneasy status, or be reduced to inevitable pattern. Furthermore, the propensity to see things symbolically can undercut the concreteness of life, with transparency sacrificing the uniqueness of each thing. Individuals in this World tend to feel alone, and as a neglected minority in modern society can be encouraged to adopt an individualistic posture toward life and others.

WORLD TWO: CONFLICT AND VINDICATION

Strength: Persons who reside in this World tend to be committed to issues of justice and freedom. They are often willing to risk personal security and gain in order to join God in the fight for vindication of what is right. This leads many to protest against the individualism and privatization characterizing current life in the United States. They appreciate the physical ingredients of common day existence, which accounts in part for their anger when the necessities of life are denied to anyone. There is a firm awareness of the corporate nature of life, and thus of the degree to which evil is basically systemic. These people tend to have a finely honed social conscience and are committed to the cost of discipleship.

Weakness: Often such persons have a difficult time enjoying life, drawn to "doing" far more than to "being." Not only are they often driven people, but there is a tendency to regard things more as means than ends. They live more for the future than the present. As a result, there can be a shallow and nonspiritual activism, on the one hand, or, on the other, a sacrifice of relationships in behalf of results. Ironically, passion for one's particular cause does not always bring with it a sensitivity to other oppressions. Anger against death can lead to an avoidance of death. There can be a cleavage between humans and nature, bringing an insensitivity that sacrifices the ecological whole to a rectification of economic impoverishment. Furthermore, the emphasis on corporate and systemic injustice can be made so central that the sin residing deeply in the self may be neglected. Likewise, concern for people can lead to a neglect of the person. Self-righteousness can also be a temptation, leading one to simplify issues by dividing groups into "good" and "bad." This can result in crusades, where the means for victory can contradict the values entertained as goals. Finally, this emphasis on goals can lead to utopianism, both in program and in personal calling, leading to burnout and/or capitulation.

WORLD THREE: EMPTINESS AND FULFILLMENT

Strength: There is a keen sensitivity in this World to how socialization can scar and marginalize the person. Inhabitants of this World understand how individuals can be lost in any structure, resulting in the self being alienated from itself. They tend to have a healthy regard for *eros:* for vitality, for feelings, for deep sharing, for a lyric love of living. Dualism is opposed, insisting, for example, on integrating right and left brain thinking, and regarding mind and body as a whole. This World is populated with persons whose eyes are honed to see possibilities, becoming awakened to one's environment as positive and hopeful. "Becoming" is a key term, with growth regarded as the natural state of things. The precious moments are often characterized by a lyric childlikeness, fascinated with the new and imaginative.

Weakness: In the passion for fulfillment, there can be a tendency to neglect or even exclude persons who are not part of one's support. There can be excessive pride in one's stage of "maturity," needing the "less enlightened" with whom to compare oneself. Because citizens of this World are often from more privileged classes, there is a tendency to overlook the negative impact of systems and the need to use power in changing dehumanizing systems. Seeing life in terms of potential, there can be a tendency to identify "winners" with personal effort, "losers" with failing to try enough. Finally, the optimism often characterizing this World can lead to a discounting of one's shadow side, blind to one's own motivations for advantage even when denying all interest in power.

WORLD FOUR: CONDEMNATION AND FORGIVENESS

Strength: Residents of this World have the courage to look at human duplicity without illusion. They see a powerful case for God in the destructive spectacle of humans playing god in the very act of denying God. Evidence of the Fall is this universal human pretentiousness. What needs to be heard is the good news that God's grace is free and available to those who repent of their arrogance and ask for forgiveness. Whereas conversion can be once and for all, there continues to be a need for ongoing confession and forgiveness, over and over. Christian life is characterized by humility, in knowing that one is sustained by grace. The response called for is one of faithful obedience, rooted in a strong distinction between good and evil and in a committed discipleship of self-denial.

Weakness: There can be a tendency for the individual in this World to be guilt-ridden. Thus one may be tempted also to put guilt trips on others. Either way, incapacitating self-images can result. Stress on sin can be so strong that it blurs whatever motives, capacities, and degrees of goodness may be present, even undercutting morality in society. In portraying the "new birth" in terms of a heavy contrast between before and after, one's inevitable shortcomings can be driven inward, creating a secret life of deception, sometimes from oneself, but certainly from others. Relatedly, the distinction between believer and nonbeliever can be so graphically drawn that rather than confessing one's shortcomings, one may be tempted to project them onto others, in acts of righteous superiority. This can occur not only in personal living, but in establishing political, economic, and national dualisms which too easily identify one's own position with God's. Such idolatry can encourage use of force to keep the "unrighteous" from prevailing. Emphasis upon response can render justification by faith, ironically, into a new form of works-righteousness, known as the Protestant work ethic, in which one is driven to prove one's worth. There can be a tendency to surround the offer of God's free and unmerited grace with so many conditions that it is no longer free.

WORLD FIVE: SUFFERING AND ENDURANCE

Strength: Residents of this World have a keen discernment of the way things are, and what it means to live as the leftovers of others. This sensitivity can bring a deep empathy for others. There is a tendency to be tenacious, strong, and shrewd, committed to living with a special brand of homey integrity. Deep loyalty and dependability for its own sake can become second nature, with a capacity to outlast with long suffering. These are the ones who remain for the long haul. They are often surprisingly open in sharing what they have, being more concerned for the quality of the little than the quantity of the much.

Weakness: Although these are the salt of the earth, the salt can lose its savor—by becoming strung out, overextended, or burned-out. Thus around the edges can lurk the shadows of depression or immobilization, even a tinge of masochism. For inhabitants of this World, closure and resolution are difficult to achieve. Also apathy toward change can become a defense mechanism. There can be a tendency to squander everything in an irrational moment, either of respite, or of gambling on a miraculous reversal. Because this World rests on life as unchanging, remaining basically what it was, is, and always will be, a resident can be undone if a reversal does occur. In finding oneself in the "up position," one can be tempted to become judgmental, even intolerant, of those with whom one had formerly identified so deeply.

CHAPTER FIVE

An Experimental Case Study
in Local Church
Variegation

Before we apply the Theological Worlds Inventory directly in developing models, structures, and functioning for the theologically conscious variegated congregation, it will be useful for us to explore how one particular church took several significant steps toward diversity. Unfortunately, there was no Theological Worlds Inventory yet available for them to ground their experimentation theologically. The reader is invited to explore how the idea of theological Worlds, in general, and the Theological Worlds Inventory, in particular, can be used creatively in such experimentation with variegation. The reader can then compare the ideas evoked by this model with the concrete explorations with which the remainder of this book will be concerned.

Several years ago, two pastors, rather than downplaying their significant differences, made a decision to emphasize them. "To that end, we developed a theological perspective that blesses differences and options and choices."[1] The church building is located in an affluent suburban municipality, but has low visibility on a non-through street. In an attempt to gain visibility, they advertised clearly and proudly that each of their services was markedly different. Each worship group was given a special name, a distinguishing symbol as logo, and a distinctive bulletin with contrasting print and picture. Each group is firmly encouraged to view itself as a unique congregation, within an inclusive whole. Although visitors are encouraged to sample the various services, each person is strongly urged finally to choose a "service home." The church currently has four of these subcongregations. "We're pretty intentional about all this. We offer persons choices of time, worship styles, leaders, preachers, and sacramental method and frequency."

The "Pilgrim's Gathering" meets on Saturday evening at 5:30 P.M.—chosen basically because there would be no required ending time. The focus is Eucharistic, within a context of "the Word read and preached." The sermon can be as long as thirty minutes, but since informality is encouraged, interruption of the sermon is welcomed as a kind of dialogue. Leadership is broadly shared by those who attend, often with children being readers and ushers. The participating clergyperson does only the Eucharistic prayer and sermon, with the laity responsible even for baking the bread. The total event normally lasts about one and a half hours, with children having an alternate activity during the first half, returning for the Eucharist. For baptisms, children are given privileged vantage points around the font or on the shoulders of the nearest adult available. There is a period after the service for child education, while adult education is a talk-back with the pastor. A covered dish is incorporated into the event once a month.

How this subcongregation resolves issues is indicative. Someone raised the question as to whether Holy Communion was just for the baptized, or for all. The next week the two pastors had a dialogue-sermon exhibiting publicly not only the theological method by which each of them had reached their conclusion, but that they were free to declare their disagreement. After congregational response, a compromise was reached. "If you feel the call of the Spirit, come; then see us afterward for training leading to baptism."

Two hundred persons attended the first night, with attendance fluctuating now between one hundred and two hundred, with visitors accounting for the fluctuation. Those most responsive to this type of service have been singles, young families, and those alienated from the church. "Fun" and "folksy" were words participants used in describing what happens. Staff members were clear about their overall goal: to foster commitment through diversity. Although each subcongregation functions more or less autonomously, each group elects representatives to the larger church administrative board.

The 8:15 A.M. service was originally designed as a looser, less structured preaching event than the later service, aimed at those interested in brunch afterward. Ironically, however, what evolved was a High Church liturgy—reverencing the altar, sung responses, monthly Eucharist, with most folks getting dressed up. Yet, surprisingly, preaching is not from the pulpit, and the passing of the peace is conversational. This service too, then, has taken on a life of its own, a life that one pastor characterized as feeling "Baptist-Catholic-Pentecostal." Here, as in all services, the lectionary is used.

The 9:30 A.M. service is best described as highly devotional—a chapel-like forty-five minute time apart. The ambience is subdued lighting, with candles used to further the atmosphere of a small, intimate, and gentle space. A variety of liturgical orders are used for Holy Communion, but in each case a meditative-type worship is observed. Whereas on Saturday night and early Sunday morning a chalice and loaf are used, here there are individual cups and wafers. On Saturday night and early Sunday morning, what is done is identified as Eucharist. Here it is always called communion. It is observed first, "so that the preaching that follows can be abbreviated, if needed—staying carefully within the promised 'shortness.'" The rationale for this most recently devised service was to provide a broader spectrum of options. "In encouraging newcomers to try our various services, and then join one subcongregation, we found a gap in what was available."

The 10:45 A.M. worship is the most traditional—formal in liturgy and decor, with preaching being central. Lay participation is at a minimum, with the same basic order repeated each week. Anthems are classical, reponses are sung by the congregation, and dress is expected to be "proper." "This is the service where 'civil religion' is observed, such as Boy Scout Sunday, Mother's Day, Memorial Day, Independence Day—complete with promotion pins and quarterly communion—the whole bit." "This one we need to play more by a feel for the demographics." This service has the largest attendance.

The professional staff is composed of an older senior pastor, a younger associate pastor, and a diaconal minister of Christian education. Every effort is made for these three to be on a par, resisting the usual hierarchical pattern. Each pastor is identified with two of the four subcongregations, for they have discovered that a ministerial identity with each group is regarded as important for laity and for the pastors themselves. The diaconal minister participates in all of the services, providing a unity of participative presence. The two pastors visit each other's services from time to time to witness support, while periodically they have dialogue sermons to model how authentic diversity can exist appreciatively within the same church.

Recently they have tried doing children's sermons for each other. In every way possible, then, each subcongregation is structured to accentuate unique diversity—different clergy robes, different ushers, different choirs, different altar arrangement, different sermons.

This whole experiment began when the senior pastor purposely sought out someone who was a genuine contrast to himself. He is liberal, with a works-oriented focus on church growth. Thus he chose a colleague who is unabashedly sacramental and orthodox, with a focus on committed discipleship. In time, the role of the diaconal staff person was redefined. Christian education became understood not simply as specialized learning activities, but as a function of the whole, with the Christian educator's uniqueness acknowledged as being activist, feminist, lay, and creatively inclusive. This mutual commitment to a functional ecclesiology transformed the administration as well. Using the Myers-Briggs Personality Indicator (which we will explore later) to identify the strengths of each staff person, interestingly the younger pastor was given responsibility for overall administration. The interactive pattern that emerged gave each a descriptive title:

—The "Shepherd" (ENFP) is responsible for new members, worship, hospital calling, stewardship, and counseling.
—The "Joan of Arc" (INFP) is responsible for concrete mission, outreach administration, education of youth and children, liturgy, and counseling.
—The "Manager" (ENTJ) is responsible for office administration, finances, personnel, committees, worship, and counseling.

It has taken time and struggle to reach this point. The pastors worked in advance on the particularly sensitive issue of jealousy—especially over preaching popularity. To their surprise they discovered that "when folks find the subcommunity where they belong, they have a surprising tolerance for mediocre preaching." The overall strain of "having everything normal be up for grabs" was severe enough for the younger pastor to become ill. "Having been the only pastor at my previous church, I found my identity taken away. I just didn't know how to be present without taking charge." In such a new situation as this, "none of us knew how to function." The saving factor was the genuine affection that the three of them had for each other. And the solution was the genuine cooperation that resulted whereby "we helped each other be happy by finding at least one subcommunity in which he or she was truly at home."

New subcongregations are being formed as the need is sensed, with lay and clergy representatives identifying the general ethos that would make for a viable alternative. Then sufficient "pioneers" are recruited who are willing to commit themselves to one year of experimentation in the new grouping. The way in which the second new subcongregation resulted was when the staff gave a selected committee the assignment to design something that would "remind folks of being at their church 'back home'—you know, rural, convenient, small, with everyone family."

None of the persons lost during the initial period of transition left for theological reasons. They left because "they could not handle folks who disagreed with them." Fundamentalists in particular were identified as being in this group. "Could you find a place for them now?" I asked. The response came quickly from the whole staff: "We've learned enough so that if there were enough conservatives who were interested, we would welcome an evanglical worship grouping."

Since this model of variegation has a history of only a few years, evaluation is somewhat premature. Yet it is possible to identify several clusters of experience that are helpful.

1. One important issue centers around how to preserve *unity within diversity*. Approaches that have been validated include these:

- Common announcements in each bulletin
- Common lectionary readings for all services, with mutually agreed upon themes for Lent and Advent
- Churchwide potluck celebrations at least twice yearly
- Special cross-congregational worship on select holy days
- Special events codesigned and cosponsored, as was their birthday party for Jesus at Christmastime
- A common church school
- Traditional churchwide activities such as prayer groups and Bible studies
- Jointly planned and executed outreach ministries
- Traditional board and committee structure, drawing representatives from each subcongregation, agreeing on the principles of age and gender diffusion. [Jokes about needing a system that

combined senate (equal) and house (proportional) representation seemed to indicate some uneasiness at this point.]
- Sacramental unity, if for no other reason than the fact the Eucharist/Communion throughout the church has increased from a total of four times to one hundred twenty times yearly

We took one session to discuss how to create a better umbrella of unity for this emerging diversity. One idea identified as needing more creativity was the planning for special events. "Our Christmas season celebrations, climaxing on Christmas Eve, could be a model for other seasons." Another possibility was a more intentional development of fellowship dinners and study groups, "perhaps capitalizing on our discovery of new festivals such as All Saints."

2. The second arena is that of *administration*. Arrangements that appear to be useful include these:

- Replacement of hierarchical arrangements with functional ones, resting on a commitment to never act unilaterally. [Their present *troika* model operates on consensus attained within weekly meetings. A role model showing how commitment within diversity can be cultivated is provided for the church as a whole by modeling administration as a process of spiritual formation.]
- Quarterly out-of-town retreats for the staff
- Staff meetings with the business manger twice monthly
- Staff meetings with the program staff (i.e., organist, choir directors) twice monthly
- Administrative Council structured to be the church arbiter, rather than the staff doing this, with committees organized so as to promote lay empowerment

3. The third arena centers around *problems that have arisen.*

- Staff time. Collegiality is not only difficult, but also time-consuming. This raises the issue of productivity through balancing means and ends. Collegiality had to be given priority during the initial year, but unless it gives rise to patterns of efficiency, burnout results.
- Work areas. As staff trust grew, willingness to delegate increased. This led to clarity about individual responsibilities, resulting in greater productivity.

- Who's in charge? Since the hierarchical model is the one that most people know, practice, and expect, there is considerable pressure to establish a senior pastor, and with it, a normative worship group around which other worship groups are regarded as experimental. They have done well in resisting this.
- Anonymity. On the churchwide level, there can be a sense of "I don't see the people I used to see." While this model is successful in expanding lay leadership, it was noted with some sadness that at the Christmas party for lay leaders, introductions were needed. What is gained in depth does entail some sense of loss in breadth. It is a matter of priority.
- Confusion. Some parishioners, feeling lost in the variety of choices, experienced, at least initially, a sense of chaos. The staff expressed an undocumented sense that this is more of a problem for persons over fifty, whereas younger persons find the options exhilarating.
- Status events. It was discovered that this model thrives best with a staff that has real differences—theological, professional, and personal—otherwise competition easily arises over such matters as who does weddings or funerals. The best solution they found was to provide choice, reflecting the worship subcongregations and personnel. The issue of who represents the church in civic events resolved itself, for one pastor is a "church" type who appreciates the broader church presence, whereas the other reflects a "sect" type, drawing satisfaction primarily in terms of the committee and disciplined communities of faith.

4. In one evaluation session, the staff was asked why they regarded the subcongregation model of variegation to be a harbinger of the church of the future. I was able to glean six reasons from their conversation.

- All of us tend to be mistaken at best, sinful at worst. Thus the staff found early the need for two contrasting types of community in order for them to function at their best: "the homogeneity of intimate support; and the 'salad bowl community' of accountable diversity." Another person added: "We often live badly in the world, so we need the church wherein to learn how to live responsibly with difference. If we can do it with theological difference, we can do it anywhere."

- Truth is no longer absolute. "There is no one right answer on anything." Diversity is "not simply a begrudging fact, but an acceptable and desirable reality." What can be more "exciting, creative, and faithful than a milieu in which things can be questioned, and an invitation to dialogue is the operating style"?
- Disagreement brings clarity of faith. "To meet those who know what they believe forces me to discover where I stand." People here "know more about sacraments then ever before, not through dogmatism but by alternative exposure. Learning inclusive language happens the same way."
- Ecclesiology insists on variegation. "Scripture and reality certainly confirm that there are many members of the Body of Christ, and the toenail and the neck bone bear little resemblance to one another." Instead of making difference a hostile fact, "the Christian call is to vicarious existence as a diverse and expanding body."
- Consistency requires diversity. "Each of us as a matter of course assumes diversity in performing our ministry, for example, in adapting counseling methods to the uniqueness of the counselee. Why not in liturgy and all of the church's functions?"
- Empowered laity demand diversity. We have long talked of the church belonging to the laity, for whom we would be consultants, but "nothing changes because we fear the chaos their dissimilarity would bring." The insistence in some churches that the clergy name(s) appear on the outside bulletin board identifies the problem. "We knew the transformation was real when we had relinquished control and visibility, not just for the buildings and grounds, but for the shape of their faith Worlds."

I was particularly concerned with this final point, in which the pastors had abrogated all responsibility for what they called "faith Worlds." The experiment, in the end, was seemingly concerned with numbers, testing if diversity would have a larger appeal than a single focus church. This is why our closing discussion was most important for our study. When pushed, the staff acknowledged that the four subcongregations were probably different theologically— but they had failed to make the theological level an underlying foundation for what they were doing. Upon reflecting on this important but missed dimension, one staff person admitted: "They must be different theologically, if for no other reason than that it is true of us pastors—and we surround each group with contrasting sermons and liturgy." Upon being pushed further, the staff, to their surprise, began remembering illustrations that pointed to contrasting theologies that have emerged, largely unrecognized. "The other pastor makes a point of using words of assurance [World One]; but for me, there must be absolution [World Four]. For one of us, the sermon is clearly a proclamation of the Word [World Four]; for the other, preaching is a shared response to that Word [World One or Three]." Whereas they affirmed that such differences had emerged, no staff person felt that the subcongregations or the church as a whole congregation recognized or understood such theological diversity.

The more the staff talked, the clearer it became to them that they did not know what to do with this emerging fact. Alarmed lest they might impose their own theologies onto the laity, they all concluded: "We need help theologically if we are to make fully intentional what we have started." That is what this book is about.

The remainder of this book will be concerned with translating the significance of the Theological Worlds Inventory and the idea of theological Worlds for developing models, programs, and ministries for the postmodern variegated church. The questions that we will explore are these: (1) How churches currently composed of more than one worshiping congregation can be made self-consciously theological in nature, so as to move beyond convenience, variety, and tolerance, to a diversity that nurtures serious and faithful commitment. (2) How the variegated church can find creative expression in the single-pastor church. (3) What models of variegation can be developed for small, even declining, membership churches. (4) How variegation can give rise to new and creative understandings and approaches to the traditional tasks of ministry.

The importance of developing variegation *theologically* becomes clear from the study we have just done of one church's experiment. Clearly, diversity is a fact, and intentionality about that fact is beginning to nudge the church into the future. But there is something *faithless* about variegation if it simply reflects whatever appeals to assorted people.

CHAPTER SIX

How to Get There from Here: Beginning Where We Are

The Seekers and the Sought

The word *diversity* means "existing in more than one form." Present responses to this phenomenon are significantly different than in the past. No longer is society or church successful in resolving diversity by becoming a "melting pot." Instead, both are functioning as centrifuges—vehicles in which at high speeds the center collapses and elements regroup in different, smaller constellations.[1] In fact, this is the state of the modern world. Baby boomers have responded by making options and choices their operating perspective. In so doing, they make more visible the fact that "the dominant reality of American experience is the choosing individual. It is this person who, for better and for worse, constitutes the pluralism with which both nation and church must deal."[2]

Yet this phenomenon is far more apparent in the behavior of individuals than it is in the response of the churches. Those who dropped out of the church in the 1960s and 1970s are returning, "looking for a religious grounding for their children and for answers to their own questions about life and its meaning."[3] What is happening is that sociological causes are so interfacing with psychological needs that theologizing increasingly renders one's pilgrimage self-conscious. In the face of societal desacralization, individuals are experiencing anew Eric Erikson's insistence that each person needs faithfulness to someone or something—resulting in a worldview with the power to foster ego formation sufficient to propel that self consistently into the future. No matter what cultural diversions flood the modern self, this primal hunger keeps returning. St. Bernard knew it would. The church, he insisted, feeds the hungry soul, not the hunger.

This accounts, in part, for why denominational loyalty is of decreasing importance in choosing a church. Bruised by past loyalties, leery of the content of tomorrow's promises, the real interest is in today—in discovering a community that can speak to a person's particular life experiences. This need, as one put it, is to open up "experiential space." Such exploration is really a confession—that the highly individualistic, utilitarian cult of modern America is unsatisfying. What persons are looking for is a warm, open, and accepting environment. Interestingly, these are the persons who, although being unsure of what it means to be religious, claim to be spiritual. To speak to these faith explorers, then, the church, as an institution of religion, must "discover religious meaning in language and metaphor. Religion is a language: it involoves learning how to talk about one's life, interpreting events and experiences, and drawing upon a legacy of beliefs, symbols, and stories, that give life meaning and coherence." [4] This is true not only of the unchurched but also of those who need to be *rechurched*. Recent studies show that those unrelated to a church involve themselves more in practices such as prayer and Bible reading than do church members. [5] What this is disclosing is that one of the largest populations for evangelism is the previously churched, who, consequently, are the religiously bruised.

The same searching, however, is true of the churched. Depending on the study, two to seven million church members regularly participate in two or more congregations each week. Efforts to touch the needs of the unchurched, churched, and rechurched are creating a dynamic that pushes toward the concept of the variegated church, in which subcongregations or alternative groupings will be functioning credos, centered self-consciously in the power of the shared story as lived. [6]

The conclusion to which I have come is this: *effective evangelism is identical with the rediscovery of the church's reason for being.* What one group needs, the other is called to become—alternative groupings or arenas in which a person is invited to share one's own story, so that one can discern its meaning in the midst of those whose common story can claim mine as a variation on the theme of "the" story. [7] Here one becomes a Christian—when the storyteller becomes the story. Put another way, real belonging occurs when I can tell the communal version as my own so that when one suffers, all suffers, and the joy of each is the excitement of all. Whether the activity we are about is evangelism, education, preaching, or worship, faithfulness means so participating in the story-as-lived that one thrives on having it told, and retold.

Whereas church leaders puzzle over the growing number of persons disinterested in the church, far more puzzling for me is the opposite—why so many persons *do* in fact participate in institutional Christianity. Recent statistics indicate that the percentage of church attendance is amazingly high, even when compared with Puritan days, the supposed heyday of American religious life. The Gallup ten-year surveys (1977–87) indicate that a consistent 50 percent of all teenagers, and 41 percent of all adults, have attended church weekly. In a more recent poll, 52 percent of teenagers and 40 percent of all adults not only attended church last Sunday but attend "almost weekly." Perhaps even more startling is the fact that over one-third of those claiming no religious affiliation attend church once or twice a month, some even more. What needs to become graphic in our minds is not the loss of membership, projected despondently into the future, rather, our focus must be on the amazing participation that is occurring, focused as opportunity. What is being exhibited is that many of the unchurched are seeking precisely what the churched profess to have found. *The tension between churched and unchurched is not in what is desired, but in how well it is being tailored to the diversity of seekers.* There is good reason to believe that it is this discrepancy that, as a matter of fact, accounts for the present membership decline.

What persons seem to be seeking is a viable theological World experienced as ethos. Ethos is the lived "feel" of shared practice, custom, belief, purpose, and procedure, which constitutes a congregation as a corporate personality. It is this interaction of memory and vision that forges the style of life of its members.[8] Thus the church's reason for being is to "model life as alternative communities in the midst of their prevailing settings."[9] This is the answer to the liberal dilemma with which we began, where intellectual assent and organizational allegiance have displaced the opportunity for personal and communal reflection upon one's spiritual journey.[10] What is needed in order to regain the commitment whose loss the conservatives rightly lament, is identical with the prescription for the church's own renewal—to become itself by offering the rich intertwining that it professes to be. "The principle of harmony and love upon which it alone can be established requires that each contribute to the community according to [one's] ability and receive from it according to [one's] need."[11] What variegated congregations can offer is

Christianity as the open-ended quest to make sense out of life. With such motivation, religion is rendered as universal as it is necessary, and the church becomes as variegated as authentic and viable diversity requires. The liberal insight is that life *is* options; the conservative contribution is that faith *is* commitment—of passionate choice. Variegation, in turn, intertwines the two with the Christian insight that the self "is both uniquely individual and a social creation." [12] Thus each life is a meaning quest for which theologizing is the intentional name, and religion the explicit practice.

Secular Groups as the Latent Church

Understanding the need, content, and rationale for the variegated congregation as the church of the future, we now face the question: How are we to get "there" from "here"? That is, what options are there for providing transition? The church's positive response to a widespread phenomenon from outside the church can provide one important avenue to variegation. Ironically, the Wednesday evening prayer meeting that I knew as a child, long discarded by the church as an anomaly, has been the model for approximately 500,000 groups meeting weekly in the United States, with an attendance of fifteen million. This reapplication began seriously in 1935 with the founding of Alcoholics Anonymous, rooted solidly in theological World Four ("Condemnation and Forgiveness"). Membership requires two assumptions: that one is powerless to change oneself, and that there is a Higher Power that can make that change possible. Within this theological context, groups provide two things for the individual that have long been acknowledged as the primal marks of the church: support in one's struggle for wholeness, and accountability for the discipline required.

The liberal church, long stereotyping World Four as archaic, fundamentalist, and guilt-ridden, has eased deep confession and absolution out of the Sunday morning worship. But, ironically, today it is sneaking in by the backdoor, reappearing on weekday evenings as droves attend alternative meetings in the church basement. *Newsweek* marvels at this phenomenon: "All of a sudden, people are pouring back into churches and synagogues with a fervor that hasn't been seen since the '50s." More amazing even than the numbers is what is happening there, for those who come religiously are "talking about their deepest secrets, darkest fears and strangest cravings." [13] After decades of liberal optimism, the shadow side of human life is reappearing. For these persons, their confession has to do with addiction to alcohol, narcotics, sex, overeating, compulsions, dependencies, prostitution, gambling, or to addiction itself. For still others, it is a World Five community in which affliction can be the bread shared—cancer, rape, AIDS, incest, depression—and unconditional acceptance is the wine drunk together. More times than not, these groups are able to bridge those societal chasms that the church finds so monumentally difficult—class, race, gender, and profession—and they do so in a manner that is neither peripheral nor short term.

Whatever the dilemma, the theological pattern remains constant and consistent. It entails confession: "there is no health in me." It entails naming: "I am an alcoholic, now and always." It entails acknowledgment: "since healing will be lifelong, we need each other for there is no 'salvation' alone." And with the "life-review" required as Step Four of each member, this pattern renders each person's whole life an open book—wounds lanced for the ongoing healing. With Step Five, one experiences forgiveness as unconditional acceptance, which is the church's definition of grace. What creativity and variety do these groups offer in order to keep persons interested? Almost none. What boggles the liberal mind is the methodical sameness of each meeting, with each program resembling an extended confessional booth. The real attraction resides internally—in urgent *need*. One is helped by helping others, thereby experiencing the healing power of community. The very meaning of "church" is close at hand. In fact, the genius for these groups is that they *are* the latent church—where "strangers gather to help one another by telling stories." [14] Autobiography is the primary focus, intersecting common stages of pilgrimage with each person's uniquely sacred self.

It is time for the church to welcome these groups as orphans-come-home and let their presence spearhead a significant intentionality in behalf of variegation. Such a prodigal welcome will entail more than providing space. Just as human needs are diverse, so the communities providing supportive accountability need to be variegated. The truth is that the problems being addressed by these groups, such as drug or weight problems, are, in reality, secondary or tertiary needs. The troublesome behavior emerges, in significant part, as unsuccessful ways for coping with deeper problems. Thus, more basic than is often acknowledged, beneath the behavioral symptoms is a dislocation for which the church can provide subcommunities, identifying and shaping one's primal theological World which can serve as a therapeutic foundation.

AA, as a model for almost all such groups, operates within a clear but latent World Four context. Yet among the diverse participants, other theological Worlds are quietly present. Consequently, many persons, for the sake of healing, are forced to push obliquely against the group's corporate World, for it is not their own. Thus these persons are being fed only tangentially. Such groups are not yet the manifest church. But in being what they are, they can open persons theologically, for beneath the negative behavior, even when coped with, is still a persistent search for a viable World of meaning.

The witness of these variegated groups is a call for the church to rediscover itself as a composite of theological alternatives, each focused by a commitment rooted in discipline. Vatican II recaptured just such a vision. "And so it happened by divine plan, that a wonderful variety of religious communities grew up. This variety contributed mightily toward making the Church experienced in every good deed and ready for a ministry of service in building up Christ's body. Not only this, but adorned by the various gifts of her children, the Church became radiant like a bride made beautiful for her spouse; and through her God's manifold wisdom could reveal itself." [15]

Stages of Local Church Transition

Stage One: Acknowledgment

We have described one societal movement which, by pressing in from the outside, can make visible witness at the periphery of the church's space to the healing power of Christian variegation. But the congregation's own first step must come with an *acknowledgment* that variegation is already an internal fact. The church does not need to decide to become variegated. It already is, like it or not. Acknowledging this can make understandable why even the choice of hymns can sometimes resemble a life and death clash. *The church's fundamental internal dynamic was, is, and will always be, the interaction of theological Worlds.* It inevitably becomes disruptive unless the church makes it creative by rendering the diversity explicit, intentional, and valuable. Unrecognized, the defensiveness that results can inflict lifelong scars.

Looking back now upon my early church experience, I suspect

that groups such as prayer partners, healing fellowships, and persons who preferred to sit in the church balcony were my first experiences of World One residents. Representatives of World Two were more often recognizable on task forces, a bit too radical for most, but tolerable for their energy in raising money and supporting causes. World Three folk found one another often around coffee klutches and fellowship suppers—even skating parties. Wednesday evening prayer meetings, revivals, and Bible studies were the recognizable haunts for World Four. And World Five people tended to be quieter, visible in support groups or serving meals from the church kitchen, and reliable in visiting the sick and elderly, faithful wherever asked, as the salt of the earth.

Diversity, then, is not only a fact characterizing today's church, it is a dynamic that works itself out inevitably in forging structures of variegation. The intriguing history of many church school classes reflects this process—such as the "Young Marrieds" composed of members who are retired, for in finding each other through the years they have found something far more than one's marriage. Time is an instrument of discernment, as like finds like, rehearsing likeness into a formative continuity that we have called a theological World. It is easier for the larger church to perceive its variegation, for it often appears as recognizable units such as multiple worship services. In midsized churches, variegation is more evident in alternative church school classes, informal groupings, and self-selecting activities. In smaller churches, often proud of their monolithic appearance as family, diversity is just as operative, but more hidden. Acknowledgment of variegation may begin here with the pastor's personal recognition of the degree to which congregational tensions or inertia, personal animosities or cliques, blockages or diversions in group process, are rooted, usually unconsciously, in the personal interaction of diverse theological Worlds. Such cleavage involves far more than conceptual differences. We must come to understand that persons are actual *residents* of their World, who actually experience life differently, see things differently, process things differently, live life differently, and thus *are* significantly different. As one mystified minister put it, "Sometimes my members don't act as if they are in the same world." Precisely. What is a problem for one member can be an answer for another. What scratches one's itch for some, rubs raw a blister for others. Thus for church leaders to begin to understand human interaction *theologically* is to take a giant step. And since small church relations often reflect configurations whose centers are outside the church, one can begin to understand decision making as informal coffee consensus—the world of the local cafe for men, select kitchens for women.

Stage Two: Discernment

Acknowledgment is the first step in the transition into intentional variegation. This is followed by *discernment*, moving toward *orientation*, and finally achieving *implementation*. The goal of discernment as stage two is to bring a congregation, or its significant leaders, to understand the *patterns* of its own variegation, and thus perceive the concrete opportunities for intentional variegation. Although there are a number of ways to do this, we will develop two.

1. Interviewing the Congregation. As a way of providing "accountable discipleship" within the "respectful limitations of pluralism," Alfred C. Krass devised a fifteen item questionnaire. Inspired by medical inventories often required by doctors of their patients, he found a spiritual equivalent in Paul's analysis of wellness as the fruits of the spirit. [16] Parishioners were asked to fill out this form during a church service. Over the next several months, the pastor arranged half hour appointments with each person to review their answers. Responding to the issues which parishioners most wanted to discuss, he found himself increasingly assuming the task of "curer of souls." The most marked questions were "those concerning growth as a Christian, life goals, the mix of personal and corporate spiritual practices, how to understand God's will in today's world, how to make use of the Bible, and what it means to bear fruit for the Lord." [17]

As over against today's myth of the autonomous individual breeding loneliness by desiring privatism, Krass discovered instead that people desire to be held accountable to their own vision—with a seriousness about forging holistic life goals. Relatedly, what he discovered from his visits was a strong interest in "the church as constituting a supportive community," with most persons interviewed being enthusiastic about such a possibility. And in this process of discovering the contours of his parishioners' interior lives, the pastor himself became excited and reenergized about the creative possibilities of ministry.

Krass now acknowledges that this interviewing was actually the "first step toward the recovery of corporate discipleship in the postmodern era." The image that emerged as pastor and congregation attempted a period of transition was of one pilgrim caring for other pilgrims. But soon a serious condition was encountered—the acknowledged need was not matched by the church's structure. Restructuring would need to begin with two features. First, each member needed a spirit friend. Second, "face-to-face primary groups [were needed] whose members would reflect biblically on their engagement in society and support one another in daily ministry." [18] Surprising was the discovery of a ready interest in having the church restructured so as to provide both ingredients. Krass insists that every church will find such a motivation present, if for no other reason than the universal human interest in talking about oneself.

When this experiment was described in *The Christian Century*, the response was an avalanche of letters reflecting a widespread need to do what he was doing. His form was actually quite simple, designed to invite dialogue about concrete topics and arenas in one's life. Any pastor could easily develop such a form. Fifteen statements invited the parishioner to respond with a number indicating the degree of agreement or disagreement. Such a tool could be drafted with only minimal familiarity of one's congregation, touching such matters as guilts, joys, disciplines, growth, goals, reading, feelings, relationships, and problems. A good one for starters might be, "How happy are you with the direction that your life is taking?" The function of such a form is to help the interviews move quickly beyond the superficial level. This worked so well that Krass decided not to interview any family that had not fully filled out the questionnaire.

Our proposal is that among the questions asked on the proposed form would be some taken from the Theological Worlds Inventory. Choices that have proved helpful include numbers 16, 19, 20, 21, 28, 43, 53, 60. Other possibilities might be numbers 3, 6, 7, 8, 15, 17, 24, 29, 33, 50. This technique is useful in clustering a congregation's diverse needs, providing a basis for restructuring. The task is neither to pigeonhole nor to instruct. It is to discern needs, gather data for a congregational profile, and create enthusiasm for experiments in variegation.

In smaller churches such interviewing is probably best done by the pastor, for while neighbors are generally friendly, they are careful about what they share deeply. In larger churches, interview pairs can be trained, as we will develop in the next chapter. They will need sufficient familiarity with the idea of theological Worlds in order for the interviews to be theologically discerning. [19] In profiling the church's configuration through these interviews, it is important to discern potential hubs for variegation in terms of the density of particular theological Worlds. With this configuration sketched out in rough form, two more things are needed. First, compare this congregational configuration with the profile of the pastor and persons central to the church's leadership. Second, examine existing groups and programs in the light of the concentration of Worlds.

2. Leadership Leaven. A second method for doing discernment would be a planning retreat for the church's lay leadership, preferably lasting several days. This method can precede, follow, or substitute for a congregational interview. The retreat might begin with the pastor's presentation concerning the polarity of diversity and commitment as issues defining the modern church's dilemma (see chapters 1-3). Then the Theological Worlds Inventory could be administered. Based on the results, five groups could be organized according to each person's primary theological World. Those whose scores are so balanced as not to give a clear perspective, can "visit around" in the groups until they find a "home." Significant time should be given for each group to enjoy their commonness through conversation. Usually such interaction is best facilitated by sharing their Inventory results with each other. Persons might compare answers to specific questions, explore differences that one's secondary or tertiary Worlds make, and share life stories that help oneself and others understand the uniqueness of their particular World. Such sharing can be done in pairs, subdivisions of the group, and/or the whole group, depending largely on the size of each grouping. Our experience has been that persons get excited by learning theologically about themselves.

The next step might be the formation of brainstorming groups, each composed of representatives from the various Worlds. Each group imagines creative possibilities for one of the church's major functions—such as worship, evangelism, education, and special programming. Facilitators can help these groups recognize and appreciate the interplay of alternative Worlds in the discussion, considering alternative ways in which these needs can be met so as to feed residents of each World.

From such imaginings, concrete suggestions from each group can be proposed, writing them on newsprint for a plenary session. These ideas can give rise to plans for particular opportunities for congregational variegation. An ongoing planning group might be formed, or ideas can be referred to existing committees. In various ways, a decision can be made to move on to the next stage, that of orientation.

Stage Three: Orientation

Orientation involves a three point process: identifying and developing theological Worlds into self-consciousness; rehearsing them through one or more liturgical communities of support; and encouraging commitment to a faith style through group accountability. The details of this stage depend on the particular congregational membership and the resources available.

If it is not feasible to begin with either a congregational interview or a leadership retreat (described in Stage Two), it may be possible to begin directly with one or more existing groups as catalysts. Another possibility would be to make use of some regular church events. For example, several church school classes could meet together in order to explore theologically the significance of their differences and similarities, as well as their preferred teaching methods, resources, supplemental activities, space appearance, and time usage. A skilled and informed group leader is a requirement with this approach.

A churchwide Advent or Lenten study series is a ready-made opportunity. One concrete theological World could be developed, illustrated, and experienced each week, complete with characteristic biblical passages, hymns, and atmosphere. A number of pastors have done this, using music, art forms, and ambience as suggested in my book, *Theological Worlds*. Another possibility would be to conduct five consecutive Sunday worship services that are constructed to capture the feel of each World—as we will develop later. Or a Lenten Series could lead to representative Holy Week services in which World Two could provide the form for Palm Sunday, with World One appropriate for Maundy Thursday, World Four for Good Friday, World Five for Holy Saturday, and World Three for Easter. Such a study series could also be used as an introduction to the church year which is itself a composite of theological Worlds.

The most intentional approach to orientation is probably through study groups. Although we will develop methods and techniques for variegated learning in the next chapter on Christian education, it will be helpful here to describe three workshop efforts in variegation that have been used in contrasting congregations.

1. The first attempt was with an *inner-city, racially mixed congregation* where educational events had seldom been held. Workshops were held on four consecutive Wednesday evenings, beginning at 5:30 P.M. with a brown bag supper. This was followed by an hour session taught by an unordained staff woman. The class, limited to eight persons, was entitled "Discovering and Naming God's Presence in Our Lives." The separate sessions were entitled: "Discovering Our Life Issues and Questions," "Naming our Problems and Longings," "Is Jesus Christ an Answer?" and "Worship and Spiritual Resources for Our Needs." A teaching chart was used to present and contrast the content of each of the five Worlds (see Theological Worlds Teaching Chart).

Half of each session was spent sharing each others' stories and experiences as they applied them to the *obsessios* and *epiphanias*. A mark of the success of this effort was the ease with which depth sharing happened and the interest in having the study offered again.

This experience suggested that dialogue might be the preferred method to be used in the inner-city context. With 80 percent of the congregation composed of single parents, and members scattered over a wide area, practical issues such as child care suggested the wisdom of dispersing the next workshop sessions in homes of the participants. These locations would also give an opportunity to create some action-reflection settings for identifying how alternative theological Worlds find expression in the context of one's daily living.

2. The second church effort was in a *rural, small town setting*. After church one Sunday, a young female pastor handed out twenty-five Theological Worlds Inventories, asking parishioners to fill them out at home, and bring them back Wednesday night to the monthly study/worship session. This was a regular event in which the pastor normally presented different topics for discussion, closing with a ritual of reconciliation and Eucharist. The theological Worlds event drew the largest attendance, and an unsigned written evaluation rated it best of all previous sessions. Several who had trouble with the terminology of the Inventory indicated that "since it was all new, an introduction would have been helpful." Nevertheless, most persons managed fairly well with the instruction to "follow your instincts and skip any question you don't understand." The pastor surmised that "in a church with more professional/educated people, this would have been no problem." The persons gathered with "high excitement," "looking forward to finding out where they were theo-

logically, comparing this with others, and exploring what this meant for them." After each person shared the results of the Inventory for them, the pastor illustrated each World with appropriate scriptures and hymns. In each case, there was surprise that these were indeed favorites of the residents in the respective Worlds, evoking genuine interest in learning why. Representatives of each of the five Worlds, in the order of Worlds One through Five, chose these as their favorites: "O Love That Will Not Let Me Go," "Onward Christian Soldiers," "Fill My Cup, Lord," "Amazing Grace," and "How Firm a Foundation."

Attention was then focused on the implications of these diverse Worlds for how worship could be changed so as to become more meaningful for each of the Worlds. Also considered was the implication of the fact that their lay worship leaders belonged within World Four, their pastor lived in World One, and there were no representatives at all from World Two. In considering the place and meaning of confession in worship, they concluded that there was need for silent confession, unison confession, words of assurance, and absolution—for each action would satisfy the particular needs of the contrasting Worlds. One of the most enlightening discussions concerned the way in which to open worship. They decided to add an invocation, for even though the pastor, belonging to World One, had no need to invoke an ever-present God, residents of World Four did.

In decided contrast to the church's leadership, most of the persons present were from Worlds Three and Five. This discernment brought clarity in discussing what persons expected preaching to be. In contrast to their pastor, the group emphasized the need to feel accepted, as this was revealed above all through Christ's suffering and endurance. Relatedly, in discussing the Eucharist, World Three folk emphasized how Christ's presence fills the emptiness within them. Their clarity in knowing what they wanted became tense at one point. World One representatives expressed the need for times of silent prayer and personal centering before worship begins. World Three persons, on the other hand, insisted that this should be a necessary time for greetings and fellowship, referring to it as "Hug Therapy Time." The compromise was to have both, understanding in a new way that the needs of each World should be clearly identified as being necessary and viable parts of worship itself. Through such sharing came a greater understanding and thus tolerance for the needs of one's fellow worshipers.

THEOLOGICAL WORLDS TEACHING CHART

Essential Rhythm	Issue	Feel	Obsessio (Human Condition)	State	Atonement	Christology	Epiphania (Salvation)
1 Separation and Reunion	Cosmos	Longing	Isolation experienced as abandonment (mystery, obtuseness, throwness, opaqueness, meaninglessness)	Alien / Orphan	Experiential (substantive, humanistic, revelational) "To mediate" Love as tearing the veil	Revealer / Evoker (to lead me home)	Coming home / Being home (harmony)
2 Conflict and Vindication	History (evil)	Anger (rage)	Normlessness experienced as chaos (enigma, wrenched, invaded, oppressed, opposed)	Warrior	Constitutive (classical, ransom, dualistic) "To combat" Love as taking our part	Messiah / Liberator	New Earth (consummation)
3 Emptiness and Fulfillment	Self	Ache (void)	Self-estrangement experienced as impotence (insignificance, self-alienation, not belonging, lost potential, invisibility)	Outcast	Enabling (subjective, representative, incorporative) "To model forth" Love as filling to overflowing	Example / Model	Wholeness (enriched belonging)
4 Condemnation and Forgiveness	Demonic	Guilt	Powerlessness experienced as idolatry (diseased, condemned, falling short, fearful)	Fugitive	Compensatory (objective, forensic, exchange) "To take away" Love as forgiving the unworthy	Savior / Redeemer	Adoption (reprieve)
5 Suffering and Endurance	Life	Over-whelmed	Meaninglessness experienced as engulfment (plagued, flooded, controlled, manipulated, wronged)	Victim / Refugee	Assumptive (subjective, reversal, cancel, anneal-ment) "To write off" Love as Outlasting with long-suffering	Suffering Servant / Companion	Survival / Endure (integrity)

At the conclusion of this session, a second retreat was planned for church school teachers, "so we can specifically look at where each teacher stands theologically, and how each can become more inclusive and responsive to the particular students they teach." The pastor has since begun using theological Worlds in her own counseling. She illustrated the pastoral value of understanding theological diversity this way. A member came to her complaining of "those depressing prayers of confession" in Sunday worship. "As an air traffic controller, I hear all week at work how inadequate I am. So I come to church to escape all that." After explaining the Worlds to him, they concluded that he belonged to World One, and what he was really seeking on Sunday was to "go home." This also gave him a new perspective for understanding why World Four folk need confession. "I suggested that he use the new silent time at the beginning of worship to let go of work, and then continue his 'alone time with God' while the rest of us moved into confession. He has been happy ever since."

The pastor expressed surprise over the continuing impact of that one evening. "When people tease each other about what World they are in, this tells me that they've integrated it and are using it." She wrote this conclusion. "The idea of theological Worlds has been an excellent means for discovering where my people are theologically, making me not only sensitive to their diverse needs, but more creative in serving them. It also creates unity and harmony as together we come to appreciate diversity rather than resent it. Above all, preparing worship has become an exciting experience for me."

3. The third church event for encouraging variegation was *suburban*. A three session, Lenten, spiritual growth event was offered by a visiting pastor. The first one hour session began by asking persons to name their favorite hymns, then the scriptures they liked best. These were written on a chalkboard. The "Self-Rating" section of the Theological Worlds Inventory was distributed and taken. Third, the descriptive teaching chart of the theological Worlds (see diagram 1) was distributed, and folks were invited to explore together the deeper meaning of the hymns and scriptures previously named. At the conclusion of the evening, the rest of the Theological Worlds Inventory was taken home to complete.

The second session began with a discussion of the individual results from the Inventory, naming any surprises from the first session. Some of the persons expressed the opinion that perhaps too much information was being supplied too quickly. As the group discussed the structure of their weekly *worship*, it turned out that an unspoken but deep resentment existed over the gathering time before worship. Here again it was the conflict between a quiet, meditative time, and a period for fellowship and vigorous greeting. For the first time, they were able to understand the issue theologically, and thus were able to resolve the anger by acknowledging that both needs were viable. Instead of choosing, diversity necessitated being more inclusive.

During the third session, theological Worlds were applied to different understandings of *prayer*. They discovered that World One persons preferred contemplation; World Two tended to contend and intercede with God through prayer as dialogue; World Three favored meditation; World Four understood prayer basically as confession and absolution; and World Five named litany as well as petition, but found it difficult to ask for things for themselves. After an experience in guided meditation, a time for intercessory prayer once again opened up the contrasts. The normal practice in this church was to take turns lifting up the names of persons needing prayer. When questioned, the World Three majority insisted that it was sufficient simply that these persons be remembered. After an insight from a World Five person, the exchange went deep. "I need to know the circumstances. If I am to take on the pain and suffering of others, just like God does, it has to become concrete. I need to feel it too." The pastor's conclusion, six months after these sessions occurred, was this. "Most of us in the local church tend to do maintenance preaching—the same basic way each week, using the same order of worship, and doing education and counseling the way we have always done it. But the Theological Worlds Inventory is making it possible for me and my parish to see and do things differently. We acknowledge our diversity now, and both of my congregations have become more tolerant and inclusive."

These are three examples of orientation into variegated ministry. The next stage is implementation.

Stage Four: Implementation

The remainder of this book is concerned with how implementation modifies significantly the church's traditional functioning—

namely how to make variegation a central feature in education, worship, preaching, administration, evangelism, and pastoral care. Yet a central issue to be raised in analyzing each function is whether or not it is wise, or even possible, to restructure the church intentionally into subcongregations or distinct groups. Each church, as it moves through this process of acknowledgment, discernment, orientation, and implementation, will need to decide the degree to which restructuring might be useful. A pastor of a small church suggested what he would do when moved to a larger church where two worship services would be likely. "I'd be inclined to orient one service toward Worlds One and Five, the other toward Worlds Two, Three, and Four." Such experiments are important, for, as we shall see, variegation is not an either/or choice, but a spectrum along which rich possibilities are diversely scattered.

If full restructuring is possible, organizing according to contrasting subcongregations, the Variegated Church Diagram suggests a model—one to which we will have occasion to refer in the chapters that follow.

The two innermost circles represent multiple subcongregations as alternative liturgical centers, formed around "vision events" as churchwide activities that provide experiences of unity in diversity. Each subcongregation is divided into "covenant groups" of eight to twelve people. These meet weekly for fellowship, characterized by support, study, and accountability, perhaps oriented around a love feast. Each person, in turn, has a "spiritual friend." Such variegation depends centrally on two functions belonging particularly to the ring marked Christian Education—those of membership and confirmation training, with a faith-sponsor from the appropriate subcongregation paired with each person. The additional rings indicate churchwide structures composed of representatives chosen by each subcongregation. The Management Board is responsible for budget and physical facilities, while the Coordinating/Planning Council both orders the diverse activities of the subcongregations and oversees representational ministries. The latter are done by Task Groups, developed as needed for the creative functioning of the church's inner life and as outreach ministries responsible for the church's external life.

An analogy might help place imaginatively in our minds the image of a variegated church. The purpose of a variegated congregation might be likened to an art museum. There would be guides, not to protect the paintings as much as to encourage their appreciation. In the lobby, not too far from the free coffee, people discuss particular styles of paintings, and gradually folks begin to find those whose choices and views are similar to their own. As these compatible groups form, they gravitate back to the particular gallery where their special kind of art is on display—coming to know each other in the process. Those who have chosen their special gallery make use of the library in the corner, studying about their favorite artists, and learning to appreciate them by knowing their place in art history. Before long, the excitement of some persons might be enough to gain permission to hold studio classes in the basement, where each helps all to practice their art. But no matter what the activities, the members of each group keep returning regularly to their favorite gallery, where they reexperience what they are about—and why. Each group begins to take on its own defining rhythm, each person settling in to what they can do best for the good of their common love. The more they enjoy what they are about, the more they realize how much they are helped by having other groupings nearby, providing overtones of contrast.

People come, and some people go. First time visitors, the wanderers and searchers, are given a map and encouraged to "see it all." They hear presentations from various persons committed to the viability of their particular approach to art. Throughout, visitors are invited to sample and see, so that they can discover the gallery that best echoes with their souls, preparing them to settle down in commitment to a particular "home base." They are even given permission to enter some of the basement workshops and play with the paint. Here the longing of visitors to paint commingles with excited invitations to participate in alternative ways of doing so. The promise is that after one learns how to mix paint and build framed canvas, the real joy is in being promoted—invited to bring one's easel into the gallery itself. There one learns to paint by imitating the great paintings on the wall. And there, among one's colleagues, one discovers that there are folks who understand one's fledgling efforts better than one does. One is particularly blessed if there is one special person who can encourage a person to become who she or he truly is. Advent and Lent are special times when one is invited to paint the best picture that one is capable of painting. These are covered with sheets. Then on Christmas and Easter mornings they are uncovered for all to see.

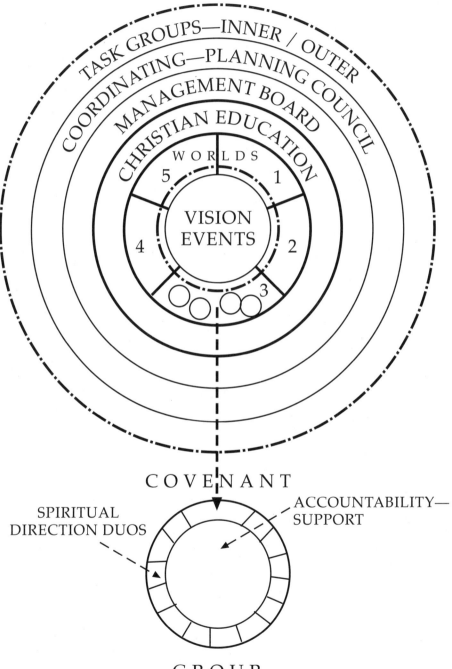

Over the whole museum is a warm fluidity, never lacking for halls where one can discuss art with others, or quiet corners to explore thoughts or to confess doubts, with open invitations to revisit other galleries, "just to be sure." From time to time there are special exhibits so that everyone can taste contrasting Worlds—El Greco (World One), Van Gogh (World Two), Renoir (World Three), Rouault (World Four), and Rembrandt (World Five). The rationale for this variegated museum would not be to show that somehow the various schools and styles are really all alike, having a least common denominator, so that new paintings will be encouraged to look alike. With such a criterion, we would know which paintings to take down and store in the closets. No, the rationale of this museum is to exhibit a rich diversity, which, together and separately, will enable us to deepen our love of art. From time to time this enthusiasm bubbles out in mutual sharing, but one always returns to the accountability and support of one's group, committed to deepening and blossoming in one's perspective. Particularly dear are those times when, after everyone else leaves, one has permission to tiptoe into one's beloved gallery, and just sit there, quietly enthralled, absorbed by the beauty. Sometimes one group or another will remember to give humble thanks to other groups and in so doing, admit that what is being enjoyed by others in alternative galleries is art too. And because of them, I can confess that I have learned my "yes" by saying "no."

CHAPTER SEVEN

Christian Education as a Variegated Enterprise: Seeing the Whole

Using Contemporary Christian Education Options

Theologizing, as we have insisted, is best understood not simply as a discursive enterprise, or as one activity among others. It is rooted in the meaning core out of which comes the motivational intent and energy for every activity. Theologizing is the process of furnishing one's World with behavior. It follows that Christian education is not simply one activity among other church activities. It is the effort to reflect upon the church's total actions so that its meaning core becomes theologically self-conscious, coherent, and pluralistically faithful for each member.

Some of today's major approaches to contemporary Christian education can become exciting if used as means to this diversified end. Unfortunately, however, these educational theories are often divorced from significant theological grounding, and thus from careful translation of their implications as *praxis*. As a result, they are wrongly made to appear as rivals, if not combatants. Our first task, then, is to show how the most creative of these present-day educational approaches become compatible when variegation is made the goal. Educator Jack L. Seymour is right in grounding Christian education in the fact that "human beings construct models, paradigms, and myths which serve as interpretive frameworks." These provide the "lenses through which the world is focused, and define patterns, experiences, and facts to which individuals must respond." By recognizing that these "define the way reality is structured," Seymour is affirming, in effect, the foundational nature of theological Worlds as basic to the task of contemporary Christian education. [1]

So interpreted, major current approaches can become strategies for developing the framework on which Christian education in the variegated church can rest. The goal for each of these approaches should be, as James MacDonald states, to help "persons understand, explore, and enhance the patterns by which they organize their meaning." [2]

1. Education as Instruction in Self-conscious Learning. *Cleros* means inheritance; *laos* means the people of God who hold the *cleros* sacred. In time, however, "clergy" came to indicate designated persons set aside to guarantee that the inheritance (gospel) is preserved by the people of God. The church has long held, rightly, that the gospel is a "given." This is why stepping over the new threshold into diversity is so difficult. Instead of prideful fighting over which version of the inheritance is the true one, our approach proposes that from now on faithfulness must be to God—the One who authors a configuration of viable alternatives, together weaving Christianity into that rich tapestry by which each unique self in its preciousness can find a home.

This understanding calls for significant changes in Christian education as traditionally practiced. First, this is a post-Christian age, in which it cannot be assumed that the average person has even minimal knowledge of scripture, faith, and practice. Second, the fact that the Christian "given" is itself a texture of perspectives, requires greater attention to self-conscious instruction than was previously needed. This task of correlating deep respect for the variety of persons with a diversity of perspectives requires a diversity of methods. This need will intensify rather than lessen as the church's concern for its inheritance *(cleros)* becomes recognized as a rich mosaic.

Put another way, variegation requires such clear encounter with viable options that choice cannot be avoided. Vague exposure, or interesting informational presentations, will no longer suffice. The subjectivity necessary for the wager that is faith, however, does not reduce the gospel to subjectivity. Rather, it identifies faith as the willingness to live and die for the gospel *as perceived and appropriated.* Thus we can see Christian education as "a 'school' in some form [that] is still important in the transmission of values, beliefs, and practices from one generation to the next." [3] For this, James Michael Lee is right in insisting upon *intentionally* structured and controlled learning environments, deliberately created for the sake of acquiring Christian behavior. [4] But in the variegated church, there is need for alternative environments and multiple methods. Together they can effect learning both within the commonality of one's own professed theological World, as well as cross-World interaction as model for living in today's pluralistic world.

2. *Education as Vision Centers*. Liturgy (as temple worship) is drama and rehearsal, as contrasted with instruction (synagogue). True education requires both. It is important to know *about* a World. But more important, and very different, is the process of walking into that World—to see, hear, smell, taste, and touch—all from within. For better or worse, each church building performs this temple function as sanctuary, proposing as sacred that which is worthy of being set apart. Such a sensual forming of space and time into a lived anatomy of meaning is crucial, for it "molds and shapes the self and its world." Thus the church's architecture, poetry, music, art, and rituals are not peripheral or external decorations. "It is through these that the basic patterns of religion are interiorized, exhibited, and transmitted." [5]

Crucial in Christian education, then, is the church as vision center—the imaginational reservoir out of which springs our thinking and acting. In the past decade, it was the mall, itself a model of unity within diversity, that so functioned for many youth. Today the vision center is fast becoming the Internet, with intense individualism in search of "belonging stations." What all of us need is an environment intentionally created to be a "pure type," a World distilled and rendered sacred with a purity and focus never actually appearing in daily life.

I remember a trip to France. My youngest daughter was having a bad morning, obstinately determined to do personal violence to every flower in front of Chartres Cathedral. I opened the huge front door, and she boisterously walked right in. She made a sudden stop. Slowly she tiptoed back to me, and reached for a hand to be held. Then we walked quietly and gently together through a World in which an occasional whisper of fascination was the only appropriate sound. A vision center is a place of focused intensity where chaotic variegation is transformed by being rehearsed and acted out as the anatomy of a defining rhythm. The church must provide this in the melody line of Ash Wednesday and of Easter, of Gethsemane and of Pentecost, of fasting and of Eucharistic banquets. Such event places are not only where eyes are honed to see the structured meaning in one's common life, but where the heart is teased by foretaste into faithfulness as the "assurance of things hoped for" (Hebrews 11:1).

Serving at the heart of the church as vision center are the sacraments and ordinances, distilled out over the centuries by the church into those points where life's density intersects with Christian vision—the seven acts of birthing, calling, forgiving, nurturing, relating, sanctifying, healing, and dying.

Thus a strong case can be made for liturgical subcongregations as vision centers of alternative theological Worlds, furnished with contrasting sacramental concreteness. Even in the small church, it is possible, as we shall see, to create both liturgical and homiletical variegation. Such vision centers, then, offer the experiential heart of each theological World, where the past is rehearsed as a critical rerembering in the present, embodying seeds for the future by virtue of a vision promised. Whatever the church's structure, the church year, in turn, provides special educational opportunities for cross-congregational vision events, as the unifying and exciting experience of celebrating richly the collective home bases of alternative Worlds.

3. Education as Faith Communities. To summarize thus far, instruction is where one "reflects on." A vision center is where one "participates within." Now faith community takes a further step into a context of accountability, whereby one becomes committed "to make it so." Wesley regarded such faith communities as so indispensable that he forbade his ministers to preach anywhere if the converts could not be organized into covenant groups before the evangelist left. One cannot be a Christian without a faith community in which one is affirmed, and before whom one stands responsible to the same horizon of meaning. Just as monastic communities entail intentional life under a "rule," so within each World there needs to be formed a group of disciplined faithfulness to the shared memory/vision. These are laboratories for Christian living in which education becomes socialization under apprenticeship.[6] John Westerhoff is correct in holding that real transmission of Christian faith/lifestyle is done by experiencing such an "intentional, covenanting, tradition-bearing faith community."[7]

Such faith groupings are both internally and externally variegated. Externally, the emphasis is on professing, even defending as viable, one's theological World, as well as learning to live tolerantly and lovingly within a diversity that is a microcosm of the church. For example, a citizen of World Two might need to defend faith as radical action in behalf of justice, while learning patience in return from those in World One, for whom faithfulness entails "being in the presence." Internal variegation is to experience accountability from those who inhabit the same World. Thus the same person, being now with those for whom social action is not debatable, is pushed beyond "talking a good game." The engagement is no longer why, but when and where and how. Such actions, in turn, are made into occasions of reflection, rendering commitment a deeper step into learning.

4. *Education as Spiritual Direction.* The fourth dimension of Christian education rests in the awareness that Christianity as faithful living is an ongoing process of personal growth in grace—with arrival not a valid category. Yet whereas faith is personal, it dare not be either individualistic or private. One cannot be a Christian alone. The "priesthood of all believers" requires that one have at least one spiritual companion for the road. Such concrete pairing retains vestiges of the idea of baptismal godparents and confirmation sponsors. The church is beginning to give these relationships depth by identifying them as spiritual direction.

When I was a child, this crucial theological individuation began with my mother's nightly supervision of my prayers. It was not long before my accountability came by being incorporated into the family unit as a whole, the home functioning as a domestic church. We even had a designated prayer corner, a mealtime offering of grace as a little Eucharist, and a family Bible recording all of the family's sacramental events (baptisms, confirmations, marriages, deaths). In this post-Christian era, such intrinsic spiritual direction within families is largely lost, even for Christians. Yet with the advent of diversity, never has the need for spiritual direction been greater. The complexity of providing variegated spiritual direction makes this a new and crucial responsibility for the church.

In ages when faith was more monolithically viewed, spiritual direction took its analogy from that of apprenticeship, the relation of novice to expert. But with the growing awareness of theological diversity, the role of director needs to be less that of expert, and more that of spiritual friend or soul companion, with whom one is committed to walk in mutual discernment of the Spirit's leadings. In a real sense, then, all congregational members are novices, needing a partner with whom to recognize that the real director is the Holy Spirit. Such pairing is provided by the mother before a child's birth. It is continued by the church when at baptism the seeds of the Spirit are planted. Godparents are partly responsible to bring that person to "harvest time"—called Confirmation, aided by an individual membership process tailored for each new member. Bishop Rueben Job is reassuring when he insists that most of us, carefully paired, are capable of participating in such a comentoring educative process. "All of us may not be gifted spiritual directors, but all of us can benefit from the skill and wisdom of another person to enable and nourish our spiritual development." [8]

5. Education as Correlation. This dimension, in being most inclusive, could well be seen as the goal, for which the other educational approaches are understood as means. Tillich's phrase, the "method of correlation," makes explicit the dialogical nature of learning. Living requires an ongoing dialogue between one's faith orientation and one's daily context. The goal of Christian education is to render self-conscious this ongoing making and living of connections.

Having considered these five educational dimensions, we are ready now to draw the implications for variegated Christian education as such. For a century, the Sunday school has been at the heart of Protestant efforts at conceptual transmission of the faith, with Roman Catholics relying on parochial education to provide the equivalent. In both cases, it has been only partially successful. In *method*, the weakness centers in the unevenness of teacher training. In *content*, its weakness centers in the theological tyranny of teacher and curriculum. What is strange is the unexamined assumption that each denomination needs a national office whose task it is to publish unending streams of curricula, which, once used, are thrown out, supposedly obsolete. With these offices tending to operate from a liberal emphasis in method, the theological posture from which a particular writer explicates the assigned subject seems left largely to that particular writer, chosen for some other reason. The result, at least in mainline Protestantism, is a curriculum of random diversity, rather than one intentionally structured to provide a coherent variegated theological foundation that poses informed, forced choices. The genius of the Roman Catholic Rite of Christian Initiation of Adults confirmation training is its reliance on shared autobiographies.

Understandable, then, is the ongoing cry of conservatives for "more Bible." The response of liberal educators is to provide more biblical stories and Bible references. But in so doing, the two theological perspectives bypass each other almost totally. What is really occurring in most denominations is that World Four persons are unable to find themselves in a curriculum characterized by a World

Three perspective. Whereas the recent resurgence of interest in spiritual formation is touching World One persons for the first time in a generation, World Two persons are experiencing this new emphasis as a betrayal of the social justice emphasis that they have worked so hard to insert since the 1960s. This crisis in Christian education pushes toward an important conclusion: *any uniform curriculum of the future must be rooted in intentional theological variegation.* The present random diversity, in contrast, is a pluralistic confusion that tends to convey theological indifference.

A solution through variegation might begin with a new approach to uniform curriculum resources. They should no longer be modeled after the analogy of dated magazines, but should center in theologically intentional, reusable texts. The present pluriformity of continuous replacement with random variety needs to be supplanted, first, with materials for use in a pattern of yearly contexts, such as Lenten and Advent studies, confirmation classes, and new member training. These need to be prepared as part of a theologically intentional whole, rather than developed, as now, by different denominational departments, using random writers, for contrasting purposes. What is needed is a consistent, intentional, and coherently variegated educational design.

Second, texts for weekly use need to approach subjects and themes from clear and identifiable theological alternatives. Such interactive materials are used not so much to evoke discussion of one's existing opinions, as they are to pose viable alternative perspectives with such force that the need to choose goes deep. I used to teach contemporary theology in such a way that for a three hour block the student was immersed, for example, in the World of Karl Barth. Fairly convinced, the students returned for the next session, only to be immersed in the theological World of Rudolf Bultmann. "Which one is right?" came the urgent question. It is at this point that real learning can occur—for the dialogue of the two depends on priorities and commitments characterizing each World. The dialogue is urgent, for next week we will lose ourselves in an alternative theological World—that of process thinkers, for example.

The third possible solution is more controversial. For decades, mainline denominations have been waging battle with many local churches. Whether the denominational headquarters is in Louisville, Cleveland, Nashville, or Atlanta, there is a concerted effort to force each church to purchase and use the denomination's usually liberal materials. The primary foe for such educators is independent conservative resources, such as David C. Cook. This conflict has been mounting until conservative caucuses are now threatening to create their own materials. This impasse is forcing a difficult decision upon the church, one with far-reaching consequences as to how deep and broad the variegation of the church of the future will be. The dilemma can be put concretely and bluntly as a question. Are mainline denominations caringly and intentionally willing to nurture those within their midst for whom the blood atonement of Jesus Christ is indispensable for life eternal? Such a question is reciprocal: are these members of World Four willing to disagree in such a way as to treat their fellow Christians as those for whom Christ also died—even if their understanding of atonement might be lived out in contrasting fashion? If the answer is "no," from either side, such unwillingness is prophetic for both church and society. But if what truly matters is serious commitment within serious diversity, the local church of the future will not need to seek outside materials. Rather, it will be the denomination's own deep responsibility, and not only that of including such conservative perspectives interactively throughout its total curriculum. It must provide, as well, in-depth study of that alternative as truly viable. To create such a variegated curriculum will entail special writers, those who, while owning their own theological home, are capable of operating imaginatively within Worlds not their own.

In addition, such variegation will require, as well, a serious use of a variegated methodology, as we shall explore in detail later. Rather than reducing method to uniform suggestions within the curricular material, variegated methodology will need to be taught to teachers who will know it so well that they will be free to make each student a unique focus. The teacher will be encouraged to master material and method together, for they will be using a curriculum that is not to be discarded, but will be used again.

Fundamental, then, to the educational program of each variegated church will be several *instructional* modules for introducing the idea of alternative theological Worlds as the formative base for the church's life, structure, and learning. After the congregation's initial transition, such modules would normally be offered as confirmation training and as a workshop for new members. This understanding would be reinforcement through special *vision events*, for example, capturing the rhythm of the church year. Throughout, the focus is not on individuals, but on the person—with the educational process being one of identifying, understanding, rehearsing, deepening, and holding each person accountable to their particular World as truly worth living with passion.

With these pieces of the church's holistic educational program in place, the church school can increasingly become an arena for correlation, for example, drawing connections. Usually the church school materials speak of group discussion, providing several questions to be used. This approach encourages a dialogue of opinions, without any "given" to wean persons from expressing and reinforcing the status quo. True correlation, however, is quite different. Once a person's orienting theological perspective has been identified, the focus can increasingly be on shared *praxis*. The intent is to broaden and deepen daily faith-action through engagement with those acting out of alternative orientations. Here spirituality and social change are partners, where "righteousness and peace will kiss each other" (Psalm 85:10).

Learning as correlation means testing the viability and application of one's World encountered with facts. Those that World Two residents might pose for residents of the other Worlds might be something like these: in the United States, one teenager commits suicide every ninety minutes, a woman is raped every six minutes, twenty-five million persons at this moment are debilitated by alcohol and drug abuse, 15 to 25 percent of elderly persons suffer from significant mental illness, half of all our marriages end in divorce, we lead the industrial world in homicides, far more persons per capita are in prison than in any other nation in the world, and we are the last major country to exercise the death penalty. "What do you do with these facts?" Each World would have, from the wealth of its stance, questions for other Worlds by which to grow and deepen.

Even if this kind of correlation did occur in today's church school, too often it would be an ongoing debate over whether the church should change people or systems. This debate would continue, but with a more genuine sense of alternatives. Furthermore, variegation makes selective involvement impossible. Church uniformity is no longer expected or even desired, either as conclusion or in strategy. Whereas the diversity of interaction will not dictate *what* to do, it will make it difficult for any group to have an excuse for inaction. Removed from any need for approval by *the* church in order to act, subcongregational action is no longer inhibited. In fact, variegation may entail contrasting subcongregations or groups from the same church acting for opposite positions, as in the case of abortion. Together they might better witness to truth's complexity, discouraging simplistic answers. Struggling together at the intersection of life's sacredness with freedom's responsibilities might be the best display of Christian faithfulness.

To summarize this variegated approach to Christian education, *vision centers* will provide contexts in which theological perspectives are rehearsed, formed, and deepened. In larger churches, these will probably take the form of subcongregations or primary groupings, self-consciously organized as pilgrims searching out together the specific calling of each.[9] Foundational for this restructuring will be *instructional* events as apprenticeships into the task of theological self-consciousness. *Covenant groups* will be where those of common orientation hold each other accountable in lived commitment. And the *Sunday school* itself will increasingly provide intentional opportunities for correlation, thereby enlarging and deepening one's faith *praxis* in the midst of similarity and contrast.

The variegated church so understood can be, in turn, an educational model for society as well. In the first place, it can witness to how persons and groups with strong but contrasting commitments can learn to live together without doing violence to each other. It shows how commitment can keep persons from being intimidated by difference into a passive conformity. A second kind of modeling for society is more complex. Commitments tend to be strongest at the point of maximum self-interest. Consequently, despite the teachings of Jesus, evidence of true self-transcendence remains rare. The willingness to sacrifice for others one's personal status, power, stability, possessions, and/or recognition is uncommon. In the variegated church, however, there is reason to hope that the interaction of contrasting subcongregations or groupings will foster *sacred embarrassment*. Through the interactive proximity of alternatives, critical thinking will be encouraged, almost naturally, exposing for each other the undue domestication of one's professed commitment. For example, citizens of World One will develop and practice their prayer life in proximity with World Two folks, whose passion for social justice makes them suspicious of prayer as escape. World Two persons, in turn, will have to justify and do their social action under the suspicious eye of World One persons, who question the motives of those who like to exercise power and be seen. With such intraexposure of alternative Worlds, there may issue forth an elemental honesty. All of us, left to ourselves, are east of Eden, still spitting out seeds.

Action-Reflection as a Way of Life

Whatever portions of this variegated approach a church may adopt, the goal needs to remain constant: to render educational the church's whole life. The task of self-conscious or intentional Christian education, then, is to see that the church's activities become actions, which reflection can turn into part of one's theologizing process. John Westerhoff is correct in identifying the educational task as rendering self-conscious, and thus intentional, the hidden curriculum of the total church life already functioning in being a community.

One way in which we disguise this holistic understanding of education is by restricting the image of teacher to workers in the church school. To counter this, a key responsibility for the variegated pastor would be to become the teacher who renders multiple church functions into intentional teaching roles. Such educative functionaries, then, would include custodian, secretary, communion steward, organist, choir director, callers, greeters, readers, ushers, choir members—until the educational "staff" increases toward including all active members.

For this to happen, all members need to be helped into theological self-consciousness. The action-reflection method is especially helpful in doing this. It could begin with guided dialogue, for either individuals or as a group, identifying the essential actions that identify their function in the church. This is followed by a "why?" question, helping persons go behind the action to reflecting on its meaning. The "why?" includes first one's ownself, then others who are touched by one's ministry. A third step is to help persons imagine the creative possibilities that could emerge if one were to render one's work theologically self-conscious. The custodian, for example, in coming to see his or her job as a theological calling, can begin to recognize the theological meaning of the various church settings for which she or he is responsible. In taking personal interest in the meaning of these environments, such persons could become practical consultants for creative settings. The choir director, organist, and pastor, on the other hand, can become a team for action-reflection learning—discerning anthems, hymns, service music, liturgy, and sermons as theologically diverse formative contexts, bringing intentionality not only in regard to words but also to placement, time signatures, rhythms, and keys. As for a secretary, it might mean discerning as a deeply theological calling the task of facilitating order, flow, and communication within the church's interaction. Theologizing needs to characterize the staff's normal processing, cutting across the whole of the church's life, modeling for all what it means to see, theologically, the color of the church door, the shape of one's family table, the disclosures haunting one's monthly bank statement, and the anatomy of one's smile.

Christian Education as Spiritual Formation: The Teaching-Learning Process

Since Christian education is intent on rendering self-conscious the church's reason for being, *its purpose in regard to each person is that of spiritual formation.* John Macquarrie puts this clearly: "Spirituality is, in simple terms, the process of becoming a person in the fullest sense." [10] Interestingly, Christianity honors the self as a sacred center, yet a center with a haunting dilemma. "Originating sin" is one way of putting it, for between the "I" and "me" lives the false self that my biological line and I have been socialized to be. This fabricated, compulsive "me," a composite of dogged expectations and ragged rejections, is awarded to me in installments, beginning before my first birthday. It is this self which the "I" increasingly resents as roommate, whether the alarming feel is that of shame, anger, resentment, envy, or deception. Superego upon ego, expectations upon failures, trusts upon betrayals, hopes upon abandonment—all this is etched into one's life tapes. Even if one gains the courage to disregard what people think, the socialized "me" never forgets the adoption papers.

Responses to this mismatched self are different in each of us, coping grimly with busyness, impotence, drivenness, or drifting. Whatever their roots, there are dangerous memories hidden in one's untamed darkness, shaped and focused as an *obsessio.* This understanding commits the variegated church to a socialization view of learning. The church's task is to help each person bring this process into self-consciousness, discerning with clarity the lively dynamic between one's *obsessio* and *epiphania*. The result will be feelings, such as satisfaction, guilt, curiosity, or disappointment. They may lead negatively to a restless struggle with alternative Worlds as a way out of one's impasse. They may lead positively to discerning the contours of a familiar World, which claims one's commitment to practice it with solid resolve. Either way, spiritual formation involves alternative socializing, in which the true self can be teased into peeping out at *epiphanias*, as gracious hints gifted from a God who is beyond, or for, or in, or as, or with us depending on one's World. Faith is the gamble that one's half-wild universe has a face. Thus whatever form Christianity takes, it is the religion of being understood by a God who makes and keeps promises.

The present dynamic with which this understanding of Christian education makes contact is this: in order "to find some sense of 'ultimate meaning' behind their particular social world and lifestyle," persons today increasingly "seek out religious organizations that seem supportive of them." [11] This support, however, as offered by most mainline churches, is simply a means for settling into conformity. Variegation, in contrast, is the insistence that spiritual formation occurs best when the socialization process happens within a context of accountability, in proximity to alternative groups whose viability forces one to exercise critical thinking. The intent is to *create congregations that provide accountable support for one's pilgrimage.*

With this educational *goal* clear, and the ingredients at hand, the task now is to develop a teaching-learning *process* appropriate for achieving this end within a variegated context. Thomas Groome's "shared praxis" model is helpful here, bringing together an action-reflection process with a restored sense of education's overall goal as spiritual formation. [12] Groome's process identifies five steps. The first is to focus the session so that each person is encouraged to name one action or experience that illustrates the issue to be considered. This is best done in a small group setting. The emphasis is not on understanding ("What do you know?") but on function ("What do you do?"). Second, the facilitator asks questions so as to invite participants to think about *why* they answered as they did. This is the reflection part of the action-reflection process, stimulating critical thinking about the presuppositions and consequences of one's action. In this interplay, reason, memory, and imagination are the ingredients that we have identified as the theologizing process. I find it helpful to have persons reflect silently for several minutes on this "Why?" question, having paper and pencil available. These results are then shared, first in pairs, followed by these pairs reflecting to the larger group what they heard each other say. The convener distills this sharing by use of a chalkboard or newsprint.

The third step, done by a resource person, entails contexting what has been happening in the group by a "handing down of what has come to us over our past pilgrimage." Here the church's story/vision is presented as it applies to the particular focus of the session. This presentation usually has a dialogical tone, whether through lecture, audiovisuals, or research assignments by group members.

The fourth phase involves dialogue between the communal story as presented, and one's personal story, discerning the ways in which the two do or do not resonate. The focus here, as throughout, is not on testing for information retention, but on discerning the meaning and implications of the "why" behind one's answers. These "why" answers are hints about what we have been calling one's theological World. For example, the focus would not be on how the church defines prayer, but on why you do or do not pray. The purpose at this stage is discovery, or what we have called discernment.

Finally, the group focuses on consequences. In light of the critical thinking involved, what actions am I willing to take, and when? Throughout, the leader should be imaged as the leading learner, for the process is that of mutual learning in which teacher and learner are exchangeable functions rather than defining roles. Groome suggests the appropriateness of a liturgical celebration as providing closure; for worship, as a primary form of socialization, is a central expression of this growth process of invitation and confrontation.

Such an action-reflection process is the educational corollary of the theological understanding we have been developing. Autobiography is theological (action); theology is autobiographical (reflection). Together they constitute the learning process intrinsic to spiritual formation—that of bringing practice into self-conscious scrutiny under the press of "Why?"

Flexibility is quite possible, so that this process could be easily used in teaching theological Worlds. As an action base, one could use a story of the East Coldenham (New York) Elementary School cafeteria disaster. It was mid-November 1989, when the sky became frighteningly black. One hundred and twenty youngsters hesitated in their eating, then gasped as in one final shiver the glass and brick wall of the cafeteria screamed in on them. The second and third graders were slashed and crushed to death. Columnist Roger Rosenblatt, surveying the community three weeks after this tragedy, concluded that "what the people of the region are doing [in their agony] is using their imaginations to survive." As he watched and interviewed, he saw them running through the established attempts to answer the haunting question of "Why?" Some found themselves surrounded by faith in God's mystery as "unintelligible to human beings" (World One). For others, there was strength in the confession that all of us are guilty of sin, so none of us dare escape the reality, that in a sense "every calamity is just" (World Four). Some took refuge in affirming that "God suffers along with those he causes to suffer," as companions in a mutual struggle (World Two). Still others saw in the courage evoked by the event that this world is a vale of soul making, a model for stretching each of us into a fullness of which we did not think ourselves capable (World Three). And there were others who stoically carried on, led by a belief that "God is only found in tragedy" (World Five). [13] A discussion of such options with a group would lead quite naturally to sharing their own stories of tragedy. This could be followed by input that would make explicit the five theological Worlds that are implicit in facing any tragedy and thus life. Implications could hardly be held off until the end.

Another of my favorite methods in evoking this action process is with collages. The assignment is not, "Do a collage that tells us who you are." That process simply takes conceptual conclusions, and finds illustrations for the obvious. Instead, this is the assignment: "Tear out anything in these magazines that catches your attention, that you like." At the end of an hour, these instructions are given: "Now take what you have cut out, and find some way of arranging them on this poster board that makes sense to you." When this is finished, input on the alternative theological Worlds is given, as each person looks at their collage to discover what theology is foundational for who they are. Then the group does discernment with each collage, seeing dimensions of different Worlds, and finally concluding on what would seem to be the primal theological World informing that collage. Usually this is so informing that the collages tend to become treasures for their creators.

With the nature of this educative process clear, Groome suggests that it is important to return to step three. He indicates that the input presentation should be couched in these words: "And that is my understanding of the tradition on this topic. What do you think?" [14] True enough, but this is misleading. The teacher must make clear that this qualifying statement is far more than a polite or rhetorical device. It is the *perspectival* nature of one's presentation that needs to be named and carefully identified as only one version among others that the hearer needs to consider. Not to do this is to have the reader inevitably hear the presentation as *the* Christian answer. To disagree one would have to think that she or he had studied the Bible more than the leader. Not likely.

We must be careful of Groome's tendency to speak about appropriating *the* story. He is frighteningly wrong if he intends this learning process to operate as if there were one proper understanding of the gospel, toward which discussion is intent on moving the group to consensus. The crucial point that must be faced unflinchingly is this: *The task of Christian education is to enable each person to discern one's own rare version of Christianity, stimulated by exposure to viable alternatives, invited into a Communal context formed by the theological World which seems most compatible, so that commitment is forged through accountability.* Such a process requires a climate of trust where each person can share the stories through which one's operative images can be identified and the implications can be drawn and tested within hailing distance of one another.

Learning Styles

In developing Christian education for the variegated church, we have thus far identified the content of Christianity as diverse, the contemporary educational approaches which are useful, what the educational goal is, and described a viable teaching-learning process. Our next task is to explore the implications of diversity for establishing personalized learning styles. Studies show clearly that individuals learn in contrasting ways, and live what they learn in alternative fashion. Thus the variegated church must be characterized not only by variegated perspectives on Christian living, but also by variegated styles of learning. I have found quite helpful what could be called a Quadrant Learning Style Theory. There are four primary modes of learning:

LEARNING STYLE QUADRANTS

IV. immersion		I. dialogue
III. testing		II. input

Type One Learners ("Dialogue") learn best by being personally involved in a dialogue of listening and sharing. They do not really know what they know, or even what they think, until they hear themselves say it with social confirmation. These persons believe in their experiences, but need *help* from others in discerning their meanings. Thus they thrive on viewing concrete situations from various perspectives. This learning style values highly the art of being in touch with one's feelings. Their favorite questions are: "How do I feel about what is going on?" and "Who am I in all this?"

Type Two Learners ("Input") are attracted by theories and data, being uneasy about the apparent arbitrariness of opinions based on personal feelings. Since they understand by gaining information, they respect "experts" who know more than they do. Such input is appraised, especially by how well the ideas presented are sequentially argued, and the conclusions logically drawn. This learning style tends to appreciate ideas more than persons, data more than experiences, input over sharing, and intellect over opinion. Their favorite questions are: "What should I know?" and "What is true?"

Type Three Learners ("Testing") are fascinated with usability and application. They are less interested in feelings and ideas than in how things work. Thus they learn best by testing hunches or hypotheses with verification through use of the senses. They appreciate hands-on experience in problem solving situations. They resent being given answers, preferring to be intrigued by the questions. Persons with this learning style are bored with ideas for their own sake, interested instead in practical consequences, and in developing skills for making things work well. Their favorite questions are: "How does it function?" and "What works?"

Type Four Learners ("Immersion"), rather than being moved by feelings, ideas, or functioning, are excited by possibilities. The skill in which they revel is the imagination. They learn best by becoming immersed in a situation, exploring possibilities through trial and error. Usually having abundant energy, they are willing to try almost anything, at least once. Preferring to process data actively by participation, they enjoy risks, arriving at conclusions more often through intuition than hard data. They prefer to make new things happen, often for their own sake, being bored by repetition. This learning style is interested not primarily in knowing but in enriching, in exploring all the nuances, and in changing how things are done. There is less interest in the past or present than in the future. Their favorite questions are: "What if?" and "What then?"

There are various learning style inventories available for identifying the preferred learning mode of each student. [15] One easy way of sensing one's learning style, however, is an exercise in which each student is given the following statement and options, numbering them in terms of which they would try first, then second if the first does not work, until all four are numbered according to preference.

If you bought a computer for the first time, you would probably:

a) *invite a friend* over and have fun sharing what you know, and in figuring it out together (Type One Learner).
b) *call for advice* from a person you know who works for a computer company; or consider enrolling in a class (Type Two Learner).
c) *experiment,* using the instruction book as a guide (Type Three Learner).
d) *play with it* to see if you can figure it out for yourself (Type Four Learner).

This exercise is particularly helpful because it identifies not only one's preferred learning style, but the sequence of styles one is likely to use, as well as the neglected styles which a person needs to develop. Unfortunately, most Learning Style Inventory Tests only identify one's primary style, rather than the learning sequence. We will indicate later how the Myers-Briggs Type Indicator can be helpful here in expanding the learning implications.

Since we have identified spiritual growth as a primary focus of Christian education, it should be clear how knowledge of each student's learning style and learning sequence enables personalized variegated learning. In addition, this Quadrant Learning Style Theory is useful as a correlate of the teaching/learning process we have described. The five steps used have at least one activity favored by each type learner, so that the whole process can appeal at some point to each person's learning strength. To illustrate, in steps one and five, *immersion* learners (Type Four) appreciate and model the use of imagination, illustrating the topic with intriguing past situations, or conceiving new contexts with likely scenarios. *Dialogue* learners (Type One) can be catalysts for group sharing such as in steps two and four. These persons are talented in discerning learning as it is occurring during the sharing of experiences. They can be helpfully paired with persons reticent to share. *Testing* learners (Type Three) function well in steps three and five in sensing the implications of the "why" questions as they are reported back by various groups, in preparing the way for input concerning key points, and in anticipating practical consequences. *Input* learners (Type Two) will thrive on step three, and in the analytic functions characterizing step two. Yet it is important that the means of doing input in step three vary from time to time, so as to appeal to various quadrants.

The fifth step, that of moving from consequences to commitment, is particularly in need of individualization. Commitment based on generalized conclusions has little staying power. Thus an educational group structured through awareness of learning styles helps each member maximize the impact of one's preferred learning method, while strengthening commitment through support sufficient for one to risk using less developed styles. For example, the Type One learner will hardly become a committed person if there is no ongoing group with whom she or he can dialogue with trust. On the other hand, that commitment will likely become sterile unless challenged and deepened by serious thinking and content that moves one beyond the data of shared feelings.

To appreciate each person as a rare and precious expression of God's creativity is the necessary foundation upon which variegated education rests. It follows that each learning group is one of a kind, unique to the particular configuration of persons by which that group is blessed.

Faith Development

We have maintained that the primary goal of Christian education is spiritual formation. In developing the variegated nature of this enterprise, our exploration of learning styles has moved us beyond corporate methodological considerations to the diverse nature of each learning group, built upon the uniqueness of each member. This brings us to a crucial question: *is spiritual development itself uniform, or is it also variegated*? Important here is the work done by such educators as James Fowler, Sam Keen, Mary Wilcox, and Gabriel Moran, built upon the pioneering insights of Erik Erikson, Jean Piaget, Lawrence Kohlberg, and Carol Gilligan. All of these persons are concerned with determining if, in addition to stages of psychological, mental, moral, and gender development, there may be related stages in the self's religious development. [16] Fowler's concern is with the *form* of faith-development, whatever the content may turn out to be. [17] He has detected stages in spiritual growth, related to each other sequentially. His orienting premise is that persons become adults in terms of some myth or image around which a life story forms, thereby defining what it means to become a complete human being.

Such a premise makes common cause with our research concerning theological Worlds. What our work suggests is that at the heart of variegated education there needs to be the interaction of faith development stages with the pluriform content provided by theological Worlds. This interaction of stages and Worlds as the inseparable functioning of form and content is what identifies autobiography as a theological pilgrimage, evoking criteria by which to understand the unique maturation of each person.

Using Fowler, Keen, Kierkegaard, Moran, Ricoeur, Gilligan, and H. R. Niebuhr as guides, we arrive at a process of six stages in spiritual development, gridded with the content of the five theological Worlds.

—The *Player* is the child in each of us, characterized by imagination and fantasy, who plays into being *ex nihilo* the seemingly unlimited needs of expansive being. Models for imitation evoke the possibilities characteristic of this stage. This resembles Keen's child stage. Fowler's intuitive projective, with early nuances of Kierkegaard's aesthetic stage and Niebuhr's "Christ *of* Culture" posture.

FAITH STAGES

FAITH STAGES	Theological Worlds				
	1	2	3	4	5
A. Player			+		−
B. Explorer	+		−		
C. Conformist		−		+	
D. Rebel		+		−	
E. Paradox	−				+
F. Saint					

- indicates undeveloped phases
+ indicates home base deepened for sainthood

—The *Explorer* emerges when self and world begin to differentiate, as one is led to explore the functional nature of otherness for the sake of the emerging uniqueness of the self. Here the givens of one's defining context serve both as support and as foil. This exploration of identity through relationship tends for males to be in terms of distinction; for females it is primarily through connection. Suggestive here are Keen's youthful rebel, Fowler's mythic literal posture, and Niebuhr's "Christ *against* Culture" stance.

—The *Conformist* stage is reached when the individual searches for reunion with the social whole, craving a belonging and affirmation which will be sufficient to ground, if at all, a second foraging forth. These second and third stages are often repeated as ongoing alternation, until either one moves on, or, as is more usually the case, an uneasy equilibrium settles in. This stage resembles Keen's adult stage, Kierkegaard's moral stage, Fowler's synthetic/conventional stage, and a more mature level of Niebuhr's "Christ *and* Culture" option.

—The *Rebel*, more infrequently seen, is the restless one, the critic, the demythologizer. Here emerges a growing recognition that the meaning promised through acquisition and conformity results instead in an aborted self, gasping truly to be born. For the male, this rebellion is most often external, for the female, internal. The growing willingness to gamble for an unknown depth resembles Keen's outlaw, Fowler's individuating/reflexive posture, and Niebuhr's "Christ *above* Culture" posture.

—The *Paradox*, representatives of which are even more infrequent, are increasingly caught in the strangeness of the "is" as it intersects the "ought." One grows suspicious of life's givens and so-called universals, which were once taught and imposed as if objective norms. It becomes increasingly difficult to quiet the nuzzling hunger for an inclusivity of opposites, for reclaiming one's strange past, and refurbishing one's impossible dreams. It feels as if one is nibbling the outside of a fortune cookie, daring to believe that in due time it will read: "Your life just might have a wholeness after all." This stage bears the shadows of Niebuhr's "Christ and Culture *in Paradox*" position, Kierkegaard's resident on the outer edge of religion type A, and Fowler's conjunctive faith.

—The *Saint* is so anchored within one's theological World as home base that one can risk all, feeling the exhilaration that comes from no longer having to clutch. Fully aware of life as a spiritual lottery, and having placed one's wager firmly on a nonrefundable ticket, one is freed to experience glimpses of a pluralistic life, lived outrageously. Integrity is the honesty of living on the edge. No longer does one feel any need to justify who one is, for living deeply and faithfully one's own World is sufficient. The *epiphania* have sufficiently bombarded one's *obsessio* for one to be honestly and thankfully at peace with one's past, now present. Then it is that the imagination is liberated to serve as plumb line for the real. This stage makes contact with that of Keen's foolish lover, Niebuhr's "Christ *transforming* Culture," and Fowler's universalizing faith.

In the Faith Stages Chart, a minus (–) indicates the stage tending to be most undeveloped (the shadow) and thus most difficult for residents of a particular World. A plus (+) indicates the stage to which the saint in each World is most likely to return for resolving his or her pilgrimage. To illustrate, residents in World One tend to avoid or remain caught in the paradoxical dualisms of life. *Epiphania* is most likely through exploring unity in terms of relations. Persons in World Two are often shadowed by an inability to find belonging (conformity), thereby tempted to remain rebels for the sake of rebelling. Saintly closure is most likely through a vision, rendering rebellion the means to a noble end. In World Three, the shadow usually involves insufficient exploration, resulting in failure to discover oneself as a unique and willing self. *Epiphania* can come through freely chosen play, where "not knowing better" becomes a lyric "nevertheless." World Four's shadow results from insufficient experience in rebellion, so that conformity comes too naturally. But on the far side of rebellion there can emerge as *epiphania* a conformity which is the gift of humility. In World Five, the stage most often skipped is that of play, giving to life the appearance of premature adulthood. *Epiphania* most often emerges as steadfast resolve, in which play is part of the paradoxical and absurd response to the strange wonder of it all.

Faith stages, then, function differently within each theological World, giving to faith development a more diverse nature than is presently understood. What is constant in each is what impels movement forward—an existential dissonance experienced as cognitive conflict. Rosenstock-Huessey understood this in observing that conversion is not so much a "choice of" as an "unwillingness to continue as is." Likewise, Kierkegaard identified pilgrimage as a "leaping from," only recognized afterward as the power of the lure "toward." The variegated methodology we are developing needs to take seriously this indirect method. In contrast to liberal mildness, Kierkegaard speaks of "wounding from behind," and of sprinkling salt on open wounds—with love. This is a graphic way of describing the intersecting of accountability and belonging—the two indispensable features of the variegated church.

Myers-Briggs and Personality as Positively Variegated

Our concern thus far in this chapter has been to explore seven dimensions of diversity necessary for a variegated program of education: content, approaches, goals, arenas, processes, styles, and stages. There is one more—that of *personality*. One must be careful in bringing faith-development stages into Christian education, for recent attempts have tended to bootleg the educator's own theological posture, unintentionally giving a normative content to each stage. Instead, variegation *as* stages must also be developed into variegation *within* stages. The content within each faith stage is diverse, for it is contributed autobiographically. That is, the content is forged as pilgrimage within the distinctive contours claiming one as inhabitant of a particular World. *This distinctiveness of content, however, is due not only to each person's particular experience and environment, but also to its intersection with personality as itself diverse.*

There are two helpful instruments for appropriating this pluralism of personality as it is useful in variegated education. The first provides *positive* dimensions and is called the Myers-Briggs Type Indicator. It is widely used and available, whether professionally administered, taken in the self-scoring edition, on the Internet, or done through informal adaptations.[18] Its implications have been developed for a host of activities, from management to spirituality. My research over the years has been in exploring the relation of diverse personalities with theological diversity. Educators who postpone theologizing until the child is "cognitively ready" not only do not understand theology, but begin far too late. By then, the pilgrimage is well underway, with a marked map near at hand. One's unique theological pilgrimage has already begun by the time one is born, when one becomes exiled from the unique beat of the womb's time, and the warm mystery of inhaled and exhaled sound.

Myers-Briggs is an inventory based on a Jungian understanding of personality, identifying each person in terms of four scales. The E-I scale indicates whether one's home base is external (extrovert) or internal (introvert). Our research shows that for the extrovert Christian (most at home with people and things), revelation is most likely understood in terms of God's mighty acts in history. Therefore, with Moses, the syntax from God is "I will . . . therefore go." On the other hand, the introvert (oriented inwardly as center) understands best Elijah's experience of revelation. God is beheld neither in earthquake nor fire, but in the "still small voice." Thereby those who "wait on the Lord shall renew their strength."

The second scale (J-P) identifies how one knows what one knows. The judger decides quickly, then verifies the wisdom of that decision through its implications for decisive organizing, regulating, and controlling. "I like this tree, therefore . . ." The perceiver, on the other hand, is concerned to gather data, risking tentative conclusions only when required, primarily for guidance, understanding, and adaptation. "This is a Chinese Maple, and . . ." Applied theologically, the first type (with Anselm as a model) tends to function deductively, the natural method being that of faith seeking understanding. For example, " Jesus Christ rose from the dead, therefore . . ." The second type (with Aquinas as example) is more likely to function inductively, the method being that of understanding seeking faith. "Each new spring, adorned with life from dead stalks, makes the possibility of resurrection understandable."

Applied illustratively to worship, "Js" find an order of worship helpful, providing predictable flow that moves toward closure. "Ps," however, can feel bound by bulletins and time restraints, favoring flexibility and spontaneity. Extraverts prefer participative worship, where things happen. Introverts welcome the silence, when "doing" gives way to "being."

The T-F scale indicates *how* a person weighs data in making decisions. Thinkers reach conclusions through rational processes, using logical analysis, and favoring objectivity—"this is true." Feelers, by contrast, weigh each situation through subjective feelings, gained often through relationships—"this feels right." Thus in sermons, "Ts" prefer facts, moving in an orderly fashion toward a convincing conclusion. "I learned something." "Fs" prefer a sharing of experiences, suggesting possibilities that appeal to the heart. "I found that helpful."

The N-S scale indicates one's preferred source of data. Intuitives ("Ns") focus on possibilities, imagining the new in terms of a larger picture, fit for the future. Sensers prefer empirical facts and are interested in the present—with how things work, focusing on tangible results. Therefore "Ns" resonate with the poetry of a "new heaven and a new earth," whereas "Ss" are unimpressed without cost-estimates and feasibility projections. They understand Thomas's caution: "Unless I see in his hands the print of the nails . . ."

On the basis of these four scales, sixteen personality types are identifiable, each characterized by the four letters used to indicate one's inner or outer orientation, one's operational stance, and a primary and a secondary mode of functioning. So described, one can begin to see a correlation between such personality types and learning styles, which in turn operate on one's environment to help forge one's perspective as a theological World. This is true both in terms of method and in shaping one's metaphorical life in terms of images, such as God, church, and redemption. Whether Jung is correct or not in holding that one's personality type is a "given" at birth, it is clear that the contours are at least latently in place at a very early age.

We can move further in projecting the implications of this personality diversity for Christian education by linking several of the scales. The introvert-thinker becomes interested in religion if it can be understood as providing special knowledge. The introvert-feeler perceives religion in terms of special experience. The extravert-thinker favors revelation as interpretative events, either in history or in nature. The extravert-feeler is attracted by communal belonging. The introvert-intuitive is drawn by the richness of poetic imagery. The introvert-senser is inclined toward visions, sensory mysticism, or physical manifestations of the Spirit. The extravert-intuitive is intrigued by pattern, being a poet of parable and story. And the extravert-senser has an eye for miracle, for consequence, and for verifiable results.

The educational usefulness of such pluriform personality theory can go still further. A person's type can even suggest the direction that one's pilgrimage needs to take within one's World. A personal illustration may be helpful. Growth comes in walking into one's weakness (shadow) so that as an ETNJ, growth for me would be in the opposite directions, toward my undeveloped side—PSFI. [19] In other words, I am an extravert whose escape from the coal mines of my birth depended on disciplining my thinking, to the neglect of my feelings (which, as most undeveloped, is my shadow). When thinking was sufficiently established academically to please Yale, my diploma identified my primary mode of self-identity (thinking). In being solidly based there, my intuition received increased permission to develop. It became so strong that I still have the tendency to redesign anything I see, so that in church I have rearranged in my mind the sanctuary, brought in new pews, chosen different scriptures, and stained the beams. I have done all this even before the first hymn is announced—a hymn that I have already changed! But since there is never enough time to realize all the imagined possibilities, I judge quickly, so as to "get on with it." This is who I am.

From these formative stages, I also know the direction which mature development needs to take—into the undeveloped sides. As a "J," this has meant realizing how my decisiveness, often blind to the feelings of others, can alienate and hurt, unless I begin to adopt characteristics of the perceiver—patient listening, openness, awareness of options. It was here that my passion for variegation was born. Lured toward the next least threatening mode meant confronting the disposition opposite my intuition—that of sensing. I remember well that new threshold, as awareness of my aging began a shift of attention from the ever-shortening future to the increasingly valuable now. Fascination with life's sacramental dimension was birthed, and my hands learned to shape and build with wood—ecstatic in just stroking the grain.

The remaining two dimensions in my pilgrimage required help, for both have been covered over with the drive for achievement. My shadow (feeling) is the most threatening for it is opposite my most developed disposition (thinking). I have an ongoing challenge to keep in touch with my feelings. And to complete the circle, that which is opposite my extraversion, would be the quiet, inner peace of one who is an introvert. Thus the strangeness of me, as an extravert, becoming a Trappist monk, known for their silence, is understandable only as the work of the Holy Spirit. It is just possible that becoming part of a monastic community is secretly the search for courage sufficient to enter the inferiority of my introvert side. Therefore to take the next step into my less developed introversion, I have built a hermitage, in whose solitude I am now writing these lines. I learn best by walking into my weakness.

Pilgrimage relates to theological World much as journey relates to locale, and time relates to space. It is no surprise, then, that as an ETNJ, my theological home base is World Two. There I am oriented outwardly by a God of history, my method being that of faith seeking understanding. My imagination insists upon hope as future, residing not in what *is* but in what *will be*. It fits.

And yet a question arises. Is one born with one's World? And can or does one's World change? My research indicates that one's World emerges quite early in life, as, in part, an interplay of personality and environment. And although change is possible, it is more likely to occur as a conversion than it is an evolution. Furthermore, in practice, one's theological World is rarely pure. It is something of a composite, in which one's primary orientation is coupled with a secondary, and perhaps even a tertiary, World. In my case, during the 1960s my theological World (Theological World Two) became as deep and broad as one's World is likely to be. It was a period of self-conscious acting out of who I had been since childhood. For as far back as I can remember, I had large pieces of butcher paper in my bedroom on which I pinned the faces of persons who had radically changed the world. Whereas this World persists as my primary one, I am less confident that I, or anyone, will ever see the consummation of this World on earth. Thus the monastic side of my life has emerged with a promise that the vision is more cosmic than temporal. The image that speaks to me is that of a Eucharistic participation of this earth in the "becoming" of God. Yet what is one to do if one has not directly experienced this mystic dimension of World One? In my case, I cling to it as pure faith—as a wager, a gamble in the face of what I see all around me. In the end, then, I am a stranger in World Five, one who persists nevertheless in the dream. In contrast, what stands as temptations to my theological pilgrimage are the other two Worlds. An undue sense of guilt (as in World Four) would draw my focus away from the cosmos to my own condition. Likewise, as seen through my eyes, faithfulness to the dream means that I can never let my longing be satisfied by the personal gratification of World Three. Thus who I am is a keeper of the dream, involving, in my particular case, a dynamic of two Worlds with the World of my primary orientation, as the other two Worlds function as temptations. So it is that each person is a resident of one World, but lives it as personalized by the interplay with other Worlds.

Interestingly, one's sequence of personality traits is also helpful in indicating the sequence of learning styles a person is most likely to use.

MYERS-BRIGGS PREFERENCES AND LEARNING STYLES

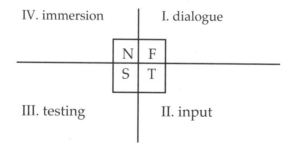

Using one's T-F and N-S scales, arrange them in order of one's most preferred to one's least developed, as indicated by one's scores. As an ETNJ, the T is my preferred way of learning, followed by the N. Opposite the N would be my S, my third preference. And the letter opposite my strongest trait (T) is my least developed (F). This diagram places an interior box into the learning styles chart we already discussed. Feeling (F) belongs with learning style Type 1;

thinking (T) with Type 2; sensing (S) with Type 3; and intuition (N) with Type 4. Thus by knowing which is your strongest personality trait on the Myers-Briggs inventory, you will identify your favorite learning style, which you will then use second if the first is not helpful, then the third, and finally your least preferred and weakest way of learning. To illustrate, in my case it means that I learn best through input (Type 2), since thinking is my preferred stance. This is followed by action-reflection immersion (Type 4) as my second preferred way of learning, corresponding with intuition as my second preferred stance. A much less preferred method would be testing (Type 3), and I have to work hard not to see dialogue (Type 1) as just an exercise in pooled ignorance.

These diverse factors we have been describing are important in showing the degree to which the variation we are advocating is, in truth, a diversity of diversities, a pluralism of pluralisms. That is, there are multiple dimensions by which alternative Worlds are molded and remolded, so that no one set of variables dare be taken as determinative. Thus the value of the MBTI (Myers-Briggs), as John Ackerman insists, is not that it reveals all the uniqueness of an individual, but that it is like a zip code, indicating that at least we are in the right neighborhood. Its educational importance is in showing how one's personality brings to the theologizing process particular attitudes, orientations, images, and needs, together forming a grid through which theological issues are both posed and heard. So it is with the grids of the other variables we have described. Each plays a part in understanding the multiple transactions called education. "God sees each of us as different, and we are called to cherish these differences."[20] And through these differences, we see God differently.

Recent studies indicate that congregations can also take on personality types which can unconsciously resist variation, even if professing openness to it. S-T inclined churches, for example, thrive on being well organized for the sake of clear and measurable goals, taking pride in offering fine facilities functionally designed for meeting immediate needs. The S-F church, oriented toward practical helping ministries, values an informal familiarity whereby each person is known and valued. The N-F church, maximizing growth with minimal structure, focuses upon relationships in which the process is open, democratic, and creative. The N-T church, oriented toward a global vision, values intellectual stimulation and exchange, with a leadership that is informed, analytic, active, and competent.[21] These values show as well the opposite characteristics about which churches might be defensive and resistive.

The Enneagram and Personality as Negatively Variegated

A second helpful instrument for understanding diverse personality types, for use in variegated education, is the Enneagram.[22] It operates on the *negative* characteristics of alternative personality types. There are nine negative or what I call "coping" types of people. (*Enneas* is the Greek word for nine.) Recently there have emerged some inventories for identifying one's type, but these inventories are not always needed. In working with congregational groups that interact with each other, all I need to do is describe a negative type and laughter indicates immediately who fits that characterization. Type 1 is the *"Perfectionist,"* who in avoiding anger, tries to be perfect so as to be accepted. Type 2 is the *"Altruist,"* who avoids having any needs by seeking acceptance through being so helpful to others that one is appreciated. Type 3 is the *"Achiever,"* who fears failure, and is therefore driven by success, which without one has little worth. Type 4 is the *"Feeler,"* who in fearing ordinariness tries always to be special. Type 5 is the *"Thinker,"* who in fearing emptiness, is driven to be informed, so as never to appear foolish. Type 6 is the *"Doubter,"* who so fears indecision that one tries to be secure in always being loyal. Type 7 is the *"Optimist,"* who in fearing pain always plans far ahead in order to avoid unhappiness. Type 8 is the *"Powerful,"* so afraid of weakness that one controls everything so as to appear to be strong. Type 9 is the *"Passive,"* who in fearing conflict tends to be nonfeeling so as to reduce one's inner tension. In understanding these types, one is able to discern the negative features of such behavior, as well as the positive attributes, providing for each a balancing goal. These in order (1 to 9) are: serenity, humility, being, equanimity, engagement, courage, commitment, empathy, and diligence. These negative and positive attributes indicate who Jesus needs to be for each person (i.e., theological World) in order not to stultify a person, but to lure and challenge them creatively.

Redemption for each type, in order are: unconditional acceptance; grace as free gift; faithful abandonment in the will of God; uniqueness through sacramental union with God; divine providence as invitation; trust in God's covenantal adoption; cocreation as total immersion; compassion for both friend and foe; and unconditional love.[23] It is fascinating how these types, based negatively according to one's original sin, as it were, are an interesting way of exploring the *obsessios* and needed *epiphanias* within the alternative theological Worlds.

Theological Worlds as Contexts for Learning

We are ready, now, to summarize and integrate the threads necessary for a holistic approach to variegated education. Christian education is an intentional exercise in spiritual formation, rendering autobiography a self-conscious pilgrimage by enfolding it within a community of support and accountability. Each person, forged by the particularized intersections of personality and social environment, learns differently, engages the stages of maturity differently, and occupies differently the space-time which shapes one's special World. Thus variegated Christian education entails maximizing the educational contexts best suited for each person and for each group by overlaying the quadrants of learning style theory, the stages of faith development, and the diversity of positive and negative personality types. This can be done in two ways.

The first way, that of *common learning communities,* has the same goals, but the groups are formed around having a common theological World. The atmosphere is much more supportive, with a trust born of collegiality in a common pilgrimage. This may be the preferred method initially, and once one is grounded in one's World, a composite type group may be attempted.

Second, then, are *composite learning groups* composed of representatives from various theological Worlds. Whatever the subject, through the interaction that results, persons learn respect for authentic variegation, perceive the distinctive implications of the Worlds in which each member is being formed, and are brought, through accountability, toward a posture of serious commitment or conversion. The atmosphere in such groupings can become confrontational. Since most of us have been socialized to have only the options of uniformity or indifference, such groups can be inhibiting. Thus the leader, at least at the beginning, needs to exercise considerable wisdom in facilitation.

Whichever way is used, it is important that leaders understand the differences entailed in working with persons of each theological World. This is crucial, for one is not dealing with ideas or opinions. One is dealing with souls—with the canon within the canon for each theological resident, that which is their very eyes of address and the platform on which they stand.

What follows is an attempt to apply what we have explored as a way of suggesting the manner in which residents of each theological World tend to learn.

1. For *World One residents,* the defining struggle is for interior depth. Thus they appreciate the opportunity to work individually on assignments, and share best in pairs or triads. Ironically, a primary motivation for these persons to join a group is the opportunity for serious sharing, yet such mutuality is often difficult for them. Deep in each member is an anxiety lest the separation they feel remains permanent—as the way things really are. In recognition of these feelings of isolation, group building exercises are useful, but only those that avoid risk of personal embarrassment. This uneasiness about being forced to relate is eased by shorter times of natural reconnecting throughout the educational process. It is important for leaders to model openness by way of their own vulnerability. Experiential exercises are useful, as long as the individual is not made to feel manipulated or singled out. Disdainful of superficiality, there is a desire for immersion, for experiencing loss of self in some sort of depth, yet at one's own pace. Sacramental situations often provide such illumination, even moments of the union they desire. Use of imagery and metaphor is more valued than systematic, conceptual information, with an appreciation for a visual supplementation of the verbal. Input is helpful if it is dialogical, for they are suspicious of extended lectures simply being a way of avoiding intimacy by "talking about" rather than being "involved in."

There is a dislike for "either/or" or restrictive definitions, with a preference being for a "both/and" approach, where similarities and harmonies are seen rather than differences and disagreements stressed. Rather than finding a linear approach helpful, these persons prefer a circular model, where things are viewed from multiple perspectives, pointing toward a common center. Use of biography and autobiography is usually welcomed, for this method suggests how various persons have appropriated meaning, rather than imposing conclusions of how things must be understood. Reflecting their christological understanding, it is important that the leader not get in the way, but become transparent, in no way pretending to be the truth, but content to point toward it. Introverts particularly welcome quiet periods along the educational path, times for personal reflection and appropriation. But the consistent priority throughout for members of this World is not so much to understand, or even to change. Their yearning is somehow to grasp and be grasped by things—down deep, behind the screen, beyond words. Consequently, retreats and retreat settings are effective, for natural surroundings maximize their receptivity to learning. The key question for these learners is, "Have I actually discovered what truly is?"

2. *World Two learners* are particularly open to an action-reflection methodology. Since their goal is committed action, they are eager to examine *praxis* critically. One begins not with "what shall we do?" but "what is being done?" Thus they enjoy case studies, accompanied by a keen interest in hearing from those with hands-on experience. Keeping current is valued, with an urgency born of knowing that in seeking a global perspective, one can never know enough about "what's going on." Examining one's own history critically is viewed as crucial for establishing a perspective from which to proclaim prophetic judgment—mostly by action. Often there is an inborn hermeneutic of suspicion, with an inclination to challenge "authorities."

Behind such critical thinking, coupled with uneasiness about anything human claiming to be sacred, is often an unspoken uneasiness that in spite of one's efforts, things may not stay better for long. Thus there is a need to hear and rehear and celebrate the vision of the gospel, lest the purpose becomes lost in the doing, and depression takes its toll. Drama and role play are helpful tools, for World Two persons thrive on rehearsing and focusing their passion. Exercises which involve the imagination are welcomed, showing excitement over new possibilities. Learning is understood as the task of linking theory and practice. Since neutrality is viewed negatively, engagement, even to the point of debate and disagreement, is preferred over detached information.

Conscientization is a favorite educational method for this theological World, in which action is evoked and through which the contradictions between ideals and performance in society are uncovered. These persons thrive on "either/or," clear definitions, and powerful images, for the intent is not informed objectivity, but, like their God, the commitment is to take sides. They can become preoccupied with identifying problems, rather than cooperating for the sake of solutions. The preferred learning environment is a busy one with posters, informational fliers, resource materials, and invitations to simulations. Closure is an important feature of every session, reflecting a linear disposition toward all of life. These persons thrive on moving progressively from a beginning to an end, through action. The key question for these learners is, "Are we doing all that we can?"

3. *World Three learners* thrive in an environment of unconditional acceptance. Whereas their favorite subject is the self, they are often uneasy about sharing deeply of themselves. The fear is in not being liked if others discover who they really are. Thus they are tempted to retreat into invisibility, believing that it is better to be quiet and belong, than to open one's mouth and be rejected. Learning needs to be gentle, beginning where each person is. A comfortable space is needed where reaching out is a natural extension of relaxing in the presence of others. This environment should be open and permissive, with gentle humor as lubricant. The effective leader needs to model permission to "mess up," for these persons are more likely to risk new behavior if "failure" is playfully made par for the course. As a result, emergence is best encouraged through positive strokes rather than through pushing.

These residents should be given ample opportunity to be pastoral with other members of the learning group—that is what they do best, having a natural identity with the underdog. Special encouragement is needed in learning to be kind to one's own self. The temptation is to escape the agony of self-discovery by denying one's self, and instead, helping others become who they are. Although they have a propensity to forgive ("for they know not what they do"), they find it difficult to forget. Thus group support needs to be balanced by an accountability, whereby persons can name their selves, and accept ownership for who they are. For this, they need to be encouraged to feel deeply, claim their hidden feelings, risk expressing them assertively, and learn to trust the self by trusting the process. Frequent use of first names has a special power in wooing the self into actuality. Keeping a journal is helpful, and by pairing writers, not only is deeper sharing fostered, but manageable goals can be set and achievements measured.

The leader, as a christological reflection, needs to be a very human role model, one who gently "does with," and kindly refuses to "do for." This posture is particularly important because the backstage temptation of these learners is to do and say what is most likely to gain approval. Thus the best environment for them is neither laid-back nor busy, as with the first two types, but warm, noncompetitive, intimate, inviting, and luring. It is important that no one feels the need to win this nurturing acceptance, for it is a "given"—as gift. Hospitality should greet each person at the door, acting out the group's gracious presupposition. Each session should share and celebrate ongoing individual and corporate accomplishments, always finding something to affirm in each person, stressing potentials rather than shortcomings. Such unconditional affirmation gives permission for persons to "try on" new behavior. Avoid all exercises in which individuals are chosen, for each harbors a secret fear that she or he will be chosen last. Throughout, the process tends to be more important than the content. The key question for these learners is, "Am I living out who I really am?"

Using Bible study to illustrate these contrasting approaches thus far, residents of World One tend to be attentive when scripture is explored poetically as metaphorical and symbolic expressions, evoking and confirming present experience. World Two thrives on scripture understood as history, calling forth obedience in behalf of liberation. World Three approaches Bible study from a meditational perspective, using guided imagery to focus on scriptural persons and relations ("What was Mary feeling when...."). World Four, to which we now turn, wants scripture to mean what it says, while World Five awakens to pungent quotes, worthy of memorization as assuring haunts of the mind.

4. *World Four persons* prefer to learn by hearing. Speaking, witnessing, and declaring are thus the central features. The working assumption is that to know something entails being able to tell someone else convincingly. Thus rotated leadership is a helpful technique. The need to "tell the story" as rehearsal provides a high tolerance for repetition. In contrast to World Three, content has priority over process. Since the source of one's current meaning is a commitment to God's acts in the past, persons who can speak with authority concerning scripture have an immediate reception. This interest in

knowing the "givens" of faith means that the preferred method is input, by lecture, sermon, or pamphlet, with regular, disciplined, private time for reading and appropriating.

Group trust for these residents is not easy. On the one hand, they are amply familiar with the universal failure of good intentions. Yet, on the other, the professed need for disciplined obedience requires that they make a clear distinction between believer and nonbeliever. Such tension can encourage a perfectionism that breeds a private fear of not measuring up. Whereas the ongoing confession of sin is recognized as important, it is also an admission of failure which one might not want others to know. Thus group interaction works best when the group is closed, so that trust can be built slowly, as everyone increasingly antes in. "The glue of mutual blackmail" is the way one member of such a learning group smilingly put it. That is, the more mutually vulnerable persons are with each other, the more likely it is that neither person will be tempted to divulge confidences. Such group interaction reflects the paradox of this World, which is that of being loved yet unlovable, forgiven yet unforgivable, now but not yet.

Whereas World Four usually shares with World Three a preference for individual over corporate concerns, the emphasis is the opposite. It is not on self-realization, but self-denial. The goal is not to be one's self but to live and witness daily in scriptural obedience. An unswerving depth of commitment is admired above all. The role of the leader thus resembles that of a trusted tour guide, who is sharing a pilgrimage known by heart. Although group dialogue can be useful, a freewheeling discussion is not trusted. The preferred interchange is a biblical presentation, drawing connections, followed by question and answer. The favored environment is one that reflects structure and clarity, reflecting a process of recognizable delegation and accountability. The key question for these learners is, "To what degree have I been faithful?"

5. *World Five residents* become anchored together as a learning community through a sharing of common struggles. The value of the group is in coming to trust that others will be there for the long haul. Thus group building, although basic, is not done quickly, or with easy techniques. It happens slowly, through the unspoken commitment of presence. Engrafting is fundamental, as each person is nurtured through becoming part of the same vine. Whereas these residents hold in common with World Three a deep appreciation for

sharing, it is not so much a means of growth as it is sharing for its own sake. Thus a characteristic response of appreciation for what is being said is not "That's helpful," but "Yes, I know." Unlike World Two, the task of encouraging action is usually not an issue. That is taken for granted. One does what one has to do. The difference that matters is the presence of those who, like God, are "there for others." This is particularly important because the unspoken uneasiness for these persons is the fear that in the loneliness one might give up. Living on the edge of burnout, the words of hope that provide the energy to continue are, "We're in it together."

There is a suspicion about neat answers and book solutions. What is to be trusted is wisdom bred of experience, from those who have paid their dues. Reflecting their understanding of Christology, leaders, to be plausible, are "wounded healers." *What* one does is not as important as *how* one does it. Integrity is what counts. The danger, however, is that since many of these persons have been told so often what to do, when placed in a structured environment they revert into passivity, as a defense called indifference. Change, experimentation, and novelty may not be valued or at least not immediately trusted. The church's importance is its long-standing stability—its sense of yesterday, today, tomorrow—faithfully the same. Truth is the residue that time distills out as worth keeping. Nothing is quite as convincing to these residents as the gentle sharing of one who has been "through it all." Forging an inner spirit and an outer smile are the high priorities. In the inner city, I have found that such learning occurred for women in someone's kitchen. For the men, there was always the same café each morning.

Such a learning group prefers not to meet somewhere special, where careful behavior or uncommon attitude is expected. It is symbolically meaningful to find time for meeting in homes, or during the day around work places. Here it is easier to "talk to the point." One's church is, in effect, the tent one carries, with the eucharist a brown bag lunch shared at noon with companions and with pigeons. Reflecting on life is often more difficult than living it. Expecting the worst comes easier than dreaming the better. Thus, at its deepest, their learning community is a mutual ministry of presence, with coffee the indispensable sacrament. The key question for these learners is the one they believe God is likely to ask in the end: "How deeply have you drunk of life?" Or, "Have you persevered to the end?"

At times I may have spoken as if to imply that one makes a rational and cogent choice of Worlds. This is misleading, for the process is one in which exposure of one particular World or another so touches one's soul that one knows it to be "home." The World itself always precedes one's awareness of the fact. Thus by recognizing the diversity of content, approach, learning process, styles, stages, personalities, and Worlds, the need for the variegated church becomes undeniable. And the future of variegated Christian education within the emerging postmodern church becomes exciting.

CHAPTER EIGHT

Variegated Worship:
Liturgical Interaction and
Subcongregations

On the night the Persian Gulf War began, National Public Radio interviewed a number of American reporters throughout the world for their response. Their interpretations were variations on the theme of positive acceptance of United States foreign policy. Seemingly unscheduled, an Islamic reporter working for a British newspaper was reached by telephone. As he spoke, the interviewers became strangely quiet. In stark contrast was heard the deep sadness of one who understood, and shared deeply from within, the Arab world. Humiliation was the word he kept using, humiliation over another presumptive solution to non-Western problems by the Western world. An upcoming radio series called "The World of Islam" was announced within a week.

A study of the concept of "everybody," as used by a typical Midwestern community, disclosed this human tendency to presuppose that one's perspective is universal. Research confirmed that "everybody" is, in fact, simply a name for "my group," as established by "the boundaries of one's conversation." [1] Such inclusive bounds determine functionally what is to be considered acceptable or unacceptable. In fact, it is such findings that confirm in social interaction the meaning of a theological World. It functions as the human tendency to idolize one's own particular time-space context, even though that World is the result of one's unique autobiographic pilgrimage. Here we approach the roots of that condition which the church calls sin. If one regards one's own World as normative for everybody, the inevitable tensions that arise are blamed on something or someone who is external. All troubles, then, become the failure of outsiders to function according to the rules of *my* World as *the* World. Ethics is the effort to negotiate the inevitable conflicts between idolized Worlds. Each sees a piece of the whole, and each sees the whole from one's piece of it.

Crucial implications follow from realizing this tendency as our universal human condition. Two implications in particular have significance for the variegated church. First, as we have shown, there are always multiple theological Worlds within every church. When this fact goes *unrecognized,* the human dilemma is not simply present, as in other institutions, but is exacerbated by being given divine sanction. Second, a church where variegation is *recognized* and made intentional can become a powerful instrument for transformation. By exploring and celebrating one's own theological World in structured proximity to alternative "everybodies," one's native suspicion regarding those who are "different" can become an invitation into interactive humility and richness.

The research previously mentioned not only illustrates the human dilemma, but identifies the church's difficulty in birthing a solution. All the churches studied receive their identity from a relatively small core group, whereas their actual membership is quite diverse. [2] Thus the key task of the contemporary church is to unleash the variegation already present within each local church by recognizing it, accepting it, rendering it intentional, and implementing it. This provides a new identity for the church, both in *perspective* and in *structure.* We will deal with churches of all sizes, but we will begin now with the larger church.

The Larger Church:
Liturgical Centers as Subcongregations

The most promising model for intentional variegation within larger churches is one that entails *alternative liturgical centers.* As Martin Marty insists, we urgently need "congregations in which alternatives to our culture can appear in the rich and transcendent messages of our theological and worship traditions." [3] What is crucial is that this richness appear as a multitextured fabric within the same church. Central for such variegation is worship, for it is there that the "biblical memory [comes] through the mediation of historic faith tradition as part of congregational remembering." [4] True, but the situation is complex. The "biblical memory" is itself diverse, and the remembrance of faith traditions is by members who bring contrasting eyes, shaped by alternative needs and autobiographic memories. Thus if Christianity, as anything worthy of the name, is to survive this period of massive secularization, the creation of intentional, alternative, and viable worship subcongregations is essential.

Such worship will entail a significant change from the present worship tendencies. In conservative churches, the theological World of a core group tends to be normative. In liberal congregations, the inclusivity of a least common denominator encourages a nontheological conformity. With alternative subcongregations, however, worship can be returned to its essential function of restoring and nurturing, by reexperiencing through rehearsal, the purity of the World in which one lives and moves and has one's being.

Whatever else a congregation may be, its Christian center is one of liturgy and sacrament. The more faithfully that center is able to express consistently and graphically the theological World of its participants, the more profound its formative impact will be. Diverse liturgy, then, follows inevitably as a central task for the modern church that takes its diversity seriously. But how can a church become such a federation of liturgical subcongregations, as it were? The first step, of course, involves identifying the theological Worlds characterizing the membership of a particular church—both individually and corporately. The easiest next step is to use the existing worship hour as a context for educating the church in how the ingredients and sequence of their present worship pattern reflect theological meaning. This could be done on a particular Sunday by interspersing reflective comments at key points throughout the worship, much as the stage manager functions within Thornton Wilder's *Our Town*.

This action-reflection method might begin, for example, by drawing attention to the theological meaning of the prelude, considering what its appearance at that point might assume about worshiper, church, and world. Throughout the service, the congregation is helped to understand the possible "why" behind the placement and interconnection of the parts. For example, this might entail exploring the difference between a call to worship and an invocation, between words of assurance and absolution. If the parts are unclear, confusing, or apparently inconsistent, the pastor's honest confession would be helpful. The sermon could reflect on the human condition which such a worship service seems to assume, the foci and climax that the pattern suggests, and the resolution being conveyed by the flow. With the help of lay input, a subsequent service could experiment with several changes to make more organic the meaning of the whole. Another service could be created that would make clear the characteristics of an alternative worship understanding—and thus make clear the pattern. The sermon could reflect upon the difference between such contrasting factors as linear versus cyclic movement, horizontal versus vertical moods, and individual versus corporate foci.

The congregation might then be ready for some workshop input that introduces theological Worlds, inviting persons to coalesce into several experimental worship planning groupings, based on the alternative Worlds around which this particular membership seems to peak. For stability, the theological World characterizing the largest number of persons might be permitted to experiment first in dialogue with the ongoing worship service at the traditional time. If the congregation is not yet ready for significant alternatives to their normal worship pattern, the planning groups should be encouraged to try out their experiments from time to time, inviting persons and/or other groups to worship with them. The task of each group would be to think theologically about its unique *what, how,* and *where*—so that the *who* is rendered visible as a corporate *why.* Within several months, it usually occurs that the meetings, interaction, and sifting between groups brings a gradual transition from being planning groups to being latent minicongregations.

Making clear that this phase is fully experimental helps to keep change acceptable and fluid. Trial worship patterns can continue to be revised by ongoing committees within each subcongregation. These committees can then respond to suggestions of the group itself. It is also helpful for representatives from each planning group to meet together, sharing their varied processes and results. Attendance at one another's experimental worship services can provide cross-fertilization. Throughout this creative time, the ministerial staff functions best as midwives. The learning patterns we have already described are useful in helping the decision-making process within each group become part of the experimentation.

As this liturgical furnishing of theological Worlds continues, correlative sacramental expressions will be encouraged to emerge. Experimentation of this sort began for others and me in the 1960s when it became acceptable to work theologically with couples in writing their own wedding vows and marriage liturgy. In the 1970s, counseling with baptismal candidates and their parents gave some of us renewed interest in sacramentals—water, banners, color, candles, vestments. The advent of the Vatican II guitar mass legitimized experimentation with the Eucharist as a family celebration in homes. More recently, this experimental emergence has encouraged ministers to help their parishioners deal with death and dying by having parishioners write their own funeral services. Such exercises provide helpful precedents, as long as it is clearly understood that these emerging worship subcongregations are *not* to be conglomerations of individual opinions and perspectives. Building upon each member's unique faith perspective, the goal of each subcongregation is to discern and establish as liturgy the unique symbolic and rhythmic shape that reflects powerfully the World of their implicit theological commonness. Part of this process would be for each theological World to claim and modify its own space. Some environments speak of a particular World so forcefully that it seems to dictate the worship type that would naturally happen there. Inevitably the issue of flexible space will arise, with the need to make provisions for different visual centering, art, seating arrangements, sacramentals— indeed, even the issue of whether table, or pulpit, or baptistery, or something else, is to be given privileged location.

If a church already has multiple services, this process is greatly simplified. But even after such planning and experimentation occurs, the church may decide to continue with only one service. If so, the work done is not lost, but can be useful in providing some alternative worship patterns for seasons or celebrative events.

Alternative Liturgies

First level theology is a name sometimes given for theology as lived. Second level theology is a name for rendering this lived-theology into conceptual self-consciousness. What we are describing requires a further step. A third level theology is the name for corporate discernment translated into common acts of rehearsal. It is at this level that variegation is able to resist the present-day tendency toward having a melting pot approach to worship.

Liturgies that are created need to be distilled within the respective planning groups themselves. And yet I have found it helpful to make available to these groups a typology suggesting liturgically contrasting possibilities for each theological World.

ALTERNATIVE LITURGIES

World	Rhythm	Question	Obsessio	Feel	Epiphania	Result	Sample Hymns
1	From Isolation to Unity	Where am I?	Stranger	Separation Longing	Coming home	Mystery Unity Peace	O Come, O Come Emmanuel Precious Lord Leaning on the Everlasting Arms
2	From Oppression to Liberation	What can be done?	Warrior	Anger Resentment	New earth	Promise Vision Commitment Focus	A Mighty Fortress Go Down, Moses Lift Every Voice and Sing
3	From Insignificance to Importance	Who am I?	Orphan	Emptiness Invisible	Personal worth	Belonging Assertive Self-realization	Breathe on Me Morning has Broken Be Thou my Vision
4	From Failure to Acceptance	Who can restore me?	Fugitive	Conscience Guilt	Forgiven heir	Accepted Adopted Claimed	Amazing Grace Just as I Am Alas and Did My Savior Bleed
5	From Survival to Integrity	Can I make it?	Refugee	Over-whelmed Weary	Enduring integrity	Annealed Befriended Strengthened	Abide with Me Lead Kindly Light Must Jesus Bear The Cross Alone

The liturgy of World One is best experienced in an atmosphere of mystery, with a taste for candles, Gothic arches, and receding shadows. This is because one faces life the way one faces death—with a sense of sacredness, touching one at the outer edges of knowing and being. Even a quiet, darkened, and peaceful room will do. An uneasiness often shadows World One, for although the ache is for "more," one is haunted by the thought that "this may be all there is." This accounts for the pensive aloneness often characterizing these residents. It is difficult, at times, to trust one's longings, but clearly they are for union, for one to be poured forth into the One, to lose one's self in a unity where dualism and separation are mysteriously transcended. The hope is that in worship one experiences more than one can know, as hints where one sees for a moment, before the veil falls again. This subcongregation thrives in a sacramental environment, in which everything purports to be more than it is.

The worshiper tends to enter a worship environment with a sense of separateness, yet with the hope of gaining a renewed sense of centeredness—not *of*, but *within* the self, and the self *within* the whole. To this end, worship is best sprinkled with intentional silence, with an intentional respect for the person's privacy and uniqueness. Whatever interaction occurs within worship needs to be by gentle invitation, for these persons resist being forced into what they regard as the embarrassment of feigned togetherness. Analogy for the harmony they value is the quiet togetherness of deep friends at fireside, beyond need for words.

Relatedly, liturgy is valued more for its poetry than its concepts, more for its capacity to lure the self out of itself than for providing information, more for evocation of deep feelings than for solutions. When leaving, the worshiper will want to have experienced a centered silence—periods of timeless peace within a promised wholeness.

Isaiah's temple experience (Isaiah 6:1-8) provides the anatomy for worship here. It is an experience of holiness, capable of being seen as filling "the whole earth," but bringing instead a sense of lostness: "Woe is me!" In humility the cleansing is made, and the invitation to respond offered: "Here I am!" But unlike World Two, the order is circular rather than linear, with alternating experiences of separation and presence. Being "high and lifted up," it is through deep inwardness that one gains a taste for "the whole earth [as] full of [God's] glory." With a focus on God's *being* more than God's *doing*, public worship and private prayer closely resemble each other. Above all, contemplation, as times of union, intertwine with the sacramental as acts of transparency. In both cases, the self becomes lost in its ground.

The liturgy of World Two suggests an ambiance in decided contrast to World One. These worshipers have a genuine uneasiness about mystery, shadows, aloneness, circularity, and silence. In heavy contrast, worship needs to be dramatic, corporate, prophetic, declarative, challenging, participatory, and active. There must be a clear linear progression, moving toward committed action. What is appealing is a vision luring the whole congregation toward a better future through provocative imagery. The hope, unlike World One, is not in transcending differences, for dualism is real. In fact, one must enter boldly into the cleavages of good and evil, of rich and poor, of us and them. Thus whereas the first World has a taste for introversion, here the temperament is strongly extraversion. An outstanding architectural expression of this is the small chapel of Coventry Cathedral, dominated by glass walls overlooking the industrial district of the city.

Whereas residents of World One yearn to be drawn into a transcendent whole, World Two sees this as escapism—a succumbing to one's unexpressed uneasiness that no matter what we do, things may not become better. Thus worship needs to touch the yearning for a vision of a *new earth,* with an emphasis on *here, now,* and *soon.* The anatomy for such worship could be the dialectic of thesis, antithesis, and synthesis. With such a lens, scripture then becomes enacted as creation, fall, and Kingdom; of Eden, Egypt, and Promised Land; of covenant, exile, and restoration. If for the first World an analogy for worship might be a quiet togetherness by fireside, that of World Two is one of drama—of prologue and epilogue, of acts and scenes, with the playwright making a guest appearance.[5]

Whereas World One might be inclined to tarry with the prelude, World Two insists on hastening to a crescendo. This might be expressed with a militant postlude, with candles not extinguished, nor remaining in the sanctuary as eternal lamp, but taken as flame out through the open doors into the world. God does not remain in some kind of quiet peace, awaiting our reverent revisit. God is already in the noisy world, beckoning. Whereas the refrain that World One continues to hear throughout the week is "Holy, holy, holy," World Two reverberates with the response, "Here am I, send me!" Uneasy about the arcane, clarity of content is important.

Imperative is crucial for the God who takes sides and rather than trust the method of evocation, we too must choose a side.

Thus the call to worship could take on the flavor of an informal reminder, with a concreteness taken from the morning newspaper.[6] The human condition is confessed graphically, with its illustrations more corporate than personal, more systemic than moralistic. The hymns are characterized by "we" and "our" pronouns, rather than "me" and "mine." Worshipers could well stand up to hear the scripture, for the intent is not meditation but address, much as a soldier might stand at attention to receive battle orders. The most cherished parts of worship might be graphic intercessions, and the Word proclaimed is done as prophetic address. Whereas the worship space for World One might be textured sacramentally with candles and icons, World Two is well-lighted, appropriately bedecked with literature racks, pamphlets, posters, bulletin boards, sign-up sheets, and detailed announcements soliciting volunteers. Pre- and postservice sharing over coffee are crucial parts of the drama. The stress throughout is on *doing* rather than *being*.

The liturgy of World Three is characterized neither by mystery nor by corporate action. Instead, worship is a warm and gentle family event, fostering a sharing that can resemble a spiritual show-and-tell. The fear which is not far beneath the surface is that one might be found out and thus recognized as of little value. This in turn would undermine confidence in the semblance of a self that one might not actually have. Thus one enters worship with a sense of being on the margin, separating self-blame and the ache to belong. The hoped for movement in worship would be toward self-affirmation, becoming reaffirmed by reexperiencing one's self as the lost sheep for whom God left the ninety and nine. The characteristic ingredients are nurture, enrichment, enlightenment, and self-actualization—those dimensions that highlight the potential of each person as a unique creation of God. Stories are deeply appreciated, as long as they are perennial variations on the theme of the missing coin that is worth turning everything on end to find; or the prodigal child kissed and embraced while still on the road; or the unwanted orphan adopted into a family that cares, joyously clothed as if being the pearl of great price.

This family gathering depends on its capacity to make persons unexpectedly welcomed, wanted, and needed. The sharing of "once I was but now I am" is expressed as encouragement through kindly invitation, luring each person from invisibility into participation. It is a worshiping community structured by acceptance so that persons dare to believe in their "selves-in-the-making." Worship is where there is no fear of rejection, and reassurance without need for approval.

There is a lyric quality about the whole, a creation spirituality more than a Lenten one, an upbeatness that leaves little place for either hierarchy or self-abasement. One feels that worship has truly occurred when the God within and the family without converge as nurture for one's true and growing self. "I was myself today" is the cherished admission, with an appreciation for the Spirit, who through community transforms individuals into persons.

The liturgy of World Four, on the other hand, is uneasy about any such self-affirmation, suspicious of it as expressing the problem more than the solution. Whereas World Three focuses on the problem of the self's fragile invisibility, the dilemma in World Four is identified as the self's obstinate determination to "get in the way." This tendency is rooted in the perennial fear of failure, and thus the apparent need to prove one's self. Persons are motivated, even driven by a determination to justify *themselves,* not only for what they do but even more for the right to even be alive. One is born with a deficit account. As a result, we become caught between the humiliation that keeps us *from* confessing, and the destructive pride that results from *not* confessing.

Worship, then, is the ongoing rehearsal of the scenario in which the good news is first heard as bad news. To "tell it like it is" is central, in which the divine "no" precedes and keeps honest any human "yes." World Three, in decided contrast, insists that it is this very process of put-downs and guilt tripping that creates the human dilemma of low self-esteem. But World Four insists precisely upon the necessity of such confession, ongoingly so, for the balloon of pride is ever in need of being punctured. The classic prayer for World Four is this: "We acknowledge and bewail our manifold sins and wickedness, which we from time to time most grievously have committed, by thought, word, and deed, against thy Divine Majesty." The center of World Four worship would be the proclamation of scripture, sermonically focused on the theme of repentance and forgiveness. This is a trinitarian declaration resting on Christ's atonement as God's objective act in history, with the Holy Spirit as God's subjective act with the heart. Without the ongoing remembrance that "once I was blind but now I see," the eyes get covered once again by spiritual cataracts. Favorite hymns are the "I" ones, for they reflect this deeply personal theme: "I love to tell the story, it did so much for me; and that is just the reason I tell it now to thee." Retelling and recalling is what worship is all about, for God's work centers in the Word whose truth adheres in the power of being proclaimed and heard.

The liturgy of World Five takes its unique flavor from an under the surface fear that one might give up. "Help Me Make It Through the Night" could well be their theme song, with the blues capturing well the abiding rhythm of the heart. In contrast with the worship of other Worlds, visitors might find the mood of this worship strange. On the one hand, an outsider might sense a stoic indifference, for in expecting little, one is disappointed seldom. Yet, on the other hand, there is a profound vulnerability—the willingness to share the little one has, which amazingly can feed many with only a few loaves and fishes.

The "prayers of the people" are crucial in World Five, raising from their midst the pains and struggles of the week. The form and intent of the prayers are not so much petitionary as participative—asking not so much for healing, but for the strength to endure and share the pain, and the courage to go on. Redeemed life means being rooted in the Spirit who "helps us in our weakness" and "intercedes for us with sighs too deep for words" (Romans 8:26). Sharing together means that no longer will one be in it alone.

The other side of this somberness, however, can be a serendipitous letting go, either as counter theme, or, at times, an emotional emptying out. One recalls a tradition in which jazz is played by black musicians as they return from the graveyard—"it is finished." But much of the time, the corporate spirit is quietly deep—of knowing and enduring the knowing again, together to 3/4 time.

Just as life itself is without much recognizable pattern, so worship for these residents has no particular order—content more with a spontaneity that flows from "the way things are." One takes what comes as it comes, without even permitting time to intrude. What does matter is that which one has control over—that is, how one will take it. Thus there is about the whole a transcendence manifested as patient waiting, for whom the classic Job would make a fine liturgist. This resistance to linear movement is really a distrust of any promised resolution. This is illustrated by a letter from a resident of World Five describing her experience at a Cursillo weekend. "It made me angry how they kept trying to move everything toward an ending that made everything 'okay.' So when they moved everyone to a high point of dancing to 'Morning Has Broken,' I started to cry. I was far more at home the night before when we did the Stations of the Cross by candlelight. The Mass that I attended at that same church a week later was far more real for me. Folks with infirmities came just as they were, right off the street. No one tried to dress up their surface selves to make a Sunday church appearance. I felt at home, for putting one's best foot forward isn't the way life is."

Visitors from other Worlds will no doubt experience World Five worship as paradoxical, but that is the way World Five people live life within their World—singing in sadness, sowing with tears, and clapping a rhythmic order for the chaos. One worships most when one feels least like doing so, for by enduring the "no" together, it becomes a "yes." The writer Flannery O'Connor made such liturgy the anatomy of her novels. She spoke of needing to cherish the world at the same time one struggles to endure it. And what makes it endurable is the gospel of divine strangeness. "What could be stranger than a God who decides to suffer with us?" In his own way, Oscar Wilde also understood by identifying sacred ground with the presence of sadness.

We have described these Worlds as liturgically distinct, and so they need to be experienced, at least sometimes. A one word characteristic of the five Worlds (in numerical order) is this: evocation, imperative, invitation, declaration, and oblation. But no World is ever lived purely, so each can be linked to a secondary World. O'Connor herself confessed this when in a letter she identified the World One dimension with her own World Five orientation. She indicated that her daily prayer always ended as a hope that heaven might be a serene and peaceful place beyond life's agonies. For her, the overlap of two Worlds fits. It had to.

Alternative Approaches to Sacraments and Sacramentals

The emergence of liturgy characteristic of each World also involves furnishing each World with corporate symbols—objects and drama as means for corporate remembering *(anamnesis)*. Three of the most powerful of these sacramental expressions for all five Worlds are baptism, Eucharist, and funeral. We will diagram them as they correlate to the liturgies just described.

ALTERNATIVE RITUALS

	Baptism	Eucharist	Funeral
World 1	Engrafted into the Whole, at Soul Depth (analogy: dew in nature; falling water)	Mystery Transparency Presence Foretaste Banquet	Death as threshold Home at last Finally to see With Christ in God All in all—union
World 2	Immersed in Victory of Christ's Death & Resurrection (analogy: the Red Sea)	Vision: when none shall go away empty Breaking of the powers & Principalities	Death as foe Fight the good fight Thy Kingdom come Commendation/Victory
World 3	Adopted into the Family as Belonging (analogy: birth)	Nourishment Family table Sharing Fellowship	Death as part of life's rhythm Commemoration Celebration
World 4	Washed Clean: New Beginning (analogy: Noah)	Sacrifice/absolution Last Supper commemoration Obedience—do it in remembrance of me Thanksgiving	Death as rightful penalty Trusting the promise Substitutionary death Final judgment
World 5	Second Birth: 1st into human pain; 2nd into the pain of God (analogy: tears)	Common cup Pledged commitment to covenantal living Incarnation Bound together	Death as the way things are The vale of soul making It is finished

Baptism. Discerning how sacramental events are best understood and observed within the uniqueness of each of the theological Worlds is a powerful educational happening. Case studies are helpful tools. And once diverse worship and sacraments are uniquely in place, the subcongregations themselves, by functioning in proximity to each other, become case studies for each other and for visitors.

An example for exploring the meaning of baptism is this case. During World War II, a S. S. officer came secretly at night to a German pastor. "I don't believe any of this Christian nonsense, but it would please my dead father if you would baptize my boy." The pastor refused. Meanwhile, on the other side of Berlin, a Christian nurse in a maternity ward was imprisoned. For over a year, unknown to anyone, she had been baptizing the new born children of S. S. troopers. Both nurse and pastor were tortured and killed—one for refusing, the other for doing it.

By wrestling with such a case study, persons are forced to choose in depth the meaning and way baptism might best be done within the contours of the World in which they are living. Having chosen, they can then help each other explore the beliefs implicit in that decision. A useful tool for enabling the transition from the "I think I would" to the "I wonder why," is to distribute the following list. Assign different members to do Bible study on one or more passages, and then together reflect upon alternative ways in which scripture images baptism.

1. Washing/cleansing (1 Corinthians 6:11; Titus 3:5)
2. Freed from death by death (Romans 6:3-5; Colossians 2:12)
3. Marked/bought with a price (Galatians 6:17)
4. Watered/growth (Genesis 1:2, 20, 29; Psalm 1:3)
5. Rebirth/born again (John 3:5)
6. Enlightened (Ephesians 5:14)
7. Flood/moral purity (Genesis 7:17; 9:15; 1 Peter 3:20-21; Hebrews 10:22)
8. Adoption/new humanity (Galatians 3:27-28)
9. Exodus/liberation (Exodus 2:10; 14:16)
10. Promised land/over Jordan (Exodus 3:8; Revelation 22:1-3)
11. Sustenance/for the Desert (Exodus 17:6; Isaiah 30:19-20)
12. Love/Anointed (Exodus 29:4; Luke 7:44)
13. Refreshment (John 4:15)

14. Healing (John 5:3-9)
15. Thirst (Revelation 21:6)

By studying these analogies, one can detect exciting theological interconnections. They make church traditions more understandable, such as why Cyril of Jerusalem would build a baptistery over the site of Christ's tomb. Even the issue of how water is to be used—as in immersion, marking, pouring, washing, sprinkling, and drinking— leads to important discussions of the alternative meanings implicit in each World. Likewise illuminating is the ancient practice of completing baptism by giving the person a cup of milk and honey.

Additionally, the issue of when baptism is best administered uncovers further contours of each theological World. Barth, as a member of World Two, insisted upon adult baptism as normative. Given the state of today's world, he says, to be a Christian entails radical commitment to a faithful minority, opposing the dehumanizing nature of present cultural values.[7] Relatedly, the post–Vatican II Roman Catholic Church is discouraging its former custom of baptizing a child early into the Catholic ethos. The emphasis now falls on adult baptism and confirmation being given together, concluding a one to three year catechumenate—exploring Catholic beliefs in regard to one's own faith journey.

In contrast, a mandated United Methodist "Committee to Study Baptism" task force recently proposed discarding the term "confirmation" altogether as giving "a misleading view of baptism." Sympathetic to a World Four understanding, their recommendation rests on understanding grace as prior to any human act. Thus infant baptism witnesses best to the fact that even before one is able to respond, God engrafts one into the Body of Christ.[8] Such an understanding would be close to what the Catholic Church once advocated, but is now attempting to discourage. The diverse anger that the United Methodist proposal evoked witnesses to the unacknowledged fact of variegation.

Meanwhile, such insistence upon baptism as a means of grace stands at odds with a proposed ecumenical model more reflective of both Worlds One and Three. Stressing the universal dimensions of acceptance and affirmation in knitting together the total human family, baptism does not give a love that the child does not otherwise have, but points to the divine love that was present in birth itself, bringing the child into a community committed to that love.[9] Being suspicious of the doctrine of original sin, World Three persons might prefer infant *dedication* rather than baptism—dedication being a congregational promise made to the child. Believer's baptism could then be encouraged, understood as an "ownership" of one's self as accepted and acceptable.

The issue of *who* should conduct sacramental acts could evoke further depth exploration in each subcongregation. For example, the tension that this question would create for World One is a way of proposing the issues for the other Worlds. On the one hand, for World One, mystery is profaned if it takes on a common day familiarity. Therefore would this not happen if sacraments become available to all, exercised by anyone, using materials readily present? Is it not important that such precious acts be cherished, protected, and using special words and utensils, celebrated by consecrated persons who have been set aside uniquely by an indelible ordination? And yet, is not all of life sacred, humans and nature united together in a cosmic sacrament? Are not all of us priests, ordained by our baptism? Is not baptism a symbolic reminder that opens us to the specialness of every shower and all washing? Rather than sacraments such as baptism being special happenings, is not sacredness so woven into the fabric of life that sacraments are symbolic action-parables that are needed to open us to see what is abundantly present all around us if only we would look?

It is important to help church people know in such deliberations that what is being solicited are *not* opinions or preferences, or the establishment of some minimal consensus. Most parishioners will have given little thought to such matters, so if they are not encouraged otherwise, their responses will be merely opinions reflecting sentiments associated with memory. Thus the variegated church must resist two extremes: unity based on the least common denominator, and diversity as disguised personal taste. Sacraments are the primal rituals of incorporation. Thus they are inevitable and necessary, characterizing for each theological World the symbolizations which touch in their own characteristic and intimate fashion the universal needs for greeting, naming, belonging, nurturing, and promising.

Eucharist. Alternative meanings for Holy Communion follow inevitably from the shape of the liturgical rhythms emerging from each subcongregation. For *World One,* the Eucharist evokes a symbolic awareness of the sacred grounding of everything—"experiencing that it is so." Our senses need to be primed to see. Thus through the bread and wine, as Tillich observes, we are enabled to see every meal as a Holy Communion, just as every shower is a baptism. Yet such universal experiences of the eternal now reside under a cloud of "not yet." There is always a deep and unfulfilled yearning. "I shall not drink again of this fruit of the vine until that day when I drink it new with you in my Father's kingdom" (Matthew 26:29).

In *World Two,* the emphasis is linear, centered in a "commitment to make it so." Understandably, then, J. A. T. Robinson calls the Eucharist a dress rehearsal for the first supper of the new age to come on earth. This makes the unconditional breaking of bread a revolutionary act. For *World Three,* Eucharist is a communal sharing, experiencing belonging as a call to make it so. In the secular world, it is common for those who appreciate each other to "do lunch" together. So it is at church. In like manner, to entertain in one's home is participation in a eucharistic event. Marjorie Suchocki also makes it clear how important the subjective is for World Three, for without appropriation there is no sacrament.

For *World Four,* Eucharist entails "receiving that which has the power to make it so." Thus Luther, while acknowledging Christ is everywhere, declared that he deigns to meet us in a special way in the bread we break in the Holy Communion. Thus we have an immediate and empowering fellowship with Christ as real presence. Often in this World, Word and sacrament are two sides of the same act—communication of the gospel in two forms. As for *World Five,* Eucharist converges in a faith remembering, as when Zwingli reflected the meaning that the word *sacramentum* had for centuries. It was the oath of loyalty a Roman legionary took as a pledge until death. Here communion is a profound recommitting, based on reremembering when and where and how and why—or if at all.

The rich and variegated meaning of this event called Eucharist is witnessed by the plethora of key words it forces upon Christians. Such terms drive toward the roots where each World is shaped and nurtured—words such as give, remove, see, defeat, promise, claim, participate, join, preserve, belong, persevere, and hope. Everything depends on which are chosen, on where the priority rests, and on what it is one is committed to. Where better to forge the unique perspective of a particular World than in a variegated church? Here, for example, residents of World Four could struggle deeply with the dilemma set by the death of an unbaptized child. Meanwhile, nearby residents of World One might be pondering the agony of Graham Greene's priest, who desperately struggles to find wine in time to give final communion to a dying person in *The Power and The Glory*.

Funeral. The creativity of having several subcongregations within one church is illustrated well by the opportunity for interparticipation in variegated funerals. As a World Two person, I regard death as a foe to be fought, gambling that at Gethsemane God took sides against death, and in the resurrection was victorious over our final foe. Yet, in an effort to comfort me at the death of my father, a resident of World One sent me this letter: "My Dear Paul, Death is our friend. May St. Francis help you at such times as these, when in his 'Canticle of the Sun' he sings affectionally to 'Sister Death.' Your father has been called home, and we celebrate his good fortune. Sickness and pain are welcomed dress rehearsals for when, through death, we will rest with Christ in God." I was not comforted. I was sadly angered. It is difficult to imagine a more stark contrast between two theological Worlds. I revel in earthly life, praying with Jesus "thy kingdom come, on *earth*" whereas this person sees life as "passing through." With that letter still in front of me, I wrote an addendum to my will, insisting that my funeral be a defiant, triumphant cry with Paul: "O Death where is thy victory? O Death, where is thy sting?"

I still remember with strong feelings the funeral of a woman neighbor who had a fatal heart attack on Christmas Eve while opening Christmas presents with her family. At her funeral, the priest declared: "We don't always understand, but of this we can be sure: God gave Lil the best Christmas gift she could ever receive!" Damn! My comforting letter writer, and this disturbing priest, disagreed deeply with me. And yet I must acknowledge that the World in which they reside has just as cherished a place in church history as does mine. Almost from the beginning of the church's life, the feast days of saints were celebrated on the date of their death—as their "heavenly birthdays."

How better a way, then, to bring persons to theological seriousness than to expose them to serious liturgical alternatives within proximity of each other? That way anger, conflict, or a sense of betrayal can be experienced as existing within and between Worlds, shared at a deeply human and caring level. In fact, it is the very existence of such subcongregations that resists theological reductionism, and, in so doing, makes neutrality increasingly difficult.

Alternative worship services can be conducted at different times within the same space. Or they can become separate places distinctively furbished, with worship held at varying times, or even concurrently. One church designed a number of 8'x 8' carpeted squares, one foot high. Since the floor of their worship area is level, it is relatively easy to slide or stack or join or separate these squares to create different worship spaces. From the first, this was precisely what they did, giving the congregation contrasting ambiences appropriate to the festival and the season. These range from traditional arrangement, to church in the round, to equal emphasis on Word and table.

Blessed are the congregations that have the opportunity for alternative settings. But it is likewise important to provide opportunities for informal interaction. This happens best in what Charles Foster calls the "in between times" of the church's life—the *before* and *after* and *during*—providing breaks for most things that are scheduled. Much of the real formation and crucial decisions occur on the church steps, or in the entry and hallways, in the parking lot, or working side by side in the church kitchen, or during shared rides, or spontaneous sharings of Sunday dinner at a favorite restaurant. [10] These are the whereabouts that need more intentional recognition and time. Yet they are the very times that keep being abbreviated and attenuated by "important" things, or the hurry to have "efficient" meetings. In most churches on Sunday morning, the lights start getting turned off soon after the benediction, with the janitor pointedly waiting with impatience to lock up. Or narrow halls force apologies for conversations that hinder traffic flow. The intentionally variegated church, however, will turn such informal and chance interactions into an operational stance as well, legitimating and facilitating such times and places.

Such sanctioned, informal sociability can be encouraged by providing an inviting environment. For example, the narthex or the space salvaged by removing unused back pews can be made into a lounging area. Sunday morning coffee can be provided at several intersecting points within the normal traffic pattern. Benches can be installed along outside walkways. Fellowship dinners, covered dish suppers, or even simple refreshments before or after regular church events have surprising magnetism. Perhaps by then a nonfattening donut may be invented!

Formally, events can be planned whose clear purpose is to encourage deep interaction between subcongregations. Some of the most successful possibilities include problem dramas or case studies that are watched and then discussed in table arrangements, debates on secular or religious issues by representatives of varying Worlds, or a film series with each film chosen by a subcongregation as particularly reflective of its perspective. This creativity focuses a central dilemma of the modern church, that the variegated church is particularly designed to confront. Folks do not know one another in such a way as to even have deep conversations.

The Smaller Church: Intracongregational Worship as Variegated

The larger church is best suited to develop alternative liturgical centers. This is true for more reasons than just space, staff, and membership size. The urban context fosters a greater sense of individualism and isolation. This not only prepares persons for diversity but also instills through absence a yearning for a community of identity. What, then, are the possibilities for intentional variegation within the smaller, often rural church? Anthony Pappas's study of the "world of the small church" identifies it as a minifolk society, or tribe. [11] It invites belonging to "a world by itself," in which there is a primacy of oral communication and expressive behavior. Relations tend to be ends in themselves, with stability and thus tradition a basic norm of truth. Time and space form an integrated pattern worth maintaining from which behavior is motivated by habit or disposition more than by intention. Meaning is held together through story or myth, in the context of which problems are dealt with intuitively more than analytically.

Since he concludes from this description that the small church inevitably resists change, Pappas sees a bleak future for it. His pessimism, however, is ill founded. Without knowing it, what he has done, and done well, is to describe functionally one *particular* theological World. All Worlds attempt to withstand change, for by their nature they resist being other than they are, whether their context is rural or urban. Pappas's mistake is in failing to acknowledge that the type of change he is advocating comes from his being a resident of a theological World other than the one that he is analyzing. In using his own World as a universal norm for judging another World, his pessimism reflects an unacknowledged contrast of Worlds, with the conflict being between the two alternative concepts of change.

Yet a real problem does exist for another reason. Many small *congregations have the form of a particular theological World, but no longer retain its functional content.* There was once a time in this country when both Protestantism and Catholicism exhibited a predilection for World Four. Within that context, time was experienced as repetitive, for the present turns primarily toward past events for its meaning, preserved by narrative and made real by rehearsal. No longer does this World claim widespread public allegiance. Instead, what tends to remain in the small church is the *posture* of that theological World, but with only vestiges of the content that once claimed such powerful allegiance.

There are some congregations, of course, for whom World Four remains vital, measured by the degree to which its configurations reflect autobiographically the nucleus of its membership. This helps to account for the elderly membership of these churches, and their penchant for memory. But many small churches that Pappas describes are a "vestige form," largely disengaged from theological content, functioning now mostly from a socio/econo/political disposition. These are a final symbol of heteronomy against further erosion of *any* kind. The old hymns, furnishings, folk customs—the old anything—are sacred harbingers of "the way it once was," against the present, experienced as loss. Even those who no longer attend these churches often support their bazaars and homecomings, and maintain a sentimental defensiveness about even the building itself, with downright hostility over hints of its being closed.

Yet the price for such theological emptying is more than a physical distancing. For many who continue to attend, the distancing is psychological. Attendance becomes more habitual, done for increasingly secondary reasons. Permitting one's own World to remain submerged is the price for such belonging. As a result, as research shows, the small church receives its identity from an increasingly small core group, although in fact the actual membership is quite diverse. Caught in this vicious circle, fewer persons are willing to continue active participation in a theological World not their own. Meanwhile, the rest appreciate it from a distance, serving as a symbolic witness of assumed stability by those who "do believe it." Even if there were no membership decline, we would still be witnessing a sad demise. The real tragedy for the mainline denominations is the loss of the small church as a *religious community.* This forfeits World Four as well, as a viable theological World, by crystallizing it in past expressions rather than letting it take on a twenty-first century variegated shape. The widespread presence of guilt as a major counseling problem today is evidence enough that World Four has a ready clientele, if only they could find each other under the banner of forgiveness.

Hope for recovery of the small church resides in the planned emergence of its own brand of variegation. Sometimes the stark reality of declining membership and attendance is sufficient to motivate serious conversations. But consideration of even the idea of alternative theological Worlds within such a congregation depends upon a careful regard of four points. First, diversity is not something to be introduced, but a concrete fact to be acknowledged—not only among the unchurched, but actually within the present dynamics of the local congregation's own life. Second, the motivation for working with this diversity must be clearly seen as not being a "liberal" scheme. That is, at every point in the process, it must be clear that this is not an attempt to deny, undercut, or in any way discredit the beliefs, practices, indeed the very hymns, of those who are satisfied and fed by the World they suppose to be universal. Thus the motive for variegation must be clearly communicated as unabashedly evangelical and spiritual, to reach the unreached and to deepen the Christian spirituality of those already reached. There should be no intimation of change or removal—only that of "making room for."

Third, success depends on creating a friendly environment in which those not accustomed to expressing themselves on such matters are invited and supported to do so, with such sharing being clearly identified as the meaning of Christian hospitality. Fourth, the key to success is the nature and quality of facilitation that is used. Sometimes the pastor can be the facilitator, but only if he or she is theologically alive, functionally skilled, and warmly regarded. Sometimes an able layperson can evoke less uneasiness, permitting the pastor room for more maneuverability. Sometimes an outside pastor, or a denominational staff person, can bring an objectivity and expertise that is appreciated. Attention is especially awarded the person who has been successful in revitalizing another congregation.

Acknowledgment of diversity can provide opportunity for some of the educational ideas we have already described. This might be through a Sunday school class, a fellowship dinner program, or a series of sermons. These function well for exploring gradually the idea of variegation. But unlike the possibilities for reorganization within larger churches, a clue for success in the small church rests in identifying where and how concrete features are already present in the regular Sunday worship. Thus what is being proposed is more intentionality in nurturing the concrete needs of the residents of particular Worlds within that congregation. Personally, I have found that the best approach is to begin with a worship committee, using some of the techniques already described for teaching the idea of Worlds. If need be, the pastor can slowly introduce certain of these elements into the worship. But at each point, explanations, either vocally or in the bulletin, are crucial whenever *any* change is forthcoming. The pastor should always resist the temptation to "slip things in." I have never had much trouble in changing things if I do it slowly; but it is even more important that I provide a clear theological rationale that makes sense. If a pastor knows and "loves the people," by far the most effective technique is to show how specific modifications, as we will see, would be helpful to persons with first names.

What follows are some possible modifications that can help minister to the needs of persons in different Worlds within the small church. The goal is to help each person forge a home base, as well as learn from one another and the Worlds what might be helpful ingredients for each of our lives.

World One is particularly appreciative of sacramentals—whose familiarity can render a room into a sanctuary. Every small church is custodian of "object memories"—some stored in the furnace room, others ill placed. And although their origins are often unknown, still, to move them is suicidal. This situation is a creative opportunity to care enough to sift through aged memories for their origins, then through them, to visually acknowledge and celebrate the church's unique history. Such a focusing can render these objects into symbols. Then, by a thoughtful arrangement of place and function, they can help to give an overarching unity that residents from World One could identify as a theological home. The goal would be to intensify the "now" by providing the sacredness of tradition as its context.

The prelude can have special importance for residents of World One. They value quiet solitude, something rare in a small church that needs to do multiple functions within a limited and common space. But whatever musical clue is needed to signal the congregation to gather, an organ or piano can intentionally provide "white sound" for the gathering. Quiet music *after* persons are in place is also a way to encourage centering, unless the pianist leaves much to be desired.

World One persons appreciate liberal amounts of silence inter-
spersed throughout the service. Their desire is to sense the presence
of a Holy Otherness, and to feel internally the impact of the whole.
Appropriate times for this silence might be after a corporate confession, and for reflection after the sermon.

The hymns these persons prefer are particularly appropriate for
the beginning of worship—celebrating God's creation ("All
Creatures of Our God and King") and the glory of the Transcendent
One ("Holy, Holy, Holy!"). The call to worship can also make special
contact with this World if it acknowledges God's abundant presence
everywhere. The "call" would be the need now for us to be called
from the tendency of taking life and God's gifts for granted. We bor-
row our life from God. Advent, with its special sense of waiting and
preparing, is a season of particular importance for World One.

Residents of *World Two* find special import in the time of corporate
confession, especially if it provides opportunity to focus on acts of
commission. Particularly meaningful is the practice of using concrete
names, places, and events to evoke images of oppression and neglect. The remembrance of saints for the day is useful, especially when
updated to the present, including persons within the church's own
locale and history. This helps to concretize the call to be followers of
"Jesus the pioneer," not alone but as participants with that "great
cloud of witnesses" who have "run with perseverance the race"
(Hebrews 12:1-2).

Another important part of worship for World Two is when the
pastoral prayer is made into the "prayers of the people." With this
change concrete intercessions from the congregation can be lifted up
in performatory language as words of commitment. The practice of
standing to hear the gospel read can gain significance here. The
hymns that World Two residents prefer are those most appropriate
as recessionals, those with militant tempo and exhortative words
such as "Marching to Zion," or "For All the Saints," when they
acknowledge "the Lord, their captain in the well-fought fight."
Perhaps at the top of their list of hymns might be "The Battle Hymn
of the Republic": "As he died to make men holy let us die to make
men free." Pentecost can be a focus time for such persons, for as the
birthday of the church, emphasis is on the Holy Spirit, who commis-
sioned and sent out the disciples to transform the earth. Epiphany
also is special, for then the good news was taken to the far corners of
the world.

World Three persons appreciate the fellowship in the narthex. The friendship of coffee and conversation before the service is really their prelude. They would appreciate special Sundays in which such conviviality could be invited to overflow into the worship itself. Even with coffee cups in hand, there could be a time of welcome, informal greetings with those sitting nearby, sharing of important happenings, announcements of church and community events, rehearsing of hymns, and passing the peace. The uneasiness such a suggestion would cause for World One folks suggests the importance of alternation. Trading off between a "silent beginning" and a "fellowship beginning" might be preferable to the present situation, which is probably neither quietness nor fellowship, but confusion.

The World Three group particularly likes the fellowship of singing, and might appreciate a period of singing favorite hymns, almost as a warm up. The words in them are not as important as the feelings evoked by the corporate singing itself. Therefore one should not be confused by the anomaly of World Three folks loving to sing gospel hymns whose words they are not about to believe. The point is that they are familiar. As for World Three favorites, "Blest Be the Tie That Binds" and "Breathe on Me, Breath of God" might be near the top. Whereas heavy emphasis on personal confession is not appreciated in World Three, the sins of omission are appreciated. In the early history of the church, only confirmed members were permitted to participate in the prayers of the people, the kiss of peace, and the table fellowship of communion. Since World Three persons are concerned above all with belonging, these elements are precisely those that are most valued, but they want them to be open to the stranger as well. These are Easter and Christmas persons, appreciative of creation as the gift of growth. World One folks might secretly appreciate incense, but World Three knows of no aroma able to match that of food cooking in the basement, hinting of the fellowship dinner to follow. A thanksgiving meal is their spiritual way of life.

For *World Four,* an invocation at the beginning of worship provides the key. All we can do is invite God, for God is the One who chooses who and what and when. Correlatively, personal confession is imperative in worship, for we are the ones who keep rejecting the divine invitation. One cannot hear the Word without the humility that comes from standing naked before the God who knows our inmost thoughts. And what needs to follow our confession is absolution of sin—not as a hope, but as a divine declaration of forgiveness.

Thus the pastoral prayer takes on the quality of a conversation with a dear friend. The heart of the service is the sermon, preaching not to communicate new information, but as an event of faithful repetition. Thus the preferred hymns are the gospel ones, with words taken seriously. This is a Good Friday World: "Love so amazing, so divine, demands my soul, my life, my all."

World Five knows the season of Lent as if it were life's road map. Here the *Via Dolorosa*, the suffering way of the One who "endured the cross, despising the shame," becomes the path of companionship "so that you may not grow weary or fainthearted" (Hebrews 12:3). For citizens of this World, the emphasis is more on the *how* than the *what*. Repetitiveness has power here. Catholics practice this in the sameness of the rosary. One feels this same power in the monastery, with identical chants to the same psalms, every three hours, for a lifetime. One experiences it in many black services, where, as the preacher "calls Aunt Jane," the congregation repeats back words of encouragement, and the refrains intensify, moving to intoxicating rhythms of repetitive clapping and singing. Many small churches still have their "Amen corner." Wherever it appears, the "how" is an emotional weaving of a pattern of togetherness, as the parts transcend into a wholeness that needs no justification beyond the experience itself. A favorite hymn is "Must Jesus Bear the Cross Alone" or "How Firm a Foundation." "When through the deep waters I call thee to go, the rivers of woe shall not thee overflow."

This transconscious sameness in World Five tends to be serendipitous, easier to detect when it occurs than to schedule. One possibility might be through the present tendency to restore "responsive readings" to their former meaning as "psalter." Psalms read or chanted antiphonally, or perhaps with repetitive responses, provide fitting rejoinders to the word anticipated or heard.

Frequent Eucharist, which could be meaningful for World Five, is usually unavailable because of residents of other Worlds who insist that frequency makes important acts commonplace. But that is what the residents of World Five really yearn for—for the commonplace to be rendered important by frequency. African American spirituals have been important in doing this well. To experience this World, one needs only sing "Were You There" or "He Never Said a Mumbalin' Word"—with service music in 3/4 time. Whereas such singing is infrequent in white churches, except at poor white storefronts, vestiges continue in its secular successor as rhythm and blues—with the chant finding its secular reincarnation as rap. One can find this World in most hymnals under the theme of passion and death, with hymns reflecting this perspective going back at least as far as the Reformation:

> Ah, holy Jesus, how hast thou offended,
> that we to judge thee have in hate pretended?
> By foes derided, by thine own rejected,
> O most afflicted. (1630) [12]

For Catholics its profound expression is found in the Good Friday Reproaches: "My people, what have I done to you? How have I offended you? I led you out of Egypt, from slavery to freedom, but you led your Savior to the cross." This deep commonness is what Henry Mitchell identifies as a central characteristic of black preaching, that of providing a habitable living space through "the establishment of a celebrative island of consciousness in an ocean of oppression and deprivation." [13] For small churches in the midst of the farm crisis, one wonders about the possibilities.

The primary opportunity for variegation in the small church, then, comes by incorporating within the common Sunday worship service aspects that intentionally touch dimensions of each of the Worlds. Likewise, a careful selection of hymns can provide variegation. One church, for example, studied its hymnal, and marked each hymn as to its appropriateness to the theological Worlds represented in the congregation. Then by choosing hymns representatively, a wider congregational familiarity with hymnody resulted, not only by creating interest in new hymns, but by having particular hymns claimed by groups and persons as "their songs."

Another approach, as we mentioned before, is to give a special emphasis to differing services, planning alternative worship patterns with representative committees. This not only ministers to different persons in special ways, but over a period of time becomes an educational venture in variegation for the whole congregation. The church year can also be used to focus on appropriate theological Worlds, giving an opportunity to practice sustained variegation.

A problem that many pastors of multiple small churches face provides an interesting possibility. Often small congregations in proximity to one another refuse to merge, despite absence of any practical reason for continuing separately. This dilemma can provide the opportunity for having the two congregations choose to take on the flavor and environmental characteristics of two contrasting Worlds. This choice not only gives to each church a special reason for being, but encourages interchurch participation, perhaps on alternating Sundays, gaining a sense of nonthreatening unity through intentional diversity. For example, with over half of the churches in United Methodism connected in charges, such variegation is a significant possibility.

Lyle Schaller once observed that the typical small church Sunday worship is attended by older persons, usually related by blood or marriage. Instead of inviting potential members to break into that exclusive group, why not organize a new subcongregation? Whatever possibilities are tried, success depends particularly on two factors. First, make very clear to the congregation the theological wisdom of trying particular changes, otherwise such changes will quickly be labeled and rejected—as being Catholic or Baptist or High Church or liberal. Second, establish a dynamic of trade-off—give a little, take a little, so that there is "something for everyone." I have been impressed with how tolerant small church worshipers can be when adaptations to the normal service take on faces. "Silence would make me uneasy, but obviously that is something Alice really misses." "Some of those gospel hymns don't make sense, but I sure got a kick out of old Jake last week—he really got into it." But the bottom line of change rarely moves far from this syntax: "I can live with that, just as long as I have . . ."

Whereas the larger church has the advantage of being able to create special spaces for alternative Worlds, it is important to recognize the degree to which smaller churches have regular spaces where, in fact, various Worlds are routinely acted out. *World One* persons thrive in quiet, sacred places, as in a prayer chapel, or where there is sunlight through a stained glass window. When not available, these persons will discover open churches where candles signal a sacramental presence, or spend time at retreat centers, or find favorite spots for sitting in the park. These persons would greatly value their church being opened at regular hours to enter without need for scheduling or explanation. Unfortunately within Protestantism, those seeking such silence are often misunderstood as being in need of counseling.

World Two persons tend to find each other in a particular church school class—one where they gain the reputation of being "do-gooders" or "cause folk," always selling tickets or recruiting for some service project. Women's weekday mission groups signal a World Two presence, whereas many can be found on weeknights in space made available for nonchurch community groups.

Residents of *World Three* are usually most numerous in or around the basement fellowship hall, planning or conducting festive meals or special activities. *World Four* locations are readily identifiable as the Sunday morning Bible class(es), often in or near the pulpit-centered sanctuary. The bulletin indicates the homes where this group will be meeting during the week for Bible study and prayer.

World Five women often know each other through working together in the church kitchen, sometimes at odds with the World Three workers who are in the dining area glad-handing people as they come and are seated. Male representatives are often those loyally involved in hands-on maintenance, with the furnace room or the toolshed their symbolic place. And rare is the church in which World Five persons are not found in the church office (or by any flat surface) stuffing envelopes or keeping attendance records, invisibly seeing that things "keep on keeping on."

I remember well a meeting of the monks of the monastery to which I belong. Fruitcakes are what we make for our livelihood, and last year had been particularly successful, selling out before the end of the year. The question they had been called together to discuss was whether we should bake one additional day each week so that we could make more fruitcakes the next year. I was proud when one of the monks settled the question this way. "Right now we are monks who happen to make fruitcakes. If we increase our production over our needs, I fear that soon we will be fruitcake bakers who happen to be monks." So it is with worship. Liturgy must be the way we live our lives, for otherwise, I fear, we will be secular folk who happen to go to church on Sunday.

CHAPTER NINE

Variegated Preaching:
Theologizing Within Intentional Contexts

Worship, as the celebration of and in a theological World, is structured by plot. Preaching takes its meaning as an inseparable event within that liturgy, rendering that plot self-conscious. Thus preaching is a "drama within the drama," providing an aperture for understanding worship as a whole. It follows that the particular liturgy serving as the context for a sermon should determine the particular structure and method of that sermon, rather than the reverse.

Some years ago at the seminary where I taught, we developed a new curriculum based confidently on an action-reflection methodology. We involved students in "exposure experiences" that would challenge their ways of living and understanding. But what distressed me was that before, during, and after these immersions, students kept asking: "What am I supposed to see?" No doubt this question reflected some resistance to strange environments, but in time I came to see their question as insightful. There is no such thing as a naked, objective experience. Things are always and necessarily seen from a particular perspective. Thus to take students to a gay worship service can bring insight, shock, information, or defensiveness—or all of them. What one sees depends on where one stands. And so it is with the sermonic event.

Preaching Within Alternative Worship

It has been said of Barth that he approached scripture as a nonfictional novel. That is how we all approach life—as searchers for the plot. In Melville's *Moby Dick,* Ishmael, as lone survivor, is bequeathed the role of reflecting back over the whole as its omniscient interpreter. Such transcendence as self-consciousness is the task of preaching. The preacher stands within the liturgical event as the agent of perspective. Thus the experience of worship must surround the homiletic task, as the air breathed by the preacher.

Paul Scherer is correct in insisting that a sermon should not begin, nor build upon, where the individual is. The human dilemma is that we do not know who we are or where we stand—or at least we are always on the edge of forgetting. [1] Thus, in contrast to Harry Emerson Fosdick's homiletical practice, worship should not begin as a subtle introit, moving persons slowly from their situation upon entering into a slightly different one when they leave. In drama, the curtain opens and one is plunged into a World structured by its own reality—not necessarily one's own. So it is with worship. And thus the preached answer is a response to the basic question, "Where are we?" Worship succeeds when for an hour a person becomes a participant resident in a particular, well-crafted theological World. Over Sunday dinner, the location of the "real world" is the question providing lively conversation. It is in sensing the actual or needed concurrence between Sunday morning and one's daily mornings that worship comes into its own—as rehearsing one's real World into the self-consciousness of growing commitment.

Worship structures a theological World into systemic clarity, and preaching, according to Nelle Morton, "discerns that World into speech." Consequently, the preacher who does not understand the homiletical task as one of grafting liturgy and sermon (homily) together is like a playwright writing dialogue without plot.

Helpful here is George Lindbeck's cultural-linguistic understanding of religion as a system of discursive and nondiscursive symbols linking motivation and action, and providing an ultimate legitimization for basic patterns of thought, feeling, and behavior uniquely characteristic of a given community or society and its members. [2] Of necessity, religion as an interpretive system embodies "myths or narratives and [is] heavily ritualized." [3] Thus just as a person becomes human by learning a language, so does one become a Christian in becoming a new creature through hearing and interiorizing the language that speaks of Christ. [4] As a result, the phrase "Christ is Lord" is true "only as it is used in the activities of adoration, proclamation, obedience, promise-hearing, and promise-keeping which shape individuals and communities into conformity to the mind of Christ."[5] Lindbeck's study confirms the direction we are moving. Christian affirmations are true insofar as they are spoken religiously, that is, preached in a context of worship. Preaching as religious speaking entails what Clifford Geertz calls "thick description," made possible within the context of an "imaginative universe in which . . . acts are signs."[6]

It is in recognizing preaching as descriptive thickness that the reality of theological Worlds makes important contact with the present recovery of narrative within contemporary homiletics. Preaching is narrative in which the sermon as story of stories is acted out and named within a ritual of rituals.

Narrative and Image

The traditional understanding of preaching as clerical instruction, exhortation, or devotion is presently undergoing severe transition. The full impact of permitting the lectionary to provide homiletic content is only beginning to be realized. But at least it means that scripture as selected illustration is replaced by the Word as unchosen address. Consequently, the first axiom in variegated homiletics is that the preacher's task is to discern the meaning of a given text "as a distinctive world, with its own unique shape and theological intention."[7] A second axiom, less recognized, is equally important. Encounter with the textual World is always done by a person living and moving and having one's being within a World that already has its own unique shape and intention. Thus each text is a World seen from a World.

Consequently, both sermonic preparation and delivery are dialogical events, most often between two Worlds. The first is the World of the concrete text within its originating context. The second is more problematic. With whose World shall the textual World engage in creating the event called sermon? The implicit assumption has been that this second World is that of the preacher. But it is this assumption that must be questioned, giving rise to a new approach to homiletics. In fact, this assumption rests on a deeper, unspoken one—that the sermon is capable of bringing into proximity the

Worlds of text and preacher, because it is assumed that there is a reality called *the* World to which both can determine correspondence. But if, as we have insisted, there is no such thing as an objective World, both the former and the current understandings of the homiletical task become undermined. Thus this question must be raised again, with greater urgency. Whose particular World will the second one be, the one which will provide the "proper" perspective? Unlike in the past, the preacher's own World-perspective no longer has legitimacy for being the omniscient interpreter. Thus the new homiletic we are developing is one in which preaching is understood as a *contextual* art, one through which the particular theological World, structuring a concrete liturgy, is brought into self-consciousness. The sermon is *a microcosm of the particular liturgical whole in which the text is being preached.* The sermonic dialogue, then, must be between the World of the text and the liturgical World functioning as present context.

In making out this case, an insight from the current narrative approach to homiletics is helpful. This theory insists that the church's own narrative self-understanding is foundational for preaching. The self comes to faith through the community's narrated tradition, rooted in scripture as its primary story.[8] Thus one sees as a Christian only when one's eyes are trained to focus—as to *how* and on *what*. This understanding is basic, and yet the narrative homiletics currently being developed from it are questionable at two points.

The first is the assumption that the discovery of one's own story "in God's story" is a monolithic process for all persons, based on the assumption that there is a "primary structure of existence" which is one, knowable, and available, through the unified communal tradition which is Christianity.[9] This unexamined assumption of a common human perspective and of a unified Christian tradition is precisely what the radical diversity of our time is bringing into severe question.

The second weakness requires more analysis. These homilists insist that narrative, being historical, renders preaching necessarily linear. That is, just as time is sequential, so must the sermon be structured. But whereas narrative is admittedly historical, history has no unified meaning in which to wrap a homiletic. History, and thus narrative, takes its meaning contextually from the particular World through which it is *imaged.*

ALTERNATIVE VIEWS OF HISTORY AND
PREACHING SERMON STRUCTURES

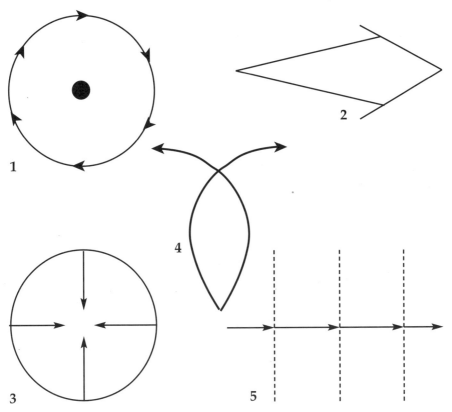

The ingredients *within* history occur sequentially, but history *as* history is not sequential. History is told meaning, richly surrounded for its thickness by imagination. To be historical is to see through eyes honed by centripetal imagery. Thus history is history only when perceived as a whole through an informing image of which linearity is only one such possibility. Put distinctly, history must be understood from within alternative theological Worlds. And each World rests on a story of stories, discerned through an image of images— and vice versa. In this relation of narrative and image, the inseparable relation of liturgy and preaching is forged.

Put another way, history is always seen through an image functioning as metaphor. Paul, for example, was one untimely born, in the sense of knowing little of the sequential history of Jesus in the flesh that the synoptics reflect. Yet he can still tell the story. Whereas

Luke's Jesus was born in Bethlehem as a blessing to the poor, Paul's Jesus was rebirthed on the Damascus road as gift to the undeserving. Struck down so as to blind his blindness, Paul's eyes were reopened to see the whole through a vow—to "know nothing among you except Jesus Christ and him crucified" (1 Corinthians 2:2). And so it is with each of us. We are all untimely born, incapable of knowing Jesus as biography but only as autobiography. And history so understood is story focused by image, and image unfolded as story. This is the dialogue through which one's World is furnished as unique pilgrimage.

This situation characteristic of Paul, and us, is true as well for the Gospel writers themselves, whose history appears at first glance to be linear. For John the historical Jesus walks a theological World characterized by realized eschatology, honed by images of seed and leaven so that the narrative itself becomes one of growth as breadth from a sacramental center. Here one enters, above all, into World One. And here it is that linear history is forfeited for chosen moments—*kairoi,* so pregnant with meaning that through them the whole is experienced as an eternal and timeless now. Mark's Jesus, on the other hand, is intensely active, harvesting for an end that is momentarily imminent. Yet for the writer of Revelation being historical entails an apocalyptic World in which sequence is reversed meaning coming from a discontinuous future breaking into an unsuspecting present. Interestingly, though both Mark and Acts are supposedly the most linear, in the best texts that we have, neither have endings.

The Hebrew Bible (Old Testament) likewise exhibits alternative views of history. For some writers, history as story is imaged through the perspective of nature's rhythmic cycles, whereas for others even this continuity dissolves into a mystic hub for the turning wheel of history. Still others, suspicious of closure, prefer narrative as a portrait of those who bridge the isolated moments with fervent acts of will. All of these images stand in heavy contrast to the prophet's view of history, which narrative homilists treat as normative—that of a rich beginning, moving convolutedly, then hopefully, toward a resolving end. Thus although the thickness of prophetic narrative is indeed a weave of linear imagery, it reflects only *one* theological World. Within scripture, then, are narratives thickened by rival images of depth, breadth, moment, height, dialectic, alternation, or spiral. History's leaven may be from within, or time may appear as the shadow of eternity, or depth discloses history's center point, or *call* renders history as outward expansion toward a transformed earth. *All of these are alternative meanings of history.*

The important conclusion to be drawn, one that modifies significantly the present understanding of narrative preaching, is this: whereas narrative is historico/temporal in nature, history is *not* necessarily sequential in meaning. Put another way, there is no *one* narrative structure to serve as normative for preaching. Instead, there are alternatives, each depending on the World that it defines for its defining motion, and by which, in turn, it is clothed.

The homiletical resolution toward which diversity pushes us is to be found in worship. Liturgy is narrative in the etymological sense of the word—to relate so as to know. Liturgy is that dramatic relating of which the sermon is the distilled *image*—through which one comes to know by beholding the whole. Thus liturgy and preaching interact much as "what" relates to "how." The result is a new approach to homiletics.

Toward Variegated Homiletics

Each theological World, curling in on its own image of history for meaning, structures uniquely the sermonic functioning occurring at its center. The sermon as microevent *is* the meaning. Whether characterized by thunderous crescendo, or silent whisper, uncanny resolution, serendipitous gasp, systematic unfolding, or intriguing guesses—it should not be reducible to mere techniques. It needs to be understood as an expression of image-event within a particular liturgy. The present rejection of the traditional "three points and a poem" sermon is not actually a critique of method, but an insistence that life can no longer be imaged by such simple order. Yet the error of narrative preaching is related. As presently understood and practiced, it assumes *one* theological World—binding scripture, preacher, and worshiper in a simple objectivity. This is theologically untenable. Instead, what is needed is a homiletic theory solidly rooted in a variegated understanding of reality, thereby providing alternative preaching methods rather than making one possibility normative.

Richard Eslinger is correct in recognizing the relation of narrative and image as a key issue needing more exploration in contemporary homiletics. His preliminary steps, however, continue to reflect the problem more than a solution. By declaring narrative of a particular kind to be primary, he continues the neglect of history seen pluralistically. He bases the primacy of narrative on the assumption that since time involves duration, plot as the necessary time line of narration imitates the very nature of human experience. [10] Thus, once again, one particular theological World is regarded as universal, rendering its linearity normative as *the* homiletical structure.

What is needed is an approach to preaching that rests on the reciprocal relation between image and narrative. Poetry provides a helpful analogy. In entering the time of a poem, one enters a dimension where sequence, even sentence structure, is no longer a reliable barometer of meaning. Here, where image is deeply at home, meaning is birthed and rooted in the metaphorical nature of language itself, with the poem's structure resident within its unique root image. Thus whereas water is a common ingredient in countless poems, the structure of each is contained within a particular image of disclosure. Thus "ocean" may disclose itself through "cycle," "fountain" as "empowerment," "well" in "depth," "ripple" through "expansion," "rain" as "nurture," or "river" in "pilgrimage." Relatedly, narrative is a foraging for image, which, once found, validates the search by becoming prelude, postlude, center, or circumference for the whole. This relation of narrative and image is what gives both literature and life its ongoing torque. Thus John Masefield invites the reader into World One with the image of a first line: "I could not sleep for thinking of the sky. . . ." With that image a soul is born, called forth to sail "a million years" in order to end where it began, "In nothing, not even Death, not even tears." [11] Narrative? In its own unique way. Linearity? Hardly.

Psalms likewise illustrate how narrative is rooted in image, and image itself is implicit in narrative. Psalm 106 is a World Two narrative, rooted in the image of call and rebellion. Psalm 136 tells the same story, without linear texture. Here the time signature of the retelling is that of World Five. Every other line is a refrain of perseverance—as ceaseless beat: "For God's love endures forever."—twenty-six times. In contrast, the lives of Trappist monks are shaped by the psalms *as a whole,* chanting 75 each week, in seven episodes each day. Here linearity fades into the circularity of ordinary days, weaving World One's timeless images—"no more than a breath," "the companion darkness," "down into the silence," "a passing guest," "walking the presence," "deep calling to deep," "a thirsty soul" for one "whose grave is home." On and on, piled on top, the images are stuffed into every crevice, until each year repeats the last and the next.

Obsessio and *epiphania* relate here, much as do narrative and image. What one sees depends on the spectacles through which one looks. Thus, as Eslinger acknowledges, certain stories evoke images which then persist as their own centers of meaning. Although he correctly resists such disengagement of image from story, he neglects the counterpart. Story disengaged from root images leaves hearers to provide their own subjective meaning. This is the particular weakness characterizing many seminary students taught in the present-day narrative manner. There is lacking a root metaphor or image. Repeating a scriptural story is very different from having the story told. Master storytellers, by contrast, provide the image in the telling. Narrative and image are deeply dialectical, grounding variegated homiletics in the dialectic of liturgy and sermon.

An illustration of this is the manner in which I do spiritual direction. I let the person "empty out," as I listen with pencil and paper. Gradually I draw lines that begin to relate words, and events begin intersecting. What is being sought is the primal image around which one's life has been taking shape, for better or worse—the unpacking of which can take a lifetime. Lives are like novels in this regard, in that at the beginning one is just as confused as the characters until a metaphor or image suggests itself, around which suddenly one discerns the plot unfolding as meaning for the whole. But whereas Eslinger correctly acknowledges the importance of narrative for providing the interpretative focus for an image's multiple inherent meanings, he neglects what is equally crucial: to acknowledge how the image itself serves "as the hermeneutical perspective from which the entire story is received," providing its point of view. [12]

This reciprocity of liturgy and sermon thus renders it a mistake to tailor the worship ingredients that precede and follow the sermon as providing a homiletical context. We have been wrongly taught that if the sermon is about joy then the hymns and prayers and all other ingredients should echo that same theme. My insistence is that the liturgy must stand firm in the integrity of its own wholeness, whatever the sermonic emphasis. Thus, for example, World Four liturgy without confession is not worship, even if the focus of the morning's sermon is on "God's good creation."

The real tragedy for the church is not so much the unchurched, but the minimally churched—those countless church-goers who have no awareness of what is going on, as to what, how, or why, even though the doing is an ingrained habit. A major cause of this superficiality is the sermon performed as if it is a disengaged ingredient, with worship functioning as a warm up, opening exercises, as it were, for the sermon as climax—a performance prepared to have a life of its own. This is a far cry from understanding the sermon as intent upon rehearsing into self-consciousness the liturgical dynamic of a particular World as a way of life.

Eugene Lowry, a master of narrative preaching, asks of the sermon what needs to be asked of the liturgy as a whole. The question is not "Did you get it across?" but "Did it happen?" The sermon, to be faithful to itself then, *must be an event within an event.* Yet, whereas he seems to understand this, the homiletical method which he develops as normative is in fact an *ordo salutis,* a distillation of the historical process characteristic of *one* particular theological World. He insists that the sermon line must be linear, until it reaches a theological dead end; there, and only through reversal, is advancement possible. The first aspect of linearity could be identified as "works." The second is the linear reversal called "grace." This homiletic method seems so self-evident to Lowry because it expresses the anatomy of his own particular theological World, to which, of course, he is deeply committed. As a friend, I know him well. His is a World in which life as it was intended to be lived has become reversed (fall as self-imposed linearity), so that only when the reversal is reversed can God's intended linearity be resolved as catharsis. Because his World, and thus his sermons, are events in time, he has no time for a sermon (and thus, apparently, any theological World) whose informing image is spatial. [13] Thus his homiletic method is, in truth, a theological statement. And because the informing image of his World is that of sequential ordering, the sermon, by definition for him, is "an ordered form of moving time." [14]

The two preaching methods Lowry identifies depend upon the basic paradigm informing the preacher—that of either time, or of space. What follows for him are two contrasting goals characterizing the sermon—either that of happening or of understanding. What Lowry apparently does not see is that his insistence on time-oriented preaching as the only valid type is not, in the end, a homiletical decision. It is a theological confession determined by the World in which he lives daily, and thus within which he pursues with skill his homiletical craft.

As a result, he identifies the methodological goal to be illumination rather than manifest declaration. The distinction between Worlds One and Four could not be summarized better. What he insists on for a sermon are images as paradigms that illumine, thereby sharpening perception about *how* to think. But how this works itself out homiletically for him becomes, in truth, a theological confession of one understanding of revelation, chosen from among other equally valid understandings—with corresponding homiletical options. His emphasis upon images as illumining paradigms should force him to recognize the unacknowledged dialectic of image and narrative, pushing toward a variegated homiletic. [15]

In spite of Lowry's insistence upon linearity alone as homiletically valid, there are persons like the poet Rilke who do indeed live deeply and fully in a World imaged by space, with a skill that shares it brilliantly. "I live my life in growing orbits. . . ." Movement for him is not into a time forward, but a depth downward, not toward a goal future, but a center which is inward—into a World where dark space broods at the center point of the wheel, in holy depth. Here he acknowledges that "I am circling around God," for years, far longer than his lifetime. Life is the search for one instant which if lived fully can contain the whole, the center around which the cities practice their foolishness.[16] Lowry and Rilke are both correct. That is what makes truth so profoundly diverse, and what forces homiletics into being a variegated art.

Preaching "As If"

If preaching is to rediscover its task as liturgical self-consciousness, two approaches must be explored. These correlate with the two models of variegated worship we have been developing—one for alternative subcongregations, the other for singular variegated worship. In either case, sermon preparation begins in exegesis, requiring that one's imagination be lured into the World of the text. This hermeneutic requires the development of one's *aesthetic capacity,* which is a relationship possible with almost anything. In the aesthetic experience, one transcends the issue of truth or falsity, by being drawn into and shaped by that which is encountered. Works of art are marked by this special capacity for magnetism. Thus one can be so drawn into the World of Macbeth that the image of stained hands makes one glance uneasily at one's own. An aesthetic relationship is one of "pure dramatic immediacy" to the point of absorption. [17] This capacity is not only at the heart of the hermeneutic we are developing for preachers, it characterizes the relation between congregation and liturgy as well.

Put another way, religion is the total response of the whole person to the hulk of life. Liturgies have been developed through the years to order these responses into alternative narrative structures by discerning resident images from which the anatomies of contrasting theological Worlds flow and are formed. Worship occurs when one's individual World becomes subsumed experientially within a corporate one. It is within this interaction that the sermon gains its functional identity. As we have suggested, the process of reading a novel provides an apt analogy here too. One stumbles along in relative confusion until confronted by an image that hints of being a prism capable of illuminating the whole. From then on, one tries on that image, experiencing the possibilities that flow from that perspective—likewise for the sermon. It functions in worship much as image relates to plot. Its task is to offer the text as prism so that the collective unconsciousness of the liturgical whole becomes reexperienced as *kairos*.

This understanding involves, as well, the aesthetic method by which the preacher needs to enter into the lectionary reading. That birthing process is to discern *within* the text an informing image by which to grasp the whole *of* the text. But two difficult questions arise. First, how broad a context for the text should one permit? If the text is Psalm 23, is the psalm itself sufficient context as a song of confidence for deliverance from one's enemies? Or should it be expanded into the larger context of temple meals? Or one could expand it still further into God's covenant community, or even further through the Near Eastern use of shepherd imagery for kings? Thus the term *context* is ambiguous. But whatever size the context, one must recognize that it is the reflection of a World.

Second, in living with the text in hope of discerning an image yearning to be born as prism for the whole, is not the preacher's own theological World central in this exchange? In a variegated church of alternative liturgical centers, the answer should now be clear. The aesthetic task of the preacher is to *open the text from within the World which is the liturgical context in which it is to function as an event.* This forces powerfully the issue of variegation upon the art of preaching. The preacher can no longer avoid the primal fact that what one sees is directly related to the World through which one's eyes look. To assume that these eyes should be those of the preacher is an unwarranted presumption.

To illustrate this homiletical approach, we can continue to use Psalm 23 as our text. Discerned from the orientation of World One, images likely to arise have to do with presence "beside still waters," restoring one's soul, anticipating one's dwelling "in the house of the Lord forever." World Two eyes focus elsewhere, perhaps on a table "prepared before me in the presence of my enemies." Residents of World Three will have contrasting ears, honed for the sounds of yearning that "I shall not want," lured forward with the promise that "my cup overflows." Christological images will likely be emitted for World Four, as "He leads me in paths of righteousness for His name's sake." The ethos of World Five, in turn, might be rehearsed in the image that "even though I walk through the valley of the shadow of death . . . thou art with me, thy rod and thy staff, they comfort me." Thus, unless one is content simply to repeat the Psalm, preaching is an event in which an informing image becomes the jewel through which nuances of the whole become an enhanced reflection. This makes the sermon an invitation to participate in a particular theological World through the aperture of a text.

If, then, the preacher is responsible for opening the text from within the liturgical context of a particular theological World, a second question follows quickly. *Can one really preach from a World not one's own?* Certainly. An actor can play Macbeth without having as his own *obsessio* the gory heights of jealous ambition. Wesley, in fact, advised doubting preachers to preach what they could not believe until they believed it.

If, then, it is possible for preachers to learn the skill of entering aesthetically into theological Worlds not their own, exhibiting the meaning of texts from within alternative perspectives, *can one in good conscience preach what one does not fully and personally believe?* Again the answer is "yes." Each of us does live partly in each of the Worlds, part of the time. Theological Worlds are not mutually exclusive. Thus one's theological World is where one begins and ends one's day, as home base. It is the home from which one wanders forth to forage in strange places, to which one brings back one's treasures, and into which one retreats in order to behold their meaning.

Thus the preacher can and needs to know much about other Worlds, and can share some of their experiences, even though one might not choose to remain there overnight. During his final week, Jesus immersed himself in truly contrasting Worlds: of triumph, anointing, purgation, nurturing, and betrayal. We see him crying over the future, countering spies, arguing theology, marveling over the poor. But "when evening came they went out of the city" (Mark 11:19). Matthew disclosed Bethany as home base, embraced by friends (Matthew 21:17). Luke surrounds him in a vigil with disciples "on the mount called Olivet" (Luke 21:37). And John, knowing home as within, described a Jesus who "departed and hid himself from them" (John 12:36).

Furthermore, no one ever lives totally in a liturgically shaped World. Each World is a dramatic pure type. In contrast, daily life as fallen testifies to the fact that the meaning-structure of one's World is rarely beheld face-to-face, but "through a glass darkly." Spectacles must be sought, exchanged, bargained for, entailing numerous fittings—some for sight, many for appearance. The power of worship is that it is an invitation to participate in clarity. A liturgical World at its best is one whose anatomy is intentional, its rhythm consistent, and its objects transparent, with the sermon functioning as the play within a play to provide an image for the guided tour. In the hour of worship, one lives the purity of an "as if." Conversion is a name for the awareness that the dress rehearsal was in fact a face-to-face participation in the hidden meaning-structure of one's own daily living.

The charisma of the accomplished preacher resides in the ability to preach "as if," so modeling the spatial and temporal parameters of a crafted liturgical World that it becomes transparent. To do this with integrity requires belief by the pastor in the power of the gospel to honor persons in their uniqueness. This is possible only when preachers are so anchored in their own personal and particular theological World that they are not intimidated or threatened into a cautious ambiguity by lively alternatives—or tempted to live vicariously by selling without buying. A friend of mine is a brilliant consultant who can enter any company structure and problem solve from within. It is as if he belongs. His recent personal crisis is a warning for those of us developing variegated homiletics. Between assignments, he experiences deep depression, for he has no identity of his own— only that of whichever business currently pays his salary. In contrast, a minister must be so anchored in a clearly identifiable and consistent theological World, that it is possible, without threat, to participate in the viable alternatives of one's parishioners. Whatever else a pastor might be, at the top of the list is a resident theologian.

Preaching from and Within Alternative Worlds

This homiletics of diversity is based on the insistence that the particular liturgical World in which a sermon is to function determines the nature of the sermonic process in its preparation, delivery, and goal. The task now is to describe concretely how this works within alternative liturgical contexts. A chart is useful.

This Alternative Preaching Chart is best used in conjunction with the worship formatting we have already done, exploring the intersections. In so doing, we can remember that the liturgical dynamic in *World One* is from the *obsessio* of isolation to the *epiphania* of unity, effected in a circular rather than linear fashion. One moves from life's periphery toward the center, one that theologically (and thus sermonically) is equidistant from any of its parts. An image for understanding this process homiletically is the experience of an optical illusion. One stares at it, and life, for a long time seeing nothing except the obvious. Then suddenly there might come a moment. Suddenly, "There it is!" With surprise comes amazement—"How could I have been so blind!" Such a moment is a *kairos*, an illumination uniting *within* and *without*. Once seen, one is able to see it again and again. But it takes practice. Understandably, then, the liturgy that renders World One organic is composed of richly sacramental words, images, gestures, things—hinting of transparency into the center. To see—that is the purpose—to behold incarnation in a piece of broken bread, fresh newness in blessed water, and illumination in a finely turned phrase. And when such profound seeing occurs there, one is opened to see transparency anywhere—each meal a Eucharist, every shower a rebirthing, each desk an altar, each conversation an invitation into miracle. The narrative structure of such liturgy, and thus the sermon, is much like that of a mystery novel. One reads for hints, followed by guesses, hoping for one clue into the hidden meaning. Like a puzzle or collage or mosaic, the pearl of great price is the missing piece that exhibits the whole as making perfect sense. Once seen, one rarely reads that book again. Knowing the clues in advance renders the linearity of reading tedious. Preaching, likewise, is like rummaging in the text for an unsuspected jewel, in the light of which the parts become reflected as nuances. The understanding involved is not argument, point logically following point, to a conclusion. It is illumination, intuition tinged with emotion, radiating from the center.

ALTERNATIVE PREACHING

	Action	Sermon	Hermeneutic	Narrative Structure	Scripture	Themes
World 1	See (illumination)	Grounding Spirit to be recognized	Sacramental event	Mystery to evoke	Song of Solomon John Ephesians Colossians Hebrews	Homesickness Exile/impermanent Pilgrim/wanderer Sacramental hints Reunion
World 2	Do (celebration)	Future promise to be acted upon	Narrative happening	Comedy to envison	Exodus Isaiah/Ezekiel/Amos Mark/Luke James/Revelation	Oppression Taking sides Anticipation Liberation
World 3	Share (socialize)	Possibilites now to be realized	Autobiographic story	Lyric to lure	Genesis/Ruth parables John/Galatians John letters	Barren/insignificant Paths not taken Birthing Becoming oneself
World 4	Hear (declare)	Remembering heard as Proclamation	Pronouncement as rehearsal	Tragedy to convert	Deuteronomy Jonah Matthew Romans	Guilt Forgiveness Rebirth Perfection
World 5	Be (empower)	Identification with, to be acknowledged	Litany of webbed participation	Pathos to encourage	Numbers/Job Ecclesiastes/Jeremiah Lamentations/Hosea 2 Corinthians Philippians	Suffer/anneal Courage Companionship Integrity

Poetry may provide the best analogy for preaching within such a liturgy. In reading a poem, images float gently through the mind's imagination, but to what meaning? It is a Sunday afternoon. A man is mowing the yard. He is almost done when he runs out of gas. He decides to lie down, funnies over his face, and let the grass grow. So? Then comes the line: "Is this all that is left of freedom?" Ah! Yes! The images suddenly reappear, this time like an open floodgate, or like parts of a firework's blast now whole. The poem's title? "June-Day Joshua." [18] Yes, of course. I should have known.

Thus a sermon fit for World One is structured as a composite of nuggets, pulled, as it were, from one's side pocket. The event is a process in which even the preacher seems to be curious as to what might be pulled out next. Then comes the jewel—"Look at that!" And we know, if only for that moment. We see. Such an *epiphania* is beyond words, resisting explanations. It is an image functioning as a storyless parable. Jesus could create such magic, in which, if the disciples had to ask for a translation, it was all over. Evaporated. It either happens or it does not and any explanation is as wrong as it is useless.

The point of the sermon is the still point of the turning wheel, equidistant from time exposed as the frantic circle of life's daily periphery. The homiletic method is analogous to staring at a painting with a friend. All one can do is point. Either one sees it or one does not. And the "it," once named, sounds very strange—the eternal now, the luminous, living the moment, tasting the depth. Space, not time, is the defining context in which images are like icons, waving motionlessly at the grounding Spirit, sacramentally present in every direction. [19] T. S. Eliot understands the dilemma of World One residents, in relation to which World One preaching finds its torque— "to have had the experience but missed the meaning."

Interestingly, while Fred Craddock's homiletic theory advocates an inductive style characteristic of World Three preaching, his actual preaching style is one that would be welcomed in World One. The little stories that he tells along the way do not really build toward resolution, or actually go anywhere. They depend for their meaning on a sudden implication that flows backwards to connect them all with an unsuspected common center. [20]

World Two residents, on the other hand, are impatient with such sermons, and thus with the liturgy of World One. The informing action that they need is not a matter of seeing but of doing. The movement that feeds them is relentlessly linear, not searching for a backward flowing image, but that which moves forward toward resolution and consummation. History, and thus the sermon, must evidence coherence, a movement from beginning toward end. Life, to have meaning, necessitates that one is getting somewhere—to a somewhere, where we have not been before, except in promise.

Consequently, the narrative structure draws heavily from the epic form. Its sweep favors a large brush—powerful, brave, and full—with a tug and lure that is daring and hopeful. Lowry's method can apply full well for preaching within this World, for here the pattern of classic narrative is normative with denouement the heart of the action. Poor preaching in this context is like telling a joke and forgetting the punch line. The most damning critique of a sermon preached in this World would be, "What was the point of all that?" Just as history is absurd if its ending is aborted, so the sermon that "doesn't go anywhere" is a homiletical travesty—"a tale told by an idiot." But the "anywhere" to which these residents are attuned is a somewhere imaging the movement from oppression toward liberation.

To understand this World Two mode of preaching, one must perceive the degree to which resolution is often ridiculed by the daily facts. In a cartoon, Ziggy looks up toward the heavens, and speaks for World Two: "Have you noticed, Sir, that the meek are still getting creamed?" Therefore, for the hour called worship, the ending must become believable, justifying each part as necessary for the reversal as resolution. This is what renders World Two worship a celebration, claiming for itself the status of foretaste.

I still remember as a boy seeing my first Saturday afternoon B movie. Near the end of the last reel, the projector ate the film. For such an indignity, our money was refunded. But I wonder to this day how the movie turned out. Actually, I know. The good guys won. But that's not the same as actually experiencing it—as experiencing closure. Likewise in World Two preaching. One needs to keep reexperiencing it, just to be sure, because in daily life, there are at least nine defeats for each victory. Shakespeare knew that "all's well that ends well."

A friend asked me why I kept participating in the monthly candlelight vigils to resist United States policy in Central America in the 1980s, and the death penalty in the 1990s. "It doesn't make any difference!" My response came quickly: "When I'm by myself, life feels like an unending defeat. But when we're together, I can believe again that things will change." It was in the 1960s that I first knew that I belonged to World Two. Father Groppe made a national appeal for representatives to join him in a civil rights march through a hostile white neighborhood of Milwaukee. During the long bus trip, I pondered the futility of going. And I was scared. I arrived to find that our "planning table" was the altar of a huge cathedral. Our "instructions" were shared bread, with the words, "The unconditional breaking of bread for all is a revolutionary act." Then a common cup was drunk as a pledge to shed our own blood "for the vision of a new earth." The benediction was triumphant singing, out into the sunlight toward angry jeers that fought the hope that "We shall overcome. . . . deep in my heart, I do believe, we shall overcome some day." We knew—and for the first time I knew that I knew. Classic preaching for World Two occurred not long after, at the Washington monument. "I have a dream!" Images of hope began. "I have a dream!" They poured forth with growing concreteness. "I have a dream!" The crescendo was an energy that left no one doubting. The dream not only will be, but we will *do something to make it so.*

Whereas *World Three* residents are not totally unfriendly toward the liturgical preaching of World Two, they can find it annoying. It tends to be too corporate, too noisy, too confident, too preoccupied with the "big picture." Instead, World Three stands between the previous two Worlds. Their liturgical movement is from insignificance to importance, from invisibility to personal worth. Therefore images such as seeds and leaven characterize their narrative structure. Pilgrimages of nurture toward maturation are the identifying marks of life. Thus preaching must itself evidence a process of organic continuity. One begins with an image, an incident, even a word, hardly anything to be regarded as promising. But from there one builds, until its breadth becomes something of uncommon beauty. "On Wednesday, while I was shopping at the mall, I noticed that my shoe . . ." Inductive building, incorporating, growing.

Samuel was told by God to go and anoint a king. "Where shall I find him?" "In the house of Jesse." So he went. He scrutinized the prospects, all seven of them, one by one. Only one he found appealing. God said, "no." "Do not look on his appearance or on the height of his stature" (1 Samuel 16:7). So, Samuel asks Jesse, "Are these the only ones?" "Yes. Well, no. There's the boy, the one who does best in being with sheep. Bring him." He comes. "Ah," says God, "arise, anoint him; for this is he." World Three never grows tired of such a plot, although the names and faces of insignificance change weekly. The favorite parables are not those with a sudden influx of reversal, nor those of vigorous triumph. The beloved ones pulse with the patterns of simple growth. A favorite has to do with a mustard seed so small that it is easily overlooked, yet "it grew and became a tree, and the birds of the air made nests in its branches" (Luke 13:19). This World has no need for World Four's proclamation of a Savior, of preaching as explicating the nature of the One who does it for us. Instead, Jesus is the one who crosses the frightening river, and from the other side beckons us to give it a try; "If I can, you can too." The characteristic homiletical style is that of the shared story. Biography as autobiography provides a mirror by which one can see one's ownself through eyes honed to detect possibility.

Existentialist philosophers working within World Three discern the human condition through the image of sleepwalking. Lost in conformity, we can exist without living. Awakening comes in a process of mirroring, not as external judgment but as self-portrait. "Oh, no!" marks the point of new beginnings. Once seen, one cannot go home again. With this tentative "therefore," life becomes possible, issuing forth in spirals of beginnings without end.

World Three's preaching style can be clarified through contrast with World Four. The threshold for the latter is marked by guilt, fostering change but first disclosing the roadblocks of our own making. Conversion is a paradox of healing effected by choice, begun by a diagnosis of apparently terminal sickness. The homiletical method of World Three is the opposite. Resisting all guilt tripping, it lures the hearer from in front, while building from behind a foundation of support for feeble steps already taken. Thus praise given to a World Four sermon might be: "You really preached the gospel." Compliments concerning World Three preaching, however, would be variations on two other themes: "The preacher knows me well," or "That sermon gave me something to live by."

In turning directly to *World Four*, we enter a World where classic narrative and preaching seem meant for each other. Yet current narrative homiletics tend to neglect this World, permitting the hostility between liberal and conservative dispositions to determine methodological considerations. For content, the liberal narrative preacher is drawn to the precrucifixion life of Jesus, in general, and the parables, in particular. Residents of World Four, however, focus upon the last three days of Jesus' life, reflecting the disproportionate time that the Gospel writers themselves give to telling that story. Even so, World Four is not satisfied with narrative homiletical method. Such preaching leaves too much to hint, suggestion, and open-ended evocation. The gospel is gospel only when the indicative becomes interrogative as an imperative.

Peter saw an incredible story unfold before him on the Sea of Galilee, but it was for naught until Jesus asked the question: "Do you love me?" And with his confession, the command followed quickly: "Follow me" (John 21:15-19). World Four homiletics is structured by this dynamic. Wesley's life is such a witness. From childhood, he knew the gospel story, focused in the image of a Christ who died for sinners. But it took thirty-five years before one night, in a preaching service at Aldersgate, he finally heard: "Jesus Christ died for *me!*" That is the hearing that makes all the difference. The sermonic goal, then, is not to see, to feel, to be illumined, or to grow. It is to hear, and decide.

This gives World Four preaching an urgency that can be understood best by contrast with World Two homiletics. First, World Two acknowledges the costliness of the corporate battle, but the end, as God's battle, is affirmed without doubt. In World Four, however, it is precisely the end that is most in question. One's eternal future depends on the hearer's decision. Thus the theological dynamic, and consequently the sermonic base line, is not linear continuity. It is radical discontinuity. The river is not mine to cross, for it is uncrossable; yet, it must be crossed. Thus preaching within World Four depends for its power on establishing this torque of the "must" and the "cannot," which births a "therefore." This theological bind becomes the mark of authentic preaching: "Work out your own salvation. . . . for God is at work in you" (Philippians 2:12-13).

One senses this reversal in the hymns imaging the *obsessio* of World Four. They are the religious versions of secular "somebody done somebody wrong" songs. There is simply no way from here to there, unless the One wronged . . . In the fullness of time, in the midst of life's dead ends, this One appears as the paradox of paradoxes. This is what preachers of World Four preach—that the majestic ruler of heaven and earth has left the ninety and nine to embrace the slobbering village idiot—and that idiot is me. Thus in every sermonic witness, there is an indicative and an interrogative. The "I am he!" must have as its sequel: "And who do you say I am?"

Such preaching thrives on its own variation of reversals. It begins with dilemma, of which the prodigal son is classic. We squander our lives away from home. But the redeeming reversal is welded to a God who refuses to wait, and, unlike the parable, sends an only Son to venture into that same far country. The resulting paradox rests in a God who says of God's son, and me: "'For this my son was dead, and is alive again; he was lost, and is found.' And they began to make merry" (Luke 15:24). The purple cloak of crucifixion becomes the best robe restoring the prodigal to sonship. The rest of humankind, one by one, peep around the corner of the barn, asking, "What does this mean?" The choice to come to the homecoming is ours. Thus preaching in this World means, at one place or another, clear and unqualified declaration of the reversal, for the measure of authentic preaching resides in the decision it evokes, again and again.

World Five is akin to World One in its uneasiness about narrative, in the classic sense. In life, and thus in preaching, there is no resolution, no denouement, no decision that reverses everything. Nor is there any forward movement toward a redeeming end. But, unlike World One, neither is there a metaphorical peephole in the cosmic canvas through which to glance a beyond. World Five is draped with "givens," so much so that the only difference preaching can make is in our reception. The theatre of the absurd, which thrives on rehearsing the *obsessio* of World Five, gives clues to the preaching style that embodies World Five.

In Samuel Beckett's *Waiting for Godot,* two characters begin act 1 in a derelict place, waiting. Act 2 begins in the same place, with the same waiting. The litany strewn throughout is a two word refrain: "Let's go." Likewise, the play ends with these words, followed by these stage instructions: "They do not move." [21] Paradox. If life is the meaninglessness of not going, does writing plays about going nowhere make sense? Not going, or going nowhere—what is the difference? The answer comes in what happens through sharing nothing/nowhere. Despite it all, integrity is birthed in enduring it together. In a Beckett play, the audience alternates between humor and pathos. Over coffee, I once asked an oncology nurse why she often laughed. "It's that, or cry." Laughter through tears is the mark of transcending the knowing—of nothing, together.

This is a clue for understanding our homiletic functioning in World Five. It can be distilled in the biblical image of the poor widow with the two copper coins. She gave more, we are told, than the rich of all the other Worlds. They gave out of the abundance of their believed-in resolutions. Of her Jesus says: "She out of her poverty put in all the living that she had" (Luke 21:4). To give all of one's living! This is to face life as it is, unflinchingly, and endure the telling with an enigmatic smile.

One characteristic of the preaching method often used in World Five is a staccato of acclamations, with congregational responses of acknowledgment. The content is not a lamenting of what used to be, or of what is going to be. One responds to what *is*—knowing that it is also what was, and what will be, world without end. So be it. Even the popular press acknowledges the power intrinsic to those able to tell it like it is. *Newsweek,* in appraising support groups for those with various addictions, concludes: "To find oneself in an imperfect situation is human. To learn that you are not alone, divine." [22] Precisely. World Five liturgy is the common acknowledgment of "being in it together," and preaching within that context is the knowing that what really matters is *how one takes it.* Viktor Frankl, drawing from his experience in a concentration camp, understood this well, insisting that although we cannot choose the circumstances of our lives, we can choose our response. The most cherished praise for the World Five preacher is: "She or he knows." And the sermon's resolution resides in being able to say it so that in its hearing, one senses that "God knows."

These descriptions illustrate the nature of variegated homiletics in practice. Just as liturgy is the distillation of a particular World into the dynamic of its informing structure, so authentic preaching is the distillation of a text as image within that World, bringing the whole to self-consciousness. I just returned from an Ash Wednesday service in which this understanding was missing. The result was a bewildering conflict of two Worlds. Most persons present were over sixty-five, except the guest minister. The call to worship was from the standard liturgy, speaking of our walk through the wilderness. The opening hymn heralded a Jesus "who for these forty days did fast and pray." The scripture from Joel was coherent, voicing God's pleading: "Return to me with all your heart, with fasting, with weeping, and with mourning" (Joel 2:12). All was in readiness for the sermon. But I knew it was in trouble, even with the opening line: "Lent should no longer be regarded as a time for giving up things, or even as a period of sadness. It should be a time of joy." With continuity he moved toward the distilling image that would pose as the centerpiece: "Ashes are what you plant seeds in, and by adding water it is where growth occurs." So anchored, he built his World Three sermon toward its conclusion as a suggestion: "Remember that you are to become all that Jesus wants you to become."

Then he came down into the congregation, and resumed the liturgy that was already lost in irony: "Remember that you are dust, and to dust you shall return." We came forward to be marked with ashes, no longer with any clarity as to why. And in dramatic collision with the sermonic imaging, all around me was being acted out a World Five event. One by one we came, slowly—some with walkers, others holding onto friends to be marked with the ashes of death—the walking wounded. The minister sensed painfully that he was in a World not his own. He quickly retreated to the chancel, and tried gallantly one last time. He canceled the final hymn, the one about the lonesome valley, and substituted one he knew from memory. He sang it alone. It was about blooming where you are planted.

Variegated Preaching in the Single Service

This Ash Wednesday incident raises our final issue. How can variegated homiletics be applied when there is only one service, rather that alternative subcongregations? An answer begins by acknowledging that every service occurs within a multi-World congregation. Simple recognition of that fact should itself render traditional preaching obsolete. John Varner identifies the temptation that results. In sensing the pluralism of their congregation, most pastors, disliking controversy, preach what is assumed to be a nonthreatening appeal to the largest number. The result is a moderate message, judged successful if it evokes neither speaking in tongues during the pastoral prayer, nor a voter registration drive afterwards in the vestibule. [23] But the consequence is that social activists begin focusing their vitality at the community center down the street, whereas evangelicals find nurture at a Sunday evening Baptist service. Pentecostals, in turn, are drawn toward a Wednesday evening cottage meeting for noncloseted charismatics, whereas moderates, ironically, share competing loyalties between church and the Rotary Club. Varner's proposal is a sequential model, alternating emphases so that over a month's time the basic theological groups will know that they have been included in the family of Christ. "After surveying the theological 'positions' of your congregation," he challenges, "you may devise your own 'format' of presentations that would speak to each group." But with the Theological Worlds Inventory, one is not left to guess about format.

One way in which this suggestion has been successfully introduced into a single congregation has been by using the natural variegation of the church year for congregational participation in contrasting theological Worlds. During Advent or Lent, alternative liturgy-contexted preaching is correlated with a congregational study of theological Worlds. From such a base, it is not difficult to schedule an alternating sequence. If this is not desirable, at least one can identify (by newsletter, bulletin, or introductory statement) the theological World from which one will be wrestling with the text on any particular Sunday.

There is another possibility. One version of the variegated homiletics that we have been developing is that of preaching as "exploring with." It entails exploring the lectionary text not *for* the congregation but *with* them. Sometimes in doing team-teaching at a seminary, I have wondered if students would not have learned much more through having eavesdropped on our planning sessions, than in taking the fully developed course. Analogously, one of the major homiletical mistakes is to preach one's conclusions, rather than how one got there. In contrast, what we propose is that the preacher's exegetical exploration of the text from alternative perspectives become a paradigm for the sermon itself. This application of variegation insists that the process of arrival is more important than the preacher's own conclusions.

Our treatment of Psalm 23 hinted of such a possibility when one could share with the congregation the process of rummaging the text in search for alternative handles of viability. This is so with the parable of the prodigal son. In one sermon or several, the preacher can plunge the listeners into variegated exegesis by exploring the drama through the alternative eyes of the father, then the owner of the pig yard, the elder brother, the servant, the younger son, or the unseen mother at the upstairs window. With such a method, a spell gets cast. Figures take on more than their own personhood, each populating, for those who would see, an alternative World unto itself.

Such an approach can function in a number of ways. The sermon can be an exercise in perceiving the text from contrasting vantages. Or it can discern and develop from within the text alternative images for interpretation. Or one can expand the context by considering a passage through the contrasting World lenses of Jesus as Logos, New Being, Messiah, the person for others, or the humanity of God.

Viewing texts from contrasting Worlds can also open the imagination to cross-textual relating. Thus if the text focuses on the Lord's Supper, levels of meaning are uncovered for World Four by looking on through the eyes of Matthew's Canaanite woman: "Have mercy on me, O Lord. . . . even the dogs eat the crumbs that fall from their master's table" (Matthew 15:21-28). Or the same text can become ignited for World Five eyes in looking from the vantage of Israel in the desert where God "fed them with the bread of tears, and given them tears to drink in full measure" (Psalm 80:5). Or one can look on with World Three's perennial question: "Can God spread a table in the wilderness?" (Psalm 78:19). For the eschatological orientation of World Two, Revelation speaks well: "Blessed are those who are invited to the marriage supper of the Lamb" (Revelation 19:9). And those of World One, "I have earnestly desired to eat this passover with you before I suffer; for I tell you I shall not eat it until it is fulfilled in the kingdom of God" (Luke 22:16).

However variegated homiletics is used, the need for it rests on three points. First, significant theological diversity is fact. Second, alternative theological Worlds are viable. Third, congregations are unknowingly composed of diverse liturgical needs, on the basis of which many individuals and subgroups remain unfed. Together, these three facts converge as an opportunity whereby the church can renew the powerful meaning of preaching.

CHAPTER TEN

Variegation in Operation: Implications for Administration, Evangelism, and Pastoral Care and Counseling

C lergy are called to the ministry of word, sacrament, and order. Having dealt with word and sacrament, we turn now to the implications of diversity for order. Administration is the skill for manifesting corporate order. Pastoral care focuses upon personal and small group order. Evangelism involves the relation of the two. Something of this meaning is being rediscovered in the church's use of the word "formation," instead of "ordering." These three functions of the church are intricately connected, so much so that Callahan identifies effective church leadership with helping individuals discover their identity through community. "We know *who we are* in relation to the community in which we have found home." [1]

Order as Administration

Order means arrangement. To administer is to hold the people of God supportively accountable to the gospel in the arrangement of their corporate life. This involves a consistency of means and ends in the "development and articulation of a shared vision, motivation of those key people without whom that vision cannot become a reality, and gaining the cooperation of most of the people involved." [2] So understood, church administration, rooted centrally as it is in vision, is directly influenced by the reality of diversity.

The most elaborate model which we have developed thus far for the variegated church, which is centered in alternative liturgical centers, is the most interesting model administratively. In one model, we indicated how subcongregations can be functionally linked through representative administrative groups. These exist for purposes of common envisaging/planning, coordination, management, experimentation, and outreach.

One might expect that a church's decentralization into subcongregations would produce a centrifugal dynamic, frustrating efforts at cooperation. This need not happen, depending on three factors. First is the depth and quality of commitment which key leaders have, to experiment with authentic diversity. The second is the spiritual maturity of these persons, for there is a direct relation between the security with which persons hold to their own theological self-identity, and their willingness to cooperate with other persons and groups. The third factor is more complex, and to this we turn. Professional administrators and lay leaders must gain a concrete understanding of how residents of each of the alternative theological Worlds are inclined to function and interact within various groupings of the church. My research is helpful not only within administrative structures of variegated subcongregations, but is valid in the tasks of administration within any church arrangement.

Residents of World One tend to be nonassertive, inclined to keep, at least at first, a cautious distance from group process. They may convey a sense of not needing others, and thus of not trusting them. Being collegial is something at which they need to work, for it does not come naturally. Each of them finds it easier to pick up a project and run with it, than to have to explain it to others. They are inclined to be intentional and disciplined, but when such tendencies are coupled with the above temptation, they can appear to be manipulative. In turn, they can become immobilized by this tension between their typical solitariness, and a feeling that they should be more interactive. Energy for tasks is often birthed by a determination simply to live in a straightforward fashion with the anxiety that is characteristic of this World. Their particular administrative style makes abundant use of the telephone, and works best in configurations of twos and threes. Characteristically intuitive, they tend to see details as less important than the larger view of things. Often these persons are more insightful than they tend to share, needing encouragement to make their contributions. They perceive well, so that the group can profit from asking them at key points what they sense is going on now, or what the group is about in larger terms. They will need to make accountable efforts at collegial and participative decision making, which does not come naturally and be encouraged to delegate responsibilities for the sake of empowering others. They like to belong, but often do not communicate this. As a result, how they act in a group is often determined and enabled by the ambience of the room and the initial feeling of the meeting. They appreciate being able to participate on their own terms, and at their own speed, without being depended on to do so. This puzzles other types who are often confused by their fine line between neglect, permission, invitation, and coercion.

World One persons function best if the group has an organic sense to it—one in which each person has a natural role and function. Attention to group process is needed so that these persons do not become either resigned or excessively individualistic. They derive particular pleasure from bringing order out of chaos, and in discerning how parts fit together to make sense as a whole.

World Two persons tend to become impatient with process, so that "let's get on with it!" is a predictable litany. They tend to wrongly interpret the silence of World One folks as indifference or blockage. Their urgency to get things done efficiently creates predictable tension with those for whom maintenance of structures is a priority. There is a natural tendency for World Two folks to function in a group as its facilitators, feeling free to suggest tasks, organize the process, and be a barometer of its progress. When there are a number of persons from this World present in the same group, there is often a competitive power dynamic. They prefer task groups to committees, and become restless when they suspect that a group is meeting for the sake of meeting. Their penchant for results can create the temptation to manipulate and they are encouraged by their native assumption that their vision is, or should be, everyone's. Their presence inevitably influences any group interaction, sometimes intimidating others without intending to or even knowing it. They can foster resentment simply by their enthusiasm, seemingly demanding of others the high intensity that seems natural to them.

Their infectious energy and commitment can spark any group, but problems arise if they are unable to hear challenges without resentment, or if devices for balance and broader focus are not in place. Their second litany is likely to be, "Here, let me do it." Thus they need help in not doing it for others. Above all, they need help in recognizing the existence of other Worlds, for in their hurry, they tend to forget this, even when they know it. When they remember, they are more willing to delegate, which permits a sharing that midwifes a more tolerant and broader vision. They particularly need to develop an appreciation of World Three persons, who can provide a creative balance to their own contributions. This is because World Three persons are more attentive to and thrive in a more gentle and inclusive process, with a sensitivity to persons more than causes.

The drivenness of many World Two persons needs accountability structures, lest they be tempted to run roughshod over others, or succumb themselves to burnout and dropout. Groups benefit from their willingness to risk and venture, even if their tendency to try anything may sometimes be embarrassing. Their dreams may become aborted if they are not given practical help in identifying the manageable parts and in predicting unanticipated consequences. Their perpetual unrest is a helpful catalyst for corporate imagination, yet they need modeling from others in learning how to enjoy what the group has already accomplished, and in valuing one's colleagues even in loss. Whereas World One appreciates ambiance, these persons function well enough with simply a table, paper, plenty of sharpened pencils, a chalkboard, and a full box of chalk. They are willing to read almost anything in advance—but need reminding when they report that facts are more than their particular interpretation. Their strength, and their weakness, is the tendency to value ends over means.

World Three residents can make excellent process persons because of their sensitivity to include every person in the group. They function best if there is time before business sessions, and within them, for fellowship and informal interaction. First names feed them. They are sensitive to and are helpful in facilitating icebreaking. Whereas these capacities can make for a good chairperson, their natural dislike of argument and conflict can cause avoidance, sometimes blunting effectiveness. They thrive on being immersed in a group that is working well together, especially in subgroups where quick decisions are not expected. They tend to be more interested in the "how" than the "what," and the quality of discussion can be given more value than the merits of the decision. Since they prefer consensus decision making, other persons may need to provide time parameters to balance the World Three apparent disdain of clocks. They can be overtrusting of relationships, and thus be oblivious to being manipulated. Relatedly, their desire for relationships can tempt them to compromise conviction for unanimity.

Residents of World Three often need encouragement in assertiveness, balancing their valuable sensitivity with a realistic facing of difficult interaction, without either flight or undue hurt. Thus it can be helpful for them to learn conflict resolution skills. These folk are particularly useful when the group is in need of peacemaking, or when a wounded refugee from a harsh meeting needs ministering. Their suspicion of institutions needs to be balanced with an appreciation for how the maintenance of structures is helpful in relieving the weight of administration through face-to-face contact.

In meetings, these persons are helpful process observers and do well in assuming fellowship functions. In leadership roles, however, they may need help in knowing when discussion is wearing out an issue, needing closure through decision. Their tendency to see parts more than wholes makes a helpful complement to persons from World One, who can help them keep the larger perspective. They can help World Two persons find joy in the task, while learning from them, in turn, the inevitableness of power, the need for strategy, and the importance of endings in avoiding excessive diversion.

World Four persons may have a tendency to trust neither themselves nor others. Their ability at forceful declaration, coupled with their tendency to see things in terms of blacks and whites, can encourage an either/or posture if they are in leadership roles, otherwise they may become critical outsiders. Their tendency to draw sharp distinctions can be divisive, and may project an image of being closed and opinionated. Group support and appreciation of them personally can ease what often appears as a need to defend their position. They have a respect for legitimate authority, and may tend to acquiesce to it. This can create a preference for hierarchical structuring, awarding special respect to those who purport to know or are authorized by their knowledge. The group can come to appreciate this penchant for authorities if experts can become regarded more as resources to be consulted than authorities to be obeyed. Reward-punishment techniques are a favored method to accomplish desired actions. These persons in World Four function in a tension between new beginnings, traditional paths, and trying again as marks of being Spirit-led.

How these persons operate in a group may depend on which part of the World Four complex is receiving attention in one's life at the time. Thus there may be a tendency to doubt that persons can find their own way, encouraging the reactive attitude of "if you want it done right, do it yourself." On the other hand, a sense of unworthiness may encourage one to assume the role of servant for the group. They need to be encouraged to delegate, and not "take it back" if the results are not what they had in mind. Although they can profit from being encouraged to trust that others will do their part, their reluctance is helpful in holding others accountable. A relaxed group environment goes far in helping these persons minimize defensiveness, feel less like a minority, and lower the posture of self-righteousness as a cover for unfulfilled self-expectations. In feeling that they are a minority, they may be inclined to witness or develop a caucusing mentality rather than contributing gladly to the group movement. Effectiveness can be enhanced if their tendencies to lament and exhort are balanced by persons inclined to stimulate by invitation and imagination.

World Four persons are particularly helpful in keeping the group faithful to its deeper reasons for being and in stimulating other persons to discover where they stand. In turn, they are helped if faith perspectives within the group can be shared so that they can experience the deep commitment of those in the group with whom they disagree. At times they may need to be gently reminded that the absence of traditional language and content by others need not mean a lack of faith.

A perspective that these persons have for flavoring a group is a cohesiveness born in knowing that all of us, as forgiven sinners, are "in it together." They are helpful in seeing that organization is developed, used, and respected. Their tendency toward pyramidal structure can be helpful for developing flow charts of responsibility and accountability, especially if functional delegation is made on the basis of competence more than doctrinal or moral conformity. Their sensitivity to the past can be an important preservative, and their memory of what has been tried and done before can help a group not begin at square zero with every new problem.

Residents of World Five function best if understood and affirmed as wounded healers. Their gift is their deep sensitivity to people's hurts. This results in realistic expectations, enabling them to overlook the foibles of others while experiencing pleasant surprise when special accomplishments do occur. Yet this tendency to live with the shortcomings of others can bring a hesitancy to hold others accountable. They tend to plod, day in and day out, with a high sense of personal responsibility for carrying through, no matter what. They are loyal, with a tenacity that hesitates to refuse or to walk out on any situation. As one resident put it, "Since I was a child, I cannot remember ever saying 'no' or 'I can't.'" On the other hand, they can become unduly dependent on what others say or expect, or on letting the situation determine things at its own pace. Since promise is basic to World Five, there is a tendency to take people at their word. Thus they can get hurt, exacerbated by their ability to forgive and assume full responsibility—seventy times seven.

They value past, tradition, and continuity, inclined to persist in what *is* rather than to start over again. Problem solving is their particular contribution, capable of infinite patience. They tend to be wise, but not inclined to dream or let one's imagination soar beyond a short string. They use opportunities well, but do not tend to make them happen. Using a chiropractic analogy, they know how to adjust the parts to keep the whole functional. Seeing things realistically, with an orientation toward the long haul, their style is that of steering, rarely inclined to change the direction of flow. Their sense of mission is to be with others in keeping at the task.

As administrators, these persons make for a manager type, with apt skills as guides. Although they are outwardly collegial, wanting everyone to be heard, they have a difficult time trusting that matters will go well. Thus they tend to control by trying things out on their own, and then coming back to everyone with tried suggestions. This preferred style of participating could make them indispensable to the group. They appreciate support and teamwork, but do not really expect it. Consequently, they can get hurt when it is not present, even though they did not ask for it. Although they can be shrewd, they are also inclined to give freely, willing to share what they have or know.

Because they internalize much, they can burn out, grow cynical, or just give up—sometimes all of a sudden. Whereas keeping on is highly valued, it can bring apathy toward genuine change, and the absence of goals can make closure difficult. This reflects their disposition to be totally in or totally out. Yet having been tempered by life, they often have a calming effect on groups. They are team players who are at their best when other members bring sufficient imagination to keep the product creative and dynamic. Often they are in jobs or situations in which obeying orders is the expected behavior, so that when they are in a context where they are invited to share their opinion, they have a difficult time believing it, or may not even be in touch with their own opinions.

Having described the strengths and weaknesses characterizing the administrative tendencies of residents in each World, we turn now to exploring how this information can be used to help variegated groups function creatively. The most significant factor is for the group to recognize that it is composed of plural Worlds. This admission helps give permission for members to own freely, honestly, and publicly their latent disagreements and unexpressed feelings. On the other hand, it fosters curiosity and interest in understanding better the unique dynamics working within their group. Simply getting this far is a pleasant contrast with most church groups. So many groups operate under an unacknowledged shroud of dishonesty about feelings, encouraged by the operating assumption that there is some monolithic theology or accepted point of view that is expected of all. Thus each person tends to feel on the outside, with the appearance of loving cooperation apparently being the only acceptable operating norm. As a result, the dynamics of church groups tend to become unusually strange, for with basic differences sublimated and thus denied, the differences inevitably appear in ways that are intrusive, and often hurtful.

The uniqueness of a self-consciously variegated congregation, then, is the refreshing axiom that *difference, disagreement, tension, and struggle are normal ingredients of the administrative process, and thus to be expected and anticipated.* This understanding marks a significant step toward restoring a biblical ecclesiology. As Bonhoeffer insisted, the New Testament questions the integrity of any church based on compatibility, uniformity, unanimity, consensus, and congeniality.[3] Regardless of what the expected appearance of modern congregations may be, the church of scripture is no fraternity or social club with rules that guarantee like-minded folk. The family is an apt analogy for the church. Members are stuck with each other, for better or worse. This is a "given." The constituency of the biblical church is a matter of divine calling, not personal selection. And as it often turns out, the most appropriate church is the most inappropriate if chosen by comfortable self-interest. Thus the variegated church rests on the belief that the will of God is more likely to be discerned in a vital mix of committed persons, than among those whose filtered sameness tends to be a defense mechanism more than a call.

The next issue to be explored is how these plural factors can be rendered creative and constructive, as over against the present tendency to avoid, sublimate, defer, and bury as the price of diversity.

Our research has identified five ways in which variegation can be helped to function well.

1. Self and Group Knowledge. The tendencies of each World for contributing and blocking the administrative process, as we have described them, need to be identified and explored together in the group, and periodically rehearsed. Since these descriptions are typological generalizations rather than judgments being made on individual performances, much group consciousness can occur within the parameters of good humor rather than a personal sense of accusation and correcting.

2. Group Composite. Each group can well be served by exploring its own particular composition, as to types and configuration. Once done, it is possible to imagine concretely what best case scenario might be encouraged, and what worst case scenario should be avoided.

3. Intentional Correctives. Depending upon a group's composition, agreed-upon checks and balances can be put in place. This accountability can range the gamut. On one end can be structural devices, such as rotating leadership, cochairs, or time limits on discussion. On the other can be individual arrangements, such as friendly nonverbal code reminders to encourage positive traits or to discourage negative tendencies at their inception.

4. Process Facilitation. At least at the beginning, a process observer can be helpful, appointed with the right to intervene when useful, to be available to illumine situations when the group becomes bogged down, and to provide feedback at the conclusion of the meeting.

5. Selective Participation. Consensus on important issues is unlikely. And since disagreement can be divisive, it may be helpful for a person with a controversial point of view to indicate that she or he is becoming a task group of one, to which she or he is inviting other interested persons in the group to join if they agree. This avoids a win/lose conflict within the whole group, as on such issues as abortion rights. Those who disagree are not expected to either participate or to oppose the rights of others to act independently. Rather, they can be encouraged to form an alternative task force (e.g., right to life). This important principle for a variegated church involves cooperation when there is agreement, and permission when conflicted.

Such techniques as these help unlock the group process by anticipating needless blockage, and by freeing representatives to contribute what each World has uniquely to provide. Theological Worlds, as necessary portions of the Body of Christ, can together weave the fabric of creative church administration. The gift of each can be summarized:

World 1: WHOLENESS—organic sense of the relation of whole and parts
World 2: VISION—drive toward what is worth accomplishing
World 3: PROCESS—dynamic toward sensitive inclusiveness
World 4: INHERITANCE—commitment to faithfulness
World 5: CONTINUITY—determination to persevere together

Order as Evangelism

The church today is obsessed with the image of growth. Stimulated by a decline in membership, this crisis mentality encourages quantity as a questionable measure of quality. Historically, effective evangelism ("to bring good news") has been a spontaneous result of those who share that they have found the pearl of great price. Conservatives, of whichever theological World, consider such sharing to be an indispensable mark of discipleship. They regard such sharing as a privilege more than a duty. But a danger endemic to such enthusiasm can be that persons are not given choices. Such an evangelist is often experienced as a determined agent for an exclusive franchise, forcing a single model, with minimal regard for the sanctity and specialness of each customer.

Liberals, on the other hand, are taking the critical brunt of the present membership decline. They are accused of indifference, if not outright hostility, to evangelism. The truth behind this accusation is the liberal's embarrassment over the conservative image of evangelism. Consequently they feel more secure attracting potential members by factors more sociological than theological. The present church growth movement is an uneasy compromise between these two tendencies. In the training sessions that abound, energetic techniques for outreach are taught. The strategy and skills taught are often drawn from secular approaches, attempting to supplement society's shortcomings by meeting personal needs. These can range from counseling, to physical fitness, to growth groups. Liberals understand this approach well, for in spite of charges, attendance has always been a primary concern, with programming being their method of choice for attracting new members.

Yet these techniques are flowing back upon both conservative and liberal efforts, disclosing some shortcomings of outreach evangelism. In contrast, authentic evangelism centers in a different question: *what is to be done with persons who do get drawn into coming to church?* The conservative endless circle is that people are recruited to recruit others to recruit others for the sake of recruiting. But the liberal perspective bogs down in its own endless circle. Persons are assimilated by giving them something to do within the organization. This way growth spawns growth, as the increased size of the church requires an increase in volunteers to help the preacher run the church, which in turn requires additional space which means recruiting volunteers for a capital campaign.

The goals of these circles vary, whether enlisting personal evangelists, stimulating reasonable attendance patterns, or recruiting effective organizational leadership. But the danger is the same for both— that of confusing means with ends, whereby evangelism as "good news" gets lost in "outreach."

Consequently, the real crisis in evangelism rests in the dilemma with which our study began. On the one hand, we identified the liberal propensity as being an openness and tolerance which holds options within a web of relativity, encouraging interest but with little theological commitment. On the other, the conservative mentality, while demanding vigorous commitment, tends to be parochial in regard to content, and hostile toward alternatives, entailing a contraction of imagination. It has been our position throughout that what is needed are variegated churches as communities both of passion and of gracious understanding composed of persons who take seriously the evangelical responsibility. This is two-fold. *Outreach,* as a point of contact, is hollow unless there is *inreach,* which is spiritual growth through theological belonging, with intentional accountability.

The true measure of authentic evangelism is what persons find once they attend. And the quality of that experience, in turn, depends on the three dimensions which constitute the ministry of order—*identity, support, and accountability.* That is, attendance is of little consequence if the church is not intent upon helping persons discover who they are, supporting them communally in that theological pilgrimage, and holding them accountable for a creative living of their World in the world. This means that evangelism and church renewal must be recognized as two sides of the same coin, with neither preceding the other.

The point of contact for evangelism is the inevitable search of persons for meaning. In a society increasingly individualistic, however, this focus tends to be experienced as the yearning to belong. Whereas this may be what initially draws people to the church, the need itself is deeper. *It is a desire to be part of that which counts*—the base hunger to know one's self as rooted in an ache for that which would constitute home. Or, as we have alluded, the yearning is for a World in which to be and to belong are one and the same. This necessitates persons who, in finding their World, can identify as important that which is gnawing at a searcher's outer defenses. Or expressed more enigmatically, the need is for that quality of support whereby one can risk losing what needs to be given away in order to become who one is—but is not yet.

As response, the variegated church can provide what has not been available before. Liberal creativity in providing entrance activities can interact with conservative seriousness about faith style. The result is a dual witness. In being able to identify concrete *obsessios* as contrasting points of contact, evangelism gains concreteness. And the church, in turn, is able to refashion church life concretely around alternative contexts for *epiphanias*.

Pastors will need to be evangelized as well. Ministers of the future must be able to affirm the viability of World Four, insisting upon the power residing within that World to absolve guilt. They will know that persons, after years of filth, can walk as forgiven creatures into the light of a future that did not exist for them before. In a variegated church, one will see it, can testify to it, and will teach it with passion to those for whom the parameters of their *obsessios* hint of the common contours within World Four. And on the way home, this same pastor can visit a hospital patient, finding himself a guest in World One. There, through deep listening, he hears a yearning for the unknown that forever eludes. And the pastor prays knowingly with the patient and for her, where the edge of fright touches gently the promise of mystery. And later, as the pastor waits at an extra long stoplight, he muses that these sacred moments, as the meeting of wayfarers under promise, must be what his early morning reading of Marcel called the "nostalgia for being." Finally arriving at the parsonage as a World Three home, later than he or she had expected, that same pastor is fed by cuddling the frightened tears of a recently adopted child. Whatever the techniques used, evangelism of the future must rest on the ability and willingness to offer the experience of alternative Worlds to those in need, whatever one's own sustaining World may be. Seeking viable commitment to *any* must be seen as faithfulness to the *One,* who through *each* transcends them *all.*

Lindbeck is helpful in supporting the approach to evangelism that we are proposing. Motivations for being attracted to the church range from ignoble to noble, being "as diverse as the individuals involved." This is why a prolonged period of *catechesis* or socialization is necessary, "in which they practice[d] new modes of behavior and learn[ed] the stories of Israel and their fulfillment in Christ." It is this intimate and imaginatively vivid familiarity with a Christian World that "made it possible to experience the whole of life in religious terms." [4] In the face of today's secular pluralism, however, Lindbeck is not optimistic about the prospects for evangelism. But by affirming the viable options of a Christianity that is itself pluralistic, we can affirm with promise his insight. By structuring a viable pluralism, encouragement is given to pilgrimage, imaginations are whetted, persons are given permission to act out dreams, and communal rehearsing brings forth that accountability in which commitment is lured over unsuspected depths.

Order as Pastoral Care and Counseling

Ordination to Word, Sacrament, and Order, means responsibility for the Word proclaimed, sacramentalized, and ordered. Thus these functions interpenetrate. Just as in faithfulness to the Word, we say the pastor *administers* the sacraments, so for the same reason we can speak of the pastor as sacramentally administering the church's organizational life. Expressed in a related way, worship provides the formal context for centering consciousness theologically, whereas administration is the form of that consciousness lived out as structured process. Such intersecting identifies the central task for the postliberal church: to "socialize their members into coherent and comprehensive religious outlooks and forms of life." [5] Thus one's theological World relates to the *what,* as administration stands to the *how.*

The church's ordering, then, should itself be a model for the Christian's own daily living. It helps Christians learn to order the diversity of impinging commitments so that they do not tyrannize each other and themselves. "To order" means bringing one's external environment—job, family, friendships, community, systems, nation, earth—into coherence with one's interior life, through that common magnetic field which we call one's theological World. Thus the call to order and the call to worship must be cut from a common cloth, having both corporate and personal sides. We have explored church administration as the corporate focus. We turn now to the more personal focus, traditionally called pastoral care and counseling.

Pastoral care and counseling have the same intent, differing in the size and circumstances functioning as the ordering context. Both entail three tasks: (1) To discern the form(s) by which a person is actually being ordered. (2) To provide contexts of socialization by which the ideal form of one's theological World can render that meaning self-conscious, consistent, and deep—or identify it as a dead end. (3) To appraise whether such maturation can be done through the church's existing vehicles of communal formation, or whether a more specialized formation is needed.

Seminaries wisely place pastoral care and counseling together professionally and curricularly. Yet the theological meaning behind this linking often goes unrecognized, and thus unexplored. As a result, the pastor is usually trained as a counselor through developing listening skills, intent upon providing a positive and nonjudgmental environment. Ideally, such support will be sufficient for the distressed parishioner to express feelings, and thereby be helped to discern the contours of the problem requiring resolution—and in so doing, be strengthened to make the appropriate decision. If this process does not seem possible, or does not occur, referral is made to a trained professional who can therapeutically probe the hidden causes inhibiting resolution. Often in seminaries, the warning about the need for referrals can outweigh and intimidate any training as to what the pastor *can* and *should do*. The price for thus imaging the pastor as amateur counselor is often at the price of neglecting that to which pastors are uniquely called to do.

The etymology of titles used for identifying clergy is illuminating. "Pastor" indicates one who feeds by "shepherding." "Minister" is one who provides "service." "Priest" is a contraction for "presbyter," meaning "older person," presumably wise. "Counselor" means one who deliberates, advises, instructs, and exhorts. By letting these various titles feed one another, this rich definition emerges: *the pastor is a shepherd of souls, who through the wisdom of those who have gone before, provides supportive and challenging care for persons as corporate and individual pilgrims.*

Yet it is such a role definition that again exposes the deep conflict between liberals and conservatives—converging in the issue of counseling. For the liberal, counseling is regarded as a value-free enterprise, thus being the vehicle for claiming freedom from the conservative emphasis on belief as the touchstone of wholeness. Conservative suspicions, on the other hand, are coming to see and insist that value-free counseling is an illusion. None of the multiple psychological techniques now available are really neutral tools. Each rests on implicit presuppositions about human nature and condition, personal capacities and motives, individual and social dysfunctioning, and the resources available for healing. In turn, these presuppositions are precisely those that the church has regarded as theological, with its own answers for the cure of souls.

Carl Rogers's client-centered therapy, more often known as nondirective counseling, has been the primary tool by which a supposedly value-free method has entered the liberal clergy's chambers. One must readily acknowledge its usefulness, *as long as one recognizes that its defining context is primarily that of World Three.* Although it can be of some use elsewhere, it is questionable whether it can provide what is basically needed by residents of other Worlds. It was with sensitivity to an alternative World (World Four) that Carl Menninger asked liberal pastors, "Whatever became of sin?"

I recall vividly the morning a person came to me, deeply distressed, despite having received professional counseling. His conversation, hinting early of World Four, increasingly made it clear that the formative context he needed was one that was quite opposite the guilt-free method provided by his counselor. The reason why healing had eluded him was that peace *for him* could only be on the far side of confession, pouring forth his past, with all its sordid details. Only then, when he was finally emptied out, was he prepared to hear the words of absolution: "May Almighty God give you peace and pardon, and I absolve you from your sins, in the name of the Father, the Son, and the Holy Spirit." It was only then that he could pick up his bed and walk. By providing a World Four context for this person, Bonhoeffer's distinction became real for him: "In the presence of a psychiatrist I can only be a sick man; in the presence of a Christian brother I can dare to be a sinner."[6] Recently a fine psychotherapist shared this conclusion with me: "At least half of the people who see me need a priest, not a therapist." Certainly a pastor is useful as a supportive presence for problem solving, or a resource for referring deeply distressed persons. But that is not the pastor's unique and irreplaceable calling. The pastor is called to the ordering of human souls—that is, to the ministry of *spiritual direction*. It is time for the church to take seriously Jung's declaration that most of his client's problems were "spiritual." It is time to understand the implications of the American Medical Association's statement that over 60 percent of the ills which doctors are called upon to treat are psychosomatic— that is, "spiritual."

Nouwen's approach to spirituality provides a point of contact for the transition that needs to happen here. The model of nondirective counseling dare not be made normative for the ministry of spiritual direction. What the pastor is called upon to provide is a space where people are encouraged to disarm themselves, to lay aside their occupations and preoccupations, and to listen with attention and care to the voices speaking from their own center. The ground of such voices is what is meant by the Spirit. The recent interest in spirituality reflects a growing rediscovery of the Christian tradition—that the Spirit dwells within, by which one is led and empowered (1 Corinthians 3:16). So understood, redemption can come to mean experiencing one's inferiority as "a friendly empty space."[7] It is from this intimate center that one's pilgrimage flows forth, and through which one's autobiography becomes domesticated as a theological World. In Carretto's words, "By spirituality we mean the way of thinking, living, and sanctifying the acts of our lives."[8]

To assume this overall task of being a spiritual director, the pastor needs to face the inconsistency hidden by the present-day tendencies to compartmentalize different pastoral functions. As a result, one's identity can be scattered, for each role tends to exist in a different theological World. It is not uncommon for a pastor to preach grace, proclaiming that without undeserved forgiveness our works are in vain. Yet this same pastor, functioning on a social justice task force, can organize around the conviction that nothing will change without a balance of power forcing concessions. And then, during an evening counseling session, that pastor may listen supportively as a parishioner works out his or her own salvation from resources native to being human. The issue here, and it is a deep one, is that of pastoral coherence. We are speaking not of the necessity of being able to enter pastorally into different Worlds, as defined by different persons, functioning in different contexts. This is important to do. The issue here, rather, has to do with the pastor's own theological World, for today's minister is often unknowingly a theological chameleon.

Yet it is precisely here that the liberal pastor begins to feel an old anxiety. When pushed toward theological coherence, will this not lead to theological domination by the pastor? It was precisely this fear, that counselees were having the theology and ethics of conservative pastors foisted upon them, that led liberal pastors to seek and insist upon value-free counseling in the first place. But we are coming to see that there is no such thing as value-free, as over against value-laden, counseling. The issue can be put concretely. A pastor operating from a World Three grounding is fearful for a pregnant teenager who is asking help from a pro-life World Four pastor—and vice versa. The issue is not value-free, but a conflict of values—of counseling done from the perspective of rival Worlds. But if in the strict sense there is no such thing as nondirective counseling, how is the pastor to counsel without imposing his or her own values?

Actually, this question goes even deeper. The question for the conservative is that unless one risks becoming doctrinaire, how is the pastor able to regain the central thrust of the gospel? Christianity is about healing—deep, transforming healing. Yet liberal pastors carefully restrict their work to "counseling," insisting on "therapy" as the work of secular professionals. But how are we to deal with the fact that the very viability of the gospel rests on its power to transform human life? Paul is firm in insisting that new life begins with a confession of sins. And his list of possible transgressions would empty out the closet skeletons of most psychotherapists. Whichever World the Christian looks out from, tradition insists on one point of agreement—that there is a universal human dilemma, with alternative expressions, which the lone individual is helpless to rectify. And from whatever alternative *epiphania* the Christian understands the process of healing, tradition insists that the gospel of Jesus Christ has the power to transform each person into the fullness of life. Weekly, Anglicans confess that "there is no health in us." Calvin's presence is still visible in Presbyterian preaching with its concern for a "diseased will." And down the street the Roman Catholic priest begins every Mass with the *Kyrie eleison*, and with the sign of the cross offers newness of life: "May Almighty God have mercy on us, forgive us our sins, and bring us to everlasting life."

It is incredible what power for transformation liberal pastors award the therapist, while being deeply confused themselves about what the pastor's unique role in healing can or should be. However it is affirmed, and however it is imaged, *Christianity is about the curing of souls*. The word "salvation" makes this indisputable, for it means "to render healthy and whole." Therefore Christian counseling should never again pose as being value-free, for it is not—and never should be. The pastor is called to the ministry of order, of which a central piece is formation and re-formation. Alan Jones calls this the task of "soul-making." This process begins in earnest when one's strategies in self-deception are forced to be abandoned, for sanctification, as "growth toward wholeness," requires the ongoing confession that we are damaged goods.[9] But the nature and cause of that damage, as well as its proper healing process, differs according to one's World. Thus its symptoms range the gamut of Worlds—as blindness, indifference, exclusion, arrogance, or cynicism.

But the question still remains. How can pastoring move beyond liberal theological tolerance without adopting a posture of judging? The answer is by restoring the church's long tradition of spiritual direction, now refurbished through an awareness of theological Worlds. The result is a new understanding of pastoral care and counseling. The archetype for spiritual direction appears early in Hebrew scripture. God walked with Adam and Eve in the cool of the evening. The Fall was the choice of self-direction, exemplified by running to hide from God and thus themselves, missing their spiritual direction appointment. The classic Hebraic spiritual directors were the prophets, functioning in this role not only for Israel in general, but for the kings in particular. Nathan's famed spiritual direction encounter with David discloses a central method—a parable as mirror. The plot of Nathan's story was simple enough, having to do with a person's hypocritical self-contradiction in regard to a lamb. David's response was quick: "The man who has done this deserves to die." Nathan's answer was just as clear: "You are the man" (2 Samuel 12:7).

A New Testament archetype for spiritual direction is the walk to Emmaus by two disciples, when Jesus, unrecognized, became a third party to the conversation. The bottom of their life had dropped out. And as they try to make sense out of it all, Jesus listens carefully, asks questions, risks rebuke, and provides a context. With their hearts burning from within, their eyes are opened. The Gospels portray Jesus as offering pastoral care for the many, but he chose a special handful with whom to do spiritual direction. "Then he left the crowds and went into the house. And his disciples came to him, saying, 'Explain to us the parable. . . .'" When he was finished, Jesus asked: "'Have you understood all this?' They said to him, 'Yes'" (Matthew 13:36, 51).

For the churches he organized, Paul provided spiritual direction by visit and by letter. In the third century, as Christianity became the official religion of the empire, and belief became a socially advantageous matter, many who were serious about faithfulness went to the deserts, where the demons lived, to fight them without—and within. As the holiness of these hermits became legendary, people came to their caves or huts, asking: "Abba (or Amma), a word for my soul." Some stayed, built huts nearby, and periodically made the same request. Such direction from an abba led to the role of Abbot, with the huts forming a monastic community. These "monks," in turn, served as spiritual directors for others, including popes and kings. In time, monastic orders created schools as places for "schola," meaning "leisure." Schools were where people were given the leisure to reflect on the meaning of life under the oversight of a wise director as guide. British universities today retain something of this idea in pairing each student with a tutor ("one who guides") who provides support and accountability in using the university's resources to particularize one's growth.

In Roman Catholic circles, something of this function has been preserved in the role of priest as confessor, providing limited affirmation and direction for one's parishioners. With Vatican II, this function was expanded, recapturing the fuller possibilities developed throughout the church's tradition. Confession is now called the "Rite of Reconciliation," where face-to-face sharing gives rise to a more holistic guidance. Priests-in-training are required to have a spiritual director of their own choosing, and are encouraged to have one throughout their ministry. Baptismal godparents and confirmation sponsors continue this basic idea.

The Protestant elimination of private confession, because of its misuse for financial gain, was understandable, but unfortunate. Ironically, Luther's intent was not to eliminate this practice but to universalize it with the "priesthood of all believers." We are to be spiritual companions to each other, in which, said Luther, "every Christian . . . can declare in God's name that 'God forgives you of your sin,' and you may be faithfully certain that your sin has as surely been absolved as if God . . . spoke to you." [10]

This universalizing of spiritual direction became a central contribution of the ministry of John Wesley. In establishing "societies," "classes," and "bands," he attempted to create spiritual renewal within the Anglican Church, primarily by providing lay spiritual direction. In this, he drew inspiration from "societies" already functioning in the Church of England, as well as "bands" organized among the Moravians by Zinzendorf. The idea was to provide a conference ("to confer") for each Christian. To be a Christian one needed to be in direction. Wesley's spiritual direction groups were characterized by *form* more than *content*, intent on providing the context by which the "means of grace" could order one's life through support and accountability. The focus was less on correctness of doctrine, and more on the quality of Christian life. Thus new members were not required to be fully converted, but to desire the "form of godliness." The church's administrative task followed closely—to provide such contexts for growth.

For this, societies were divided into classes of twelve persons each for weekly mutual accountability. Each group had a lay spiritual director, and these directors, in turn, met regularly with Wesley as their spiritual director. The pastoral care process used was one of listening and guiding, under supervision. The intent of such face-to-face contact was for members to "bear one another's burdens," to "care for each other," to feel free to be open with one another, and thus able to "speak the truth in love." [11] Although these groups were formed geographically, in time "bands" were created for more intense sharing and accountability, organized by age, gender, and marital status. David Watson claims that these class leaders were "as skilled a group of spiritual mentors as the church has ever produced," combining "spiritual discernment with the practical disciplines necessary for accountable discipleship in the world." [12]

In present-day Protestantism, however, little remains of this central function of spiritual direction—except the name "pastor," meaning spiritual shepherd of the flock. Roman Catholicism has done better. With Vatican II declaring the wisdom of direction for every Catholic, the upheaval that followed had to do with how this was to be done, and thus what it might mean. Previously, the stress had been on the director, the person who had the authority to form another's beliefs and morals, much as an apprentice relates to a master craftsman. But as a more collegial spirit emerged, an uneasiness about this former approach extended even to finding more appropriate names. "Soul friend" or "spiritual companion" are often preferred. [13] As a consequence, spiritual direction is losing both the implication of instruction, and the aura of authority. Instead, the interpersonal process is one of mutual discerning of the Spirit's luring, identifying the plot-in-the-making which constitutes one's life as pilgrimage.

This means knowing that the real director is the Holy Spirit. "I will bless the Lord who gives me counsel, who even at night directs my heart" (Psalm 15:7 Singing Version). Thus the director's relationship is not that of being *for* or *to*, but *with*. Central is discernment as a creative listening for the Spirit, in which the director is an invited guest into a unique World that may not be his or her own.

A consensus is emerging regarding this new understanding of spiritual direction. This may be seen best by sorting through representative definitions by key persons in the field. [14] Spiritual direction is:

—facilitating another's fulfillment of spiritual needs, through a search for meaning and love in relationship with the self, others, God, and nature. (James M. Raddle, S.J.)

—providing a companion in the life of spirit, who counsels, supports, discerns, and encounters, in one's intellectual, emotional, social, cultural, and spiritual contexts. (St. Meinrad's Program)

—exploring everyday ordinariness for the presence of God and the workings of grace, by finding a friend in a theological context. (Eugene Peterson)

—receiving help in exploring every path, where the errors lurk, where the moods have their hiding places, how the passions understand themselves in solitude; knowing where the illusions spread their temptations, where the bypaths slink away. (Kierkegaard)

—relating to a mature Christian to whom we choose to be accountable for our spiritual life, and from whom we can expect prayerful guidance in our constant struggle to discern God's active

presence in our lives. The ingredients are our fears and anxi-
eties, guilts and shame, sexual fantasies, greed and anger, our
joys, successes, aspirations and hopes, our reflections, dreams
and mental wanderings, and most of all our people, family,
friends, and enemies—all that make us who we are. (Henri
Nouwen)

—responding to God's initiative through dialogue, discerning
where one has been, what one is looking for, cares about, feels
strongly for, and wants to go. It means helping a person face the
demons, and thread a path through one's illusions. (William
Connolly)

—growing in awareness as to how death and resurrection function
in one's life, thereby deepening one's self-identity. (Eugene
Merz)

—relating to one who can help the individual unmask self-decep-
tions in order to be totally receptive to God's instructions.
(Damien Isabell)

Within this growing consensus regarding direction, a similarity is
appearing as to how a *director* is to be understood:

—a companion, while the Directee is pilgrim, with an emphasis on
now. The one is a sacrament for the other, evoking rather than
compelling, as they walk in the Spirit together. (James
McCready)

—one who helps in the quest from inferiority to personal authenticity, maintaining a growth orientation. (Sandra Schneider)

—one who can penetrate beneath the surface of a person's life, to
get behind the facade of conventional gestures and attitudes
which he or she presents to the world, and to bring out his or
her inner spiritual freedom, inmost truth, which is what we call
the "likeness of Christ in one's soul." (Thomas Merton)

—a gifted presence to help a gifted self emerge, as a self in faith.
(Jean Laplace)

—one who deliberately attempts to accompany others on their
journeys into God, sharing what one has learned in making
one's own journey. (Morton Kelsey)

—the Christian who watches in amazement the marvels of God as
they unfold in the heart. (St. John of the Cross)

—a person who mediates the divine action. (St. Ignatius)
—the one who speaks healing words at the proper season. (Cicero)

Although we can clearly hear the analogy of different Worlds operating as a basis for such definitions, there is still something of a consensus emerging. *Direction is a mutual detection of the operative meanings informing a person's life, discerning these into the self-consciousness of a wholistic World, holding the person's behavior accountable as a resident, and reflecting back alternatives by which one's shadows appear in bas-relief.* Gervais Dumeige rightfully insists that God never leads two souls along the same path. And even if the paths were the same, the rhythm of the gait would be different. Thus a spiritual director is one who so knows your song that she or he can sing it back when you forget the words.

To become a spiritual director, which is what the pastor is called to be, necessitates training in the art of "midwifing." The needed ingredients to be learned are creative listening, deep caring, open vunerability, intimacy as "being with," openness to alternatives, ability to confront, being theologically informed, being capable of discerning what is behind the apparent, and freedom to encourage others to do things their way. For these, the pastor must have a sufficient sense of self-acceptance; security from easy intimidation by anger, silence, or rejection; detachment from excessive ego needs; be at home with and excited about one's own theological World; understand oneself as a Christian on a pilgrimage; be a person of God; and have one's own spiritual director.

Any analogy of the director as engineer, as though working from a uniform blueprint of the Christian life, is to be strongly avoided. Plurality must infect creatively one's entire calling. A better analogy for the director's role might be that of an artist—one who in refusing to manipulate the material, skillfully lets it unfold itself into a creation of beauty. Yet in this process the artist is not passive. It requires a practiced sensitivity to discern form in the apparently formless, plot in the seemingly directionless, and intentionality in the obsessively restless. Such discernment is not for the sake of telling, but as a guide in sensing how best to provide verbal and nonverbal contexts of support, disclosure, and accountability.

Two personal stories may be helpful. The first is my original coming within hailing distance of spiritual direction. A colleague asked me for an appointment. I assumed by the request that my role would be that of counselor. In counseling, I find that the first shoe usually drops rather quickly, with the second held tightly until near the end of the session. An affair? Cancer? He talked freely without needing to be encouraged, and continued to do so for a long while. Then he stopped. Not even the first shoe had fallen. "I could say more," he said, "but that's enough. What do you hear me saying?" There were certainly no hints of deep hurt, suggesting a therapeutic situation. There was no pronounced problem suggesting that he needed me as a counselor. So what was this? What he was asking was for me to walk with him down his path, sharing what I saw, and thus helping him discern where his steps seemed to be leading. I still remember his words that provided the clue. "You know, you only go around once; what a shame for me to get to the end and find out that I had lost my trail." This was my first intentional invitation to be a spiritual director.

The second story involves me as an unknowing directee. I was a heavy smoker for years. So was my friend. My self-deceptive games masked my inability to stop. So did hers. "I'll stop if you do!" That was a safe wager—I knew she could not stop. "OK, you're on!" Had I been on my own during the bad weeks that followed, I know I would have been ingenious in game-playing, beginning with, "Just one won't matter." But I could not. *I had promised.* I would have been able to deceive myself, but it would be wrong to betray her. Besides, we called daily to report in. I could not lie. I quit. Not one cigarette for over ten years. She moved away. One day she was passing through town and called. "How about a cup of coffee?" "Sure!" We met. "Nice place." She pulled out a pack of cigarettes, "my" brand! Never have I had such a surge of anger, nicotine seizure, and impotence, all at once. I excused myself, and could not return. What I regarded as overcome, what I thought had been rendered a past event by my own willpower, was instead rooted for its strength in promise—giving me accountability. Runners, musicians, Christians—these are the ones who know the impossibility of ordering one's vocation without disciplined accountability. "Going on to perfection" was the goal of Wesley's spiritual direction; to "run the good race" was Paul's way of putting it. One cannot be a Christian alone. Without the support and accountability of at least one other human being, no one can be trusted to become an authentic self, for it means going down the road less traveled.

How, then, does spiritual direction differ from psychotherapy and counseling? A chart of key characteristics may be helpful.

THE UNIQUENESS OF SPIRITUAL DIRECTION

	Psychotherapy	Counseling	Spiritual Direction
Issue:	Pain	Problem	Need
Model:	Medical— diagnostician (wounded)	Pedagogue— clarifier (confused)	Guide— companion (incomplete)
Process:	To restore (emotional connections)	To solve (conflicting (options)	To discern (the Spirit's leadings)
Termination:	Freedom (to cope)	Resolution (viable decision)	Never (ongoing pilgrim)
Types:	➤ psychoanalytic ➤ behaviorist ➤ humanistic ➤ transpersonal	➤ "nondirective" ➤ "directive"	➤ Informal (friendship) ➤ Communal (affirming) ➤ Group (intentional) ➤ One-with--one (contract)

—*Psychotherapy* is required when emotional pain, for reasons deep and hidden, pushes daily coping beyond one's tolerable strength. By establishing the emotional connections between past and present, sufficient freedom is gained for life to be livable.

—*Counseling* focuses on a problem for which support is needed in order to recognize and explore options, and to make a viable decision.

—*Spiritual direction* arises from the fact of one's humaness. To be is to be on a pilgrimage, impulsed by the question of "why?"

Through help in testing the anxiety marking one's tension between "is" and "ought," "was" and "might be," one attempts to discern the direction of divine nudgings.

Whereas psychotherapy is greatly dependent upon the diagnostic skills of the therapist, the counselor's contribution is in providing positive space for the counselee to mobilize his or her own powers for clarity and decision. But in spiritual direction, the real director is the Holy Spirit, whether understood as ground, lure, presence, companion, or impulse. The question is not what can be done for the person, or what they can do, but what is God about with them. Such a process never ends, for it begins months before one is born, and continues, it would seem, after death. The educational model we developed has, as its last step, disciplined accountability, leading directly to spiritual direction. And our different models for the variegated church call for both group accountability and one-with-one mutual direction for each member.[15]

Whether the context for spiritual direction is paired or group, there are a number of methods possible.

1. *Existential.* Here the point of contact is the here and now, exploring intentionally the state of one's soul. It often begins by taking seriously the greeting, "How are you?" Journaling uses the same method of self-dialogue. Selected sharing from one's journal with a director or group can be helpful—even to the point of drawing a vertical line on one's journal pages, leaving the right side for one's director, if asked. Recorded dreams provide additional clues and leadings.

2. *Autobiography.* An important spiritual exercise is to write one's theological autobiography, attempting, with the perceptions of a director, to discern the connections and patterns giving direction to one's life.

3. *Scripture.* Direction can center in daily scripture reading, consecutively or by lectionary, with an anticipation of being addressed by the Spirit through the Word. The results are shared for mutual discernment.

4. *Prayer.* Often persons ask for direction to help with their prayer life. Growth occurs through sharing one's experiences in prayer, meditation, guided imagery, and/or contemplation. Interestingly, Origen, Gregory, and Clement all used the word

homilia for prayer. Its five meanings correlate well with the theological Worlds: to be as one, to battle, to converse, to become friends, to keep company with.

5. *Apostolate.* A helpful practice in direction is the *"examen* of consciousness." At the beginning of each day, one prepares with the Spirit to meet each scheduled event—with optimum openness and creative compassion. In the evening, one reviews the day—thankfully, confessionally, and with resolution. By sharing the results, one is helped to perceive patterns, opportunities, and repetitions, both critically and supportively.

6. *Christology.* Thomas à Kempis's *Imitation of Christ* is classic in using the portrait of Jesus as a model for the Christian's life. "What would Jesus do?" has been the liberal equivalent. Theological Worlds can provide alternative christological perspectives. World One knows the Jesus who went alone into the mountains to pray (Trappist). World Two is more Franciscan, drawn by a Jesus who went about doing good, armed with only a staff. World Three, more Jesuit in approach, follows One who is immersed in the multitudes, providing enlightenment as the situation requires. World Four focuses upon Jesus as the one who lives the gospel which he proclaims (Dominican). World Five knows the persevering Jesus of the wilderness (the Desert Fathers). Thus the spiritual director, in knowing the person who is asking direction, can help midwife as *epiphania* a Jesus who is respectively revealer, liberator, example, savior, or suffering servant—as like ministers to like.

7. *Church year.* The church year is divided twice into the triadic pattern of anticipation, gift, and response. This rhythm provides opportune times for intense direction, as Advent, Christmas, and Epiphany, or Lent, Easter, and Pentecost.

8. *Rule.* Monks attempt to live faithfully by being held responsible to a rule. Every person is a creature of habit, which functions as an implicit rule. Spiritual direction is a vehicle of transformation by making one's rule explicit, modifying it accordingly, and becoming responsible in relation to it. A group rule is also helpful.

We began this explication of spiritual direction as a way of resolving the dilemma exposed by the liberal-conservative tension, transforming the practice of pastoral care and counseling. We are ready now to draw the implications. First, a multiform approach to spiritual direction frees the pastor from the illusion of being value-free, without making his or her own theological parameters normative for the person with whom he or she is working. Instead, the pastor, functioning within an explicit variegated context, is able to discern the particularized dynamic of healing needed within the parameters of the particular World in which a person is living. Each theological World is a pure type, providing its own conditions and contours of opportunity, with its adequacies for each person determined by the quality of interchange between that person's *obsessio* and *epiphania* as manifested in personal and social behavior.

Second, with spiritual direction so understood, a primary skill required for spiritual direction is the imaginative, informed ability to enter the World of another person as guest. Pastoral calling provides more than an analogy. It is like entering a person's house for the first time, trusting one's feelings. Is this truly a home, or could it be; or has it the strangeness of rented space? Pastoring requires the skill to help others "name the name." It involves discerning the semblance of a World serving as one's arena, which has hope of becoming "home"—with the process of pilgrimage stirring between the two.

We turn now to applying this art of spiritual direction more directly to theological Worlds. As we have explored, the dynamic of a World is formed around two poles—a negative configuration called *obsessio,* and a positive one called *epiphania.* An *obsessio* is "that which so gets its teeth into a person that it establishes one's life as plot"— seeking resolution. [16] Whereas in one sense each person has a number of *obsessios,* early on they establish themselves as variations on one (perhaps several) themes. An *epiphania,* for which each life then yearns, is "that which keeps the functioning of obsessio fluid, hopeful, searching, restless, energized, intriguing, as a question worth pursuing for a lifetime. It keeps one's obsessio from becoming a fatal conclusion that signals futility." [17] Thus all theology is autobiography—as a way of life rooted in the impulsing logic emerging as dynamic between these two poles.

Whether the *obsessio* or *epiphania* is predominant determines one's temperament. I identify temperament Type A as present when the *epiphania* is primary. Such persons tend to perceive their Worlds optimistically, the universe lively and immanent with meanings. Type B is more drawn by the claim of the *obsessio.* As a result, the *epiphania* is less a constant and more a hope—one that gives shape to the search. In doing spiritual direction, one must be concerned not only to help persons discern their World, but attentive to which end of the dynamic one is tending to live. Each temperament has its own temptations. The first, for example, can breed superficiality by taking things for granted. In the second, the depth of neediness can entangle hope in a web of cynicism.

Conversion is the name for a positive tipping of the polar balance, suddenly or gradually. There are two marks for its occurrence. On the one hand, moments of *epiphania* are no longer sucked into one's *obsessio* as if into a bottomless pit—and the edges of futility take on the tint of "maybe." On the other hand, one's *epiphania*, no longer glossing the *obsessio* of self-deception, takes it honestly into itself, and bored self-satisfaction takes on the spaciousness of adventure. Depending on the temperament, both of these are experienced as reversals (conversions), in which there is reciprocity between the two poles rather than domination by one.

Conversion is the beginning. T. S. Eliot speaks of *epiphanias* as "the unattended Moment, the moment in and out of time," which serves as "hints followed by guesses." Hints and guesses of *epiphania* in their interaction with *obsessio* is half of what spiritual direction is about. Eliot knows the other half as well. It rests in "prayer, observance, discipline, thought, and action." [18] Accountability as discipline is this other side, as a way of keeping open the luring of the Spirit toward open channels.

Spiritual direction can occur either individually or in groups. Henri Nouwen describes group spiritual direction as a community of Christians who commit themselves on a regular basis together to "listen with great care and sensitivity to the One who wants to make the healing presence known to all people." [19] This is done by providing "protective boundaries within which we can listen to our deepest longings." [20] Here we recognize the powerful convergence of spirituality and our call to social mission. Formation means to be "healers of persons" by giving "a place [World] to those who have none." [21]

Group direction has special opportunities for different kinds of discernment. Not restricted to verbal sharing, members can be literally assigned to accompany each other. As a companion, a guest is present to discern how one negotiates traffic, what paintings one has on one's wall, one's CD, tape, and book collections, favorite haunts and rooms, characteristic food and clothing, telephone style, and characteristic humor. Since one's "doing" emerges from one's "being," by observing one's doing, a spiritual friend can help discern who one is—and might be.

Individual spiritual direction should become normative to a congregation, pairing Christians in mutual direction—with difficult situations calling for special attention by the pastor. If blockage persists, therapeutic referral may be necessary. Signs of such need include undue preoccupation with the past; inability to pass beyond certain persons or events that begin to function as distractive; unidentifiable factors that continue to sap energy; deeply fluctuating moods; or immobilization over an issue when a decision needs to be made. Even then, spiritual direction should continue simultaneously with the therapy. Otherwise, therapeutic help, in coping, can divert one from being lured through the dark night as a sacred act. Many of the saints were faithful neurotics, likely to try the patience of any pastor.

Among the tools available for spiritual direction, the Theological Worlds Inventory is particularly useful. This Inventory indicates not only one's preferred theological World, but indicates the strength of alternatives, the order of choices, and specific questions that can be used in sharing and probing. With experience, one can learn to detect subtle variations within the *obsessio* of each World—hints of separation, conflict, emptiness, condemnation, or suffering. One also gains an intuitive sense for hints of *epiphania*—reunion, vindication, fulfillment, forgiveness, and endurance—in fact or in hope. Above all, one learns when such discernments are best acknowledged and affirmed, and when they are best left unrecognized—for the time being or until one is strong enough to hear it.

Variegation has powerful implications for both church and parishioner. It brings recognition that Christian faith is a gamble of living "as if." Homiletics entails the art of preaching "as if." And pastoring, as spiritual direction, means vicariously living another's "as if"— together. Once this diversity of alternative Worlds begins providing eyes for such formative ministry, even one's choice of comics is not exempt from the discerning eye. The preference for "Ziggy" (World One), "Doonesbury" (World Two), "Kathy" (World Three), "Andy Capp" (World Four), or "Peanuts" (World Five), is itself an exercise in theological Worlds.

CHAPTER ELEVEN

A Glance Backward,
with Realism

Since the denominational structure of Roman Catholicism and mainline Protestantism is hierarchical in nature, the natural movement is usually one of control from the top down, striving for uniformity. Although nodding benevolently toward diversity, in truth, leaders tend to treat it as if it is in disarray. Consequently, the momentum from national, diocesan, or conference offices is toward providing a common missionary strategy, a uniform approach to educational curriculum, a unified theological statement, and a conformity of congregational structure.

But against such tendencies, what is needed today is a frank insistence that it is not pluralism that is pulling apart these mainline churches. Rather the crisis is deeply and legitimately theological. Liberal educators can no longer act as if they can placate conservatives by "putting more Bible" in the curriculum. To be concrete, the clash is primarily between advocates of Worlds Three and Four. Likewise, the dilemma cannot be resolved by adding additional representatives from one World or another to the mission boards, so that the perspective moves a bit more toward the right or the left. The missionary cleavage is the conflict between World Two and World Four. And growing uneasiness over the new emphasis today on spirituality is not resolved by fine-tuning the amount of social justice programming permitted. The "foes" here are residents in World One versus World Two. When the deep reason for such massive failure of communication goes unknown or unacknowledged, suspicion arises concerning the motives and loyalties of these contrasting groups, establishing an unacceptable win/lose situation. This need not be so.

In fact, we simply need to identify that the present polarization over membership loss and how to respond to it is rooted in the contrariety of Worlds One, Three, and Five. To see this would go far in opening possibilities for a creative strategy.

The task to which the church is presently called, then, is not that of taking sides in a political battle between liberals and conservatives. This polarization is a dated conflict that has outworn its usefulness. Since there are liberal and conservative variations within each of the theological Worlds, it is a mistake to take such primal theological orientations and label any of them as being "conservative" or "liberal." Rather, *the real issue of our times is ecclesiological.* The question can be put bluntly: *is the Christian vow of love deep enough to establish a hospitality for alternative Worlds within mainline Protestant and Catholic churches?* Can theological Worlds be so understood and structured that firm commitment to one does not entail attacking and undermining the *obsessios* and *epiphanias* of others? If so, many of the church's present obstacles and struggles become opportunities. What is needed is a commitment to variegation and with it, the significant reinterpreting of evangelism, discipleship, social concerns, education, missions, preaching, and worship. This need is more than adopting a passive tolerance for diversity. What is required is nothing less than a profound and eager commitment to it.

It is time to summarize. The dilemma that we have explored has two poles. On the one hand is the liberal propensity toward a theological tolerance, holding options within a web of relativity in which interest is encouraged but commitment is dissolved. On the other hand, the conservative perspective, although encouraging vigorous commitment, tends to defend a parochial content in which the resulting hostility toward viable alternatives can contradict the graciousness of the gospel it confesses.

Our effort has been to invert this problem, celebrating diversity as a rare opportunity. By developing viable Christian alternatives worthy of lively commitment and competitive zeal, destructive pluralism *between* churches and groups can become a creative variegation *within* the local church, and within each denomination. Church renewal and evangelism are inseparable. The variegated church of the future will be one dedicated to drawing persons into life as pilgrimage, evoking powerful commitment through interactive participation within viable theological alternatives.

A Theological Epilogue

Perhaps the reader will permit me to describe my thoughts in more strictly theological language. If not, move to the final "Personal Epilogue." Truth is relational, for it is always from a perspective. Thus objectivity, at best, is subjectivity confessed—naming and owning the vantage point from which one is gambling on the meaning of life. Such a confession renders one's assumed circle of meaning a theological enterprise. The more self-conscious such theologizing becomes, the more direct and intense becomes the excitingly painful examination of one's past as a theological autobiography birthing the present. Life, then, is a dynamic of faith seeking understanding by testing one's orientation in terms of the livability of that World in the making. Imperative to this process is a group that can provide supportive accountability within a context of viable options. The goal is the movement from unconscious assumption to knowing commitment—releasing a momentum toward greater depths, and luring one toward greater inclusivity.

This much we have made clear. But one question continues to shadow these pages. "What is truth?" asked Pilate. Can truth have any meaning within a variegated church of competitive "truths"? Can truth, in the end, really permit alternatives? Our study has taken us to an important conclusion. *Truth resides within one's World*, to be measured by four factors: (1) the degree to which one identifies clearly, feels deeply, and faces with minimal deception one's impelling *obsessio(s)*; (2) the amplitude of freedom and creativity birthed by the relation of one's *obsessio(s)* and one's *epiphania(s)*; (3) the faithfulness by which one lives that World as pilgrimage—honestly, deeply, tolerantly, and with eager breadth; (4) the consistency with which one permits others the right to a World as sacred as the World that one is wagering as one's own. The golden rule finds resonance here.

Theologizing begins in earnest by owning who one is, encouraged by support and accountability to live with consistent behavior. This process of becoming who one is may lead to excitement and a sense of peace. Or anxiety may intensify, with a dark edging of judgment, as the price of trying to become who one thought oneself to be. Such strain can evoke a hunger for conversion. If this occurs, it is likely to be a convergence of sterility from behind, and the lure of an alternative World from in front. Faith, at its best, is the courage to gamble on a vision too good to be true, but which has the wrappings of gift.

We are stepping over a threshold into an age where, for the first time, diversity must be recognized as both conclusion and premise. This pluralism cannot be transcended. No universal, uniform World will ever again be available. The dream of universal truth may die slowly, for some with a frightening death, but for all it must die. I remember graphically when it did for me. It was a Monday afternoon at 4:35. I was in a seminar in ethics at Yale. The teacher, professor Brand Blanshard, the last in a great line of absolute idealists, paused. I had never before heard his gentle voice even tremble, but this time it broke: "If the subjectivism of a Kierkegaard is true, if there is no absolute truth before which we can all knowingly stand, then there is only darkness facing us." A deep silence followed. There was no mistaking the import of what he said. He reached for his answer into the past, clutching it as absolute against the demise he feared. The rest of us could not. There was no going back. Instead, as the fourteen of us glanced around the room, I sensed that there were alternative Worlds in that room, wrapped in the silence of the growing dusk.

Yet if we accept alternative Worlds, is there not at least one theological World better suited for most persons than the others? No. Is not one World more Christian than the others? No. Are there not some Worlds less exploitative than others? For better or worse, the answer must remain a steadfast no.

Ours is a time of unparalleled oppressions—systemic as well as serendipitous. Yet, despite the view of many, the cause is not that of a pluralistic breakdown of values. The reverse is closer to the truth. Ours is a time of Worlds in conflict because each claims the right to function as *the* truth. Commitment to authentic variegation has prophetic urgency at this threshold into the postmodern era. This is foundational. *Each of the Worlds has seeds leading to oppression, and each has resources potential for freedom.* Thus in World One there is an otherworldly tendency which can tempt neglect of the socio/econo/political dimensions of life, as if they lacked full reality. Yet from the heart of that World emerges a Merton whose *Raids on the Unspeakable* can excite the most radical activist. To lose oneself in the Whole can entail discovering oneself as soul-friend with every living particle of creation.

Likewise, in World Two, there is a struggle for justice that entails food without price for every orphan, widow, and sojourner. Yet warriors called by such a World have authored crusades and cheered the flames that burned "witches" and "faggots." World Three might seem more gentle, inviting all who are empty to find fullness. Yet those who gain such satisfaction can become a pampered elite. When the self is made primary, one can be tempted to justify class distinctions and ethnic deprivations as "deserved," because others have not worked hard enough.

Then is World Four more promising, insisting as it does upon the guilt of all of us in prideful exploitation of each other? Standing condemned before God, there can be born a humility of gentle thankfulness. Yet this World can also give birth to dogmatic self-righteousness, with claims of personal and/or national perfection arrogant enough to populate both purgatory and hell.

What then of World Five, where suffering forges endurance, and endurance a primal dignity—a willingness to share one's only crumbs with the most lowly? Yet in rising to the middle class, these persons can emit a surprising disdain for those whom they have left behind. The portrait of a "have not" who has won the sweepstakes can be frightening.

With the dilemma so understood, Christians are called to a dual commitment. On the one hand, the church must lead the way to a place we have never been before—insisting upon diversity as an undebatable "given." On the other hand, the church must reclaim its unique call to spiritual formation—the accountable nurturing of persons within a community of viable alternatives toward a commitment that alone provides the passion worth living. It is no small matter to help each other stare down one's *obsessio* with disciplined steadfastness and a knowing smile.

A Personal Epilogue

We have been intent on providing a theological base for alternative subcongregations and groups, exploring how variegation can become an intentional way of transforming the church. But a very personal confession is in order for our closing. A major stumbling block to the vision we have developed is the attitude of many pastors and lay leaders—beginning with me. I confess my goal, beginning with my first parish. Whereas I prided myself on being theologically open, the truth is I was intent on discrediting the congregation's favorite "I" hymns, insisting on theologically "acceptable" ones that they did not know and had no desire to learn. I badgered them into dividing an already crowded chancel, and "maturing" their folksiness with an inflexible order of worship. My stellar victory was in getting the tiny choir to stumble nobly over a Bach anthem for Easter.

In later parishes, my passion for social change grew, until my underground mission was to avoid Mother's Day sermons, ease the American flag out of the chancel, and in general, make Republicans uncomfortable. For all my pride in my liberal tolerance, I can confess now a heavy dogmatism was really at work. Liberals can be as doctrinaire in idolizing their own faith-style as they like to condemn conservatives of being. It was late for me to be learning something as basic as the faithlessness of denying others the right of pilgrimage in their own attempt at faithfulness. I am to love my enemy. Then surely I can enable my sisters and brothers in Christ to live out *beside me* their viable alternatives—with passion.

I no longer believe that tension between pastor and congregation is a creative stance. Living together in affirmed diversity is far more effective. My conversion to a variegated perspective began by falling in love with a saintly woman of eighty-three. Not only did she teach me to play "The Old Rugged Cross" on her harmonica, but had me accompany her on the piano, while she sang for the Mother's Day service at the Home. If she can recognize my attempt at playing as an act of love, perhaps she will at least wink at me before calling all "protesters" Communists.

I think I am confessing for many of us pastor-types. In my case, I had to settle something in my own mind, once and for all: that a Southern Republican homemaker, who has an American flag and pink flamingos in her junky front yard, who whistles "How Great Thou Art" through her front teeth, who actually enjoys eating grits, whose granddaughter is a high school pom-pom girl, and whose son belongs to the National Guard—such a woman might just make it into the Kingdom before me. From then on, variegated ministry as "loving the folks" seemed to flow naturally.

APPENDIX

A Clarification of Terms

Philosophy has always been concerned with the relationship between the One and the many. Technically, pluralism is the view that there are numerous kinds of irreducible reality. Monism is the opposite belief, that all is reducible to one principle or entity. Kant transcended this polarity, however, by holding that humans perceive all that is according to the way in which the mind is structured, but the thing or things in themselves *(noumenon)* is beyond our human understanding to know. Neo-Kantianism (e.g., Ernst Cassirer) expanded these categories of the mind into symbolic forms that organize experience in any period as expressions of the needs of that age. Hans Vaihinger's philosophy of "as if" refers to matters of theology as "useful fictions" which we construct to make life more manageable. These constructs have no truth in any objective sense. But he claims to know too much, for to declare something as a pure fiction one would be able to know the *noumenon*—things independent of our particular way of perceiving them. Closer to our way of thinking is William James, who insists that the "as if" results from the "will to believe." One gambles on meaning (such as faith in God) because one trusts that the risk is worth taking. The position underlying our use of the idea of theological Worlds in this book is that *faith is the supreme human act*, taken and sustained at the ongoing intersection of psychic, social, and cultural needs. Therefore, when at times we may use the terms "pluralism" or "pluralistic," it is not in the philosophic sense of reality being composed of many ultimate constituents, for this cannot be known. We use it in the Neo-Kantian sense of multiple perspectives—with truth being the quality of relationship between reality and the autobiographic uniqueness of each person, socially formed by support and accountability. The term *variegation* seems best able to carry our meaning, in that it refers to being varied in appearance, or existing in more than one form. This means being pluriform or multifaceted, as in being a "patchwork of contrasting colors." The word *diversity* is quite useful too, meaning "variety." Our concern is to avoid the popular but philosophically misleading use of the word "pluralism." What we are exploring is the pluriformity or plurality of different understandings of the meaning of Christianity. Still other synonyms may help point to the situation we are exploring—terms such as "variety," "array," "multi-plicity," "polychrome," "mosaic," "kaleidoscopic," "multifarious," or "protean." Together these words can help point to the situation of Christianity today, and to its nature.

NOTES

1. A Frightened Glance Forward, with Excitement

1. Henri Nouwen, *Reaching Out* (Garden City: Doubleday, 1975), p. 15.
2. Karen Greenwaldt and Warren Hartman, "A Generation Coming of Age," *Discipleship Trends* 3, no. 4 (1985).
3. Kennon L. Callahan, *Effective Church Leadership* (San Francisco: HarperCollins, 1990), p. 112.
4. Gabriel Fackre, *The Christian Story* (Grand Rapids: Eerdmans, 1984), p. 219.
5. Frederick Buechner, *The Alphabet of Grace* (New York: Seabury, 1970), p. 3.
6. This meaning context we will later identify as theological World Three. For a full development see W. Paul Jones, *Theological Worlds: Understanding the Alternative Rhythms of Christian Belief* (Nashville: Abingdon, 1989), p. 70.
7. Ibid., This is theological World One. p. 45.
8. Mary Jo Leddy, "Beyond the Liberal Model," *The Way Supplement,* Heythrope College, University of London (summer 1989): 40-53.

2. Theological Diversity in Today's Church

1. Garrison Keillor, "Laying on Our Backs Looking Up at the Stars," *Newsweek* (July 4, 1988): 33.
2. Jack Seymour and Donald Miller, eds., *Contemporary Approaches to Christian Education* (Nashville: Abingdon, 1982), p. 69.
3. Ernst Troeltsch, *The Social Teachings of the Christian Churches,* vol. 2 (New York: Harper & Bros., 1960), p. 1007.
4. Ibid., p. 1010.
5. Ibid.
6. Jürgen Moltmann, *The Crucified God* (New York: Harper & Row, 1974), p. 11.
7. Jerry L. Walls, *The Problem of Pluralism; Recovering United Methodist Identity* (Wilmore, Ky.: Good News Books, 1986), p. 28. See Henry C. Sheldon, "Changes in Theology Among American Methodists," *The American Journal of Theology* 10 (January 1906): 51-52.
8. Walls, *The Problem of Pluralism,* p. 37. See also p. 60.
9. Ibid., p. 63.
10. Walls's analysis draws two conclusions: (1) The differentiation between revelation and response is merged by the liberal. (2) The differentiation between substance and consequence. Whereas the liberal might be inclined to declare Jesus the Christ because of personal results, the conservative insists that the reverse is essential.
11. Jerry L. Walls, "What Is Theological Pluralism?" *Quarterly Review* 5, no. 3 (fall 1985): 52.
12. Walls, *The Problem of Pluralism,* p. 93.
13. Ibid., p. 98.
14. Dean Kelley, *Why Conservative Churches Are Growing* (San Francisco: Harper & Row, 1972).

15. Walls, "What Is Theological Pluralism?" p. 61.

16. Walls, *The Problem of Pluralism,* p. 103.

17. Richard Wilke, *And Are We Yet Alive?* (Nashville: Abingdon, 1986), pp. 69-79. Bishop Wilke's more liberal response is from within the denominational structure. Lamenting the impotence signaled by severe membership decline, he concludes that much to be blamed is the cultural milieu in which "Americans are immunized by religious talk, coated with a Christian veneer that keeps us from becoming strongly converted" (p. 53).

18. Douglas Meeks, *Oxford Institute Papers,* fall 1987.

19. W. Widick Schroeder, "The Quest for Denominational Identity and the Limits of Pluralism," *CTS Register* 75, no. 2 (spring 1985): 14-28.

20. Anthony B. Robinson, "Theology in the Church: 'Open' to What?" *The Christian Century* (Jan. 20, 1988): 46-47.

21. John MacArthur Jr., "Uniqueness Amidst Unity," *Fundamentalist Journal* 5, no. 5 (May 1986): 16-17, 64.

22. Edward Dobson, "Unity and Diversity: Contradictory or Complementary," *Fundamentalist Journal* 3, no. 5 (May 1984): 10.

23. Rodney Sawatsky, "Commitment and Critique: A Dialectical Imperative," *Conrad Grebel Review,* 1, no. 1 (winter 1983): 1-12.

24. Ibid., pp. 4, 11.

25. Ibid., p. 12.

26. Rachel Richardson Smith, "Swordplay in Sunday School," *Newsweek* (Dec. 21, 1987): 9.

27. Carl W. Lindquist, "Facing St. Louis: A Plea for Forbearance," *Challenge to Evangelism Today* 20, no. 2 (fall 1987): 3.

28. F. Gerald Downing, "Perhaps the Greatest Heresy," *Modern Churchman* 28, no. 2 (1986): 49-54.

29. Ibid., p. 53.

30. "Where Do People Go to Church?" *The Parish Paper* (Naperville, Ill., 1988).

31. Daniel Yankelovich, *New Rules: Searching for Self-fulfillment in a World Turned Upside Down* (New York: Random House, 1981).

32. Nancy Ammerman, *The Fundamental World View: Ideology and Social Structure in an Independent Fundamentalist Church,* unpublished dissertation (New Haven: Yale University, 1983).

33. Ibid.

34. J. Robert Nelson, "The Inclusive Church," *The Christian Century* (Feb. 20, 1985): 183-86.

35. Oscar Cullmann, "Unity Through Diversity," reprinted in *International Christian Digest* 2, no. 1 (Feb. 1988): 15-17.

36. Ibid., p. 17.

37. Moltmann, *The Crucified God,* p. 28.

3. The Variegated Church

1. Robert S. Ellwood, Jr., *Introducing Religion from Inside and Out* (Engelwood, N.J.: Prentice-Hall, 1978), pp. 1, 11.

2. Rueben P. Job, *A Journey Toward Solitude and Community* (Nashville: Upper Room, 1982), p. 49.

3. "Book Says 'Mega Churches' Attract 'Boomers' Best," *The United Methodist Review* (July 7, 1989): 4.

5. An Experimental Case Study

1. For a description, see Jeff Blackman, "Initiating Weekly Communion: One Church's Story," *Sacramental Life* (December 1988/January 1989): 24-26.

6. How to Get There from Here

1. Wade Clark Roof, "The Church in the Centrifuge," *The Christian Century* (Nov. 8, 1989): 1012-14.

2. David S. Steward, "Why Do People Congregate?" in C. Ellis Nelson, ed., *Congregations: Their Power to Form and Transform* (Atlanta: John Knox Press, 1988), p. 79.

3. Roof, "The Church in the Centrifuge," p. 1012.

4. Ibid., p. 1013.

5. Steward, "Why Do People Congregate?" p. 84.

6. Max Stackhouse, *Ethics and Urban Ethos* (Boston: Beacon Press, 1972).

7. See Thomas H. Groome, *Christian Religious Education* (San Francisco: Harper & Row, 1980); Sara Little, *To Set One's Heart* (Atlanta: John Knox Press, 1983).

8. Nelson, *Congregations,* pp. 7, 8.

9. Bruce C. Birch, "Memory in Congregational Life," in Nelson, p. 26.

10. James Anderson and Ezra Earl Jones, *The Management of Ministry* (San Francisco: Harper & Row, 1978), p. 125.

11. H. R. Niebuhr, *The Social Sources of Denominationalism* (Hamden, Conn.: The Shoe String Press, 1954), p. 281.

12. Gaylord Noyce, "Mandate for the Mainline," *The Christian Century* (Nov. 8, 1989): 1018.

13. Charles Leerhsen, "Unite and Conquer," *Newsweek* (Feb. 5, 1990): 50.

14. Ibid., p. 53.

15. *The Documents from the Vatican II Council* (New York: Guild Press, 1966), p. 467.

16. Alfred C. Krass, "Growing Together in Spirituality: Pastor and Parish Have a Check-Up," *The Christian Century* (April 1, 1987): 311-14.

17. Ibid., p. 312.

18. Ibid., p. 313.

19. Jones, *Theological Worlds,* pp. 42-43.

7. Christian Education as a Variegated Enterprise

1. Jack L. Seymour and Donald E. Miller, *Contemporary Approaches to Christian Education* (Nashville; Abingdon, 1982), p. 13.

2. Ibid., p. 15.

3. Ibid., p. 169.

4. James Michael Lee, *The Flow of Religious Instruction: A Social Science Approach* (Mishawaka, Ind.: Religious Education Press, 1973).

5. George Lindbeck, *The Nature of Doctrine* (Philadelphia: Westminster, 1984), pp. 34, 36.

6. Within Protestantism, see David Watson, *Accountable Discipleship* (Nashville: Discipleship Resources, 1984). A Roman Catholic version appears in Father Arthur Baranowski, *Creating Small Faith Communities: A Plan for Restructuring the Parish and Renewing Catholic Life* (Cincinnati: St. Anthony Messenger Press, 1989).

7. John Westerhoff, III, *Will Our Children Have Faith?* (New York: Seabury, 1976), pp. 49-50.

8. Rueben P. Job, *A Journey Toward Solitude and Community* (Nashville: Upper Room, 1982), p. 50.

9. See Charles Winquist, *Practical Hermeneutics* (Chico, Calif.: Scholars Press, 1980); James and Evelyn Whitehead, *Method in Ministry* (New York: Seabury Press, 1980); Verna J. Dozier, *The Authority of the Laity* (Washington: Alban Institute, 1984).

10. John M. Macquarrie, *Paths in Spirituality* (New York: Harper & Row, 1972), p. 47.

11. Jackson W. Carroll, "The Congregation as Chameleon," in Nelson, *Congregations,* p. 51.

12. Groome, *Christian Religious Education,* p. 214.

13. Roger Rosenblatt, "When the Wall Blows Down," *Life* 13, no. 3, (Feb. 1990): 23.

14. Groome, *Christian Religious Education,* p. 215.

15. See David A. Kolb, *Learning Style Inventory,* McBer and Co., 137 Newbury St., Boston, Mass. 02116. H. A. Witkins, C. A. Moore, D. R. Goodenough, and P. W. Cox, "Educational Implications of Cognitive Styles," in *Review of Educational Research* 47, no. 1 (winter 1977). Charles A. Claxton and Yvonne Ralston, *Learning Styles: Their Impact on Teaching and Administration,* AAHE-ERIC/Higher Education Research Report, no. 10, 1978.

16. James Fowler, *Stages of Faith* (New York: Harper & Row, 1981); James Fowler and Sam Keen, *Life Maps: Conversations on the Journey of Faith* (Waco: Word Books, 1978).

17. James Fowler, "Toward a Developmental Perspective on Faith," *Religious Education* 69, no. 2 (March/April 1974): 211.

18. Psychological Publications, Inc., 5300 Hollywood Blvd., Los Angeles, Calif. 90027 (for qualified users); most recently a Form G Self-Scorable Edition is available. An abbreviated version appears in David Kiersey and Marilyn Bates, *Please Understand Me: An Essay on Temperament Style* (Del Mar, Calif.: Prometheus Nemesis Books, 1978); Gordon Lawrence, *People Types and Tiger Stripes* (Gainesville, Fla.: Center for Application of Psychological Types, 1979). Isabel Briggs Myers and Peter Myers, *Gifts Differing* (Palo Alto, Calif.; Consulting Psychologists Press, 1980). Isabel Briggs Myers, *Introduction to Type* (Consulting Psychologists Press, 1980).

19. Currently types are most often listed according to a mechanical ordering. My preference is after the E or I to indicate one's dominant function next, with the secondary function following. See W. Paul Jones, "Myers-Briggs Type Indicator: A Psychological Tool for Approaching Theology and Spirituality," *Weavings* (May / June 1991): 32-43.

20. John Ackerman, *Cherishing Our Differences* (Pecos, N. Mex.: Dove Publications, n.d.).

21. L. Ronald Brushwyler, "Congregations Have Types," in *Commentary*, Sept. 1988, a newsletter of the Midwest Career Development Service.

22. Maria Beesing, Robert Nogosek, and Patrick O'Leary, *The Enneagram: A Journey of Self Discovery* (Denville, N.J.: Dimension Books, 1984).

23. Don R. Riso and Russ Hudson, *Personality Types* (New York: Houghton Mifflin, 1996).

8. Variegated Worship

1. Herve Varenne, *Americans Together: Structured Diversity in a Midwestern Town* (New York: Teachers College Press, 1977), pp. 92-95.

2. Ibid., pp. 99-100.

3. Martin E. Marty, "Filling the Gaps in Liberal Culture," *The Christian Century* (Nov. 8, 1989): 1022.

4. Bruce Birch, "Memory in Congregational Life," in C. Ellis Nelson, ed., *Congregations: Their Power to Form and Transform* (Atlanta: John Knox Press, 1988), p. 32.

5. See Bernard Anderson, *The Unfolding Drama of the Bible* (Philadelphia: Fortress Press, 1988).

6. David F. Lehmberg, "Use Sunday Papers for Opening Worship," *Circuit Rider* (Nov./Dec. 1983): 3.

7. Karl Barth, *The Teaching of the Church Regarding Baptism* (London: SCM Press, 1948).

8. Working draft from the Committee to Study Baptism of the United Methodist Church, revised January 10, 1991.

9. Robert L. Browning and Roy A. Reed, *The Sacraments in Religious Education and Liturgy: An Ecumenical Model* (Birmingham: The Religious Education Press, 1985).

10. Charles Foster, "Communicating: Informal Conversation in the Congregation's Education," in Nelson, pp. 228-32.

11. Anthony G. Pappas, *Entering the World of the Small Church: A Guide for Leaders* (Washington D.C.: Alban Institute, 1988), pp. 1-52.

12. Johann Heermann, "Ah, Holy Jesus" in *The United Methodist Hymnal* (Nashville: The United Methodist Publishing House, 1989), p. 289.

13. Henry H. Mitchell, *The Recovery of Preaching* (San Francisco: Harper & Row, 1977), p. 57.

9. Variegated Preaching

1. Paul Scherer, *The Word God Sent* (New York: Harper & Row, 1965), p. 54.

2. George Lindbeck, *The Nature of Doctrine* (Philadelphia: Westminster Press, 1984), p. 62. He makes use of Clifford Geertz, *The Interpretation of Cultures* (New York: Basic Books, 1973), p. 90.

3. Ibid., p. 32.

4. Ibid., p. 62.

5. Ibid., p. 68.

6. Ibid., p. 115.

7. Richard Eslinger, *A New Hearing* (Nashville: Abingdon, 1987), pp. 7-8.

8. Stanley Hauerwas, *The Peaceable Kingdom* (Notre Dame, Ind.: University of Notre Dame Press, 1983).

9. Michael Goldberg, *Theology and Narrative; A Critical Introduction* (Nashville: Abingdon, 1981), pp. 213, 244. Cited in Eslinger, *A New Hearing*, p. 173.

10. Eslinger, *A New Hearing*, p. 177.

11. John Masefield, "Lollingdon Downs" in *Poems* (New York: Macmillan, 1929), p. 401.

12. Eslinger, *A New Hearing*, p. 178. Eslinger keeps fluctuating so that a consistent portrait of reciprocity, which at one point he declares, keeps being undercut by the reiteration of the primacy of narrative.

13. Eugene Lowry, *The Homiletical Plot: The Sermon as Narrative Art Form* (Atlanta: John Knox Press, 1980), pp. 6, 12.

14. Eugene Lowry, *Doing Time in the Pulpit: The Relationship Between Narrative and Preaching* (Nashville: Abingdon, 1985), p. 8.

15. Ibid., p. 48.

16. Rainer Maria Rilke, *Selected Poems of Rainer Maria Rilke* (New York: Harper & Row, 1981). p. 13.

17. Elijah Jordan, *Essays in Criticism* (Chicago: University of Chicago Press, 1952), pp. 51, 75-77.

18. Warren Molton, "June-Day Joshua" in *Bruised Reed* (Valley Forge: Judson, 1970), p. 11.

19. Eslinger, *A New Hearing*, p. 179.

20. Fred Craddock, *Preaching* (Nashville: Abingdon, 1985).

21. Samuel Beckett, *Waiting for Godot* (New York: Grove Press, 1954).

22. Charles Leerhsen, "Unite and Conquer," *Newsweek* (February 5, 1990): 55.

23. John D. Varner, "Pastors Should Offer 'Pluralistic Pulpits,'" *Missouri West United Methodist* 134, no. 3 (n.d.): 2.

10. Variegation in Operation

1. Ken Callahan, *Effective Church Leadership*, (San Fransisco: HarperCollins, 1990), p. 112.

2. Lovett H. Weems, Jr., *Leadership* 1, no. 1 (Sept. 1990): 2.

3. Dietrich Bonhoeffer, *Life Together* (New York: Harper & Row, 1954), pp. 17-39.

4. George Lindbeck, *The Nature of Doctrine* (Philadelphia: Westminster Press, 1984), pp. 132-33.

5. Ibid., p. 126.

6. Bonhoeffer, *Life Together*, p. 119.

7. Henri Nouwen, *Reaching Out* (Garden City: Doubleday, 1966), p. 54.

8. Carlo Carretto, *Letters from the Desert* (Maryknoll, New York: Orbis, 1972), p. 99.

9. Alan Jones, *Soul Making* (San Francisco: Harper & Row, 1985).

10. Martin Luther, *Luthers Werke*, vol. 2, p. 716. Quoted in William H. Lazareth, *Luther on the Christian Home* (Philadelphia: Muhlenberg Press, 1960), p. 91.

11. John Wesley, "A Plain Account of the People Called Methodists," *The Works of John Wesley*, vol. 8 (Grand Rapids: Zondervan, 1959), pp. 253-54.

12. David L. Watson, "Methodist Spirituality," in Frank C. Senn ed., *Protestant Spiritual Traditions* (New York: Paulist, 1986), p. 232.

13. See, e.g., Tilden Edwards, *Spiritual Friend: Reclaiming the Gift of Spiritual Direction* (New York: Paulist, 1980); Kenneth Leech, *Soul Friend: The Practice of Christian Spirituality* (New York: Harper & Row, 1980).

14. These are quotes collected over a number years from a number of sources.

15. David L. Watson, *Accountable Discipleship* (Nashville: Discipleship Resources, 1984).

16. W. Paul Jones, *Theological Worlds* (Nashville; Abingdon, 1989), p. 27.

17. Ibid., p. 28.

18. T. S. Eliot, "Four Quartets," *The Complete Poems and Plays of T. S. Eliot* (New York: Harcourt Brace Jovanovich, 1952), p. 136.

19. Henri Nouwen, "Spiritual Direction," *Worship* 55 (1981) p. 404.

20. Henri Nouwen, *Reaching Out*, p. 109.

21. Paul Tournier, *The Meaning of Persons* (New York: Harper Bros., 1957), p. 96.